ANALYST
OF THE IMAGINATION

ANALYST OF THE IMAGINATION

The Life and Work of

Charles Rycroft

edited by

Jenny Pearson

KARNAC

LONDON   NEW YORK

Copyright Acknowledgements

Chapter 9: John Turner, "A Brief History of Illusion: Milner, Winnicott and Rycroft", *The International Journal of Psychoanalysis*, 83 (2002): 1063–1082; reprinted by permission.

Chapter 14, pp. 230–232: Robert Mullan, extract from *Mad to be Normal: Conversations with R. D. Laing*. London: Free Association Books, 1995; reprinted by permission of Cathy Miller Foreign Rights Agency on behalf of Free Association Books Ltd.

Chapter 14, pp. 238–240: Vincent Brome, "Tangling with Freud", *The Guardian* (1 June 1998). © The Guardian; reprinted by permission.

Chapter 14, pp. 234–237: Peter Fuller, extract from *Psychoanalysis and Beyond* by Charles Rycroft and edited by Peter Fuller published by Hogarth Press. Used by permission of The Random House Group Limited.

Chapter 15, Charles Rycroft, "Reminiscences of a Survivor: Psychoanalysis 1937–93", *British Journal of Psychotherapy*, 11 (No. 3, 1995), reprinted by permission.

First published in 2004 by
H. Karnac (Books) Ltd.
6 Pembroke Buildings, London NW10 6RE

Copyright © 2004 by Jenny Pearson

British Library Cataloguing in Publication Data

A C.I.P. for this book is available from the British Library

ISBN: 185575-904-7

10 9 8 7 6 5 4 3 2 1

Edited, designed, and produced by Communication Crafts

Printed in Great Britain

www.karnacbooks.com

For Charles,
with love and gratitude

CONTENTS

ACKNOWLEDGEMENTS

M y warmest thanks to all the authors who have contributed chapters or parts of chapters and stayed patiently with the processes of editing and proof-reading; to Hilda Padel and Catherine Peters for permission to include chapters by their late husbands, John Padel and Anthony Storr, and for writing biographical notes; and to Jutta Laing, widow of R. D. Laing, for help with his biographical note.

I am indebted to Paul Roazen for his encouragement, which got me started on the book and helped to keep up my enthusiasm, and to Margaret Arden, Robin Higgins, Lesley Murdin, and Dudley Young for support along the way. I would especially like to thank Charles's three children, Julia Jama, Catherine Merriman, and Frank Rycroft, and his sister Alice Harvey, for their confidence in me as an editor and for contributing personal memoirs to the biographical chapter "Glimpses of a Life"; also Rosemary Gordon, Judith Hubback, and Pearl King, who knew Charles at different points in his early life and gave generously of their time to look back and remember.

I thank Vincent Brome for an enjoyable interview and for permission to include a slightly edited version of his *Guardian* obituary in the second biographical chapter, "Further Glimpses". And I am happy to acknowledge my debt to Paul Barker, former Editor of *New Society*, for the book's title, which is based on the headline he wrote for Maryon Tysoe's profile of Charles in 1985. Part of this is also included in "Further Glimpses".

I am particularly conscious of a debt of gratitude to my own family and to many friends and colleagues for their patience and support during the long time that I have been caught up with planning, writing, and editing. I thank them all for their tolerance and kindness. In particular, I would like to thank Emyr and Ti for all the happiness they give me; my analyst Dennis Duncan, for being there; Frankie Armstrong, who has brought laughter and inspiration to our home for many years; James Roose-Evans, for friendship and a second home at the beloved Bleddfa Centre in Wales; Bevis Hillier, for a lifetime of friendship and encouragement; Ann Gilmartin, who has kept my garden going; and my good friends Mary Smail and Chris Woodland, for emails and creative adventures that have lightened the path.

The foundation chapters for the book—chapters 3, 4, 5, 6, and part of chapter 13—were originally presented at a memorable conference on the legacy of Charles Rycroft, organized by the *British Journal of Psychotherapy* and the Freud Museum in 2001. My thanks to Jean Arundale, editor of the Journal at the time, for encouraging me to include them after their publication in the *BJP*, Vol.18, No. 2, and to the Freud Museum for their hospitality, both then and for our book launch.

Finally, my thanks to Oliver Rathbone at Karnac for his faith in the project and to our editor Leena Hakkinen for her care and patience with the work in progress.

EDITOR AND CONTRIBUTORS

Margaret Arden graduated in medicine in 1953 and worked as a psychiatrist until 1962, when she became an associate member of the British Psychoanalytical Society. She retired to bring up a family and worked part-time as a child psychiatrist 1970–78, was in private psychoanalytic practice from 1976 until 1992, and a training analyst for the British Association of Psychotherapists. Her personal analysis with Charles Rycroft encouraged her tendency to think for herself rather than accepting ready-made theories. When starting work as an analyst, she was acutely aware of the gap between theory and practice, and she began to write as a way of clarifying her ideas. "Infinite Sets and Double Binds" (1984), her first paper, connected the work of the anthropologist Gregory Bateson with Ignacio Matte Blanco's theory of bi-logic. The second, "Psychoanalysis and Survival" (1985), was her response to the holistic world view of the physicist and philosopher David Bohm. Both papers were attempts to reformulate psychoanalytic theory without Freud's scientific reductionism. Each subsequent paper represented a stage in the development of her thinking. She argued for the broadening of theory to include, e.g., a synthesis of Jungian

xii EDITOR AND CONTRIBUTORS

and Freudian ideas, the importance of the integrity of the personality, and the spiritual dimension. Margaret Arden's collected papers, *Midwifery of the Soul: A Holistic Perspective on Psychoanalysis*, were published by Free Association Books in 1998.

Harold Bourne discovered when he was a medical student that he had inadvertently chosen a career path to psychoanalysis and psychiatry, which, along with Marxism for a while, had fascinated him since sixth-form days. He was initiated into army psychiatry and so escaped basic formation in medical institutions, subsequently surviving his junior post in one and flourishing in another for subnormal children. He then published his paper that demolished the accepted insulin treatment for schizophrenia, fled to academe in New Zealand, and published the first account in the British Commonwealth of a course in psychology for medical students. He spent much energy on psychiatric service reform, liberalizing the law on sexual offences, promoting psychotherapy, and turning out thirty or so papers. Back in England, a fellow of the Royal College of Psychiatrists, an NHS Consultant Psychotherapist, and a teaching-hospital Consultant in Child and Family Psychiatry, he found the therapeutic community. He considers it, when inspired by psychoanalysis, to be the most potent of all forms of psychotherapy. Since emigrating again in 1989, he enjoys practice and life in Rome, with two younger children growing up there and now approaching university. His older children, one from his first family, take part, tolerate, and try, along with the younger ones, to give him guidance.

Vincent Brome, author and journalist, was a friend with whom Charles shared many dinners and conversations at the Savile Club over some twenty years. His writing spans a wide range of subjects and genres, including novels, plays for stage and radio, and articles for the press, contributing to *The Times*, *Sunday Times*, *Observer*, *Guardian*, *New Statesman*, *New Society*, *Encounter*, and *Spectator*. His most serious work is researching and writing biographies: he reckons to spend about five years on a biography. His biographies include *Clement Atlee* (1947); *H. G. Wells* (1951); *Aneurin Bevan* (1953); *Freud and his Early Circle* (1967); *Jung: Man and Myth* (1978); *Havelock Ellis: Philosopher of Sex* (1981); *Ernest Jones, Freud's Alter Ego*

(1963); *J. B. Priestley* (1988); and *The Other Pepys* (1992). A man of great charm and style, he continues to profess and practise his love of women into his nineties while consistently arguing the case against marriage. In *Who's Who* he gives his recreations as "writing plays and talking".

Susan Budd is a psychoanalyst and member of the British Psycho-analytical Society and the Independent group. She lives and works in London and Oxford. She was trained as a sociologist at the London School of Economics and was a member of the faculty there and at the London School of Hygiene and Tropical Medicine, where she taught sociology to doctors. Her publications include *Sociologists and Religion* (1973), *Varieties of Unbelief: Atheists and Agnostics in English Society, 1850–1960* (1977), and *The Healing Bond: The Patient–Practitioner Relationship and Therapeutic Responsibility* (1994), with Ursula Sharma. More recently, she has published "Ask Me No Questions and I'll Tell You No Lies: The Social Organiza-tion of Secrets", in *The Presentation of Case Material in Clinical Discourse* (1997), and "The Shark Behind the Sofa: Recent Develop-ments in the Theory of Dreams", in *Dreams and Society* (2004). She is external adviser to the Training in Psychoanalytic Psychotherapy at the West Midlands Institute of Psychotherapy and is a member of the London Management Committee of the Freud Museum. She is a member of the editorial boards of the *IJPA* and the *BJP*.

Peter Fuller, art critic and editor of the quarterly magazine *Modern Painters* from its foundation in 1988 until his untimely death in 1990, was a younger friend whose company Charles enjoyed hugely and whose death in a car accident at the age of 43 was a source of great sadness to him. The son of a Baptist minister, Peter became a Marxist at Cambridge and was strongly influenced by the Marxist art critic John Berger. His lifelong passion for art had him writing articles about it from an early age: initially showing an interest in minimalism and conceptualism, he went on to develop strong and deeply held values of a very different kind, arguing for the continuing importance of Ruskin's view of art for our own time. Ruskin is the subject of his last book, *Theoria*. Reviewing it, Richard Dorment wrote in the *Daily Telegraph* (18 November 1988): "Like his hero, Fuller cares fervently about the visual arts, and writes about them with a fervour refreshing in today's art world. All good critics struggle to evaluate and respond to painting; Fuller' s great strength is that he inquires into its meaning and purpose." Waldemar Januszczak, in his *Guardian* obituary, called Peter "the most important art critic working in Britain at this time" (*Guardian* Obituary, 30 April 1990). In the memorial edition of *Modern Painters* (Vol. 3, No. 2, Summer 1990), Nicholas Serota paid tribute to him as "a difficult and uncompromising adversary".

Peter described his unhappiness as a young man and his long, painful, and ultimately successful analysis in an autobiography, *Marches Past* (1986). His *Art and Psychoanalysis* (1980), published by the Writers' and Readers' Cooperative, was dedicated jointly to his long-term analyst Kenneth Wright and to Charles. Peter's Introduction to *Psychoanalysis and Beyond*, which he also edited, draws on interviews with Charles as well as familiarity with his published writing.

Robin Higgins is a musician and a psychiatrist. He was a choral scholar at King's College, Cambridge, where he read Natural Sciences and Music (Pt.1.Cl.1). He went on to sing in the Purcell Singers under the baton of Imogen Holst and to complete his BMus some thirty years later at University College, London. In the meantime, he qualified as a medical practitioner, specialized in psychiatry, and had a short spell at the Tavistock Institute of Human Relations, exploring, amongst other things, the nature of perfumes and olfaction. Then for many years he was a consultant psychiatrist to two metropolitan and family health clinics and a visiting psychiatrist to Goldsmiths College and to two boarding special schools. Latterly, he ran seminars and lectures to the art and psychotherapy unit at Goldsmiths College, and to the dance movement therapy unit at the Laban Centre. His publications include many articles on children and childhood, poems, short stories, two books—*Approaches to Case Study* (1993) and *Approaches to Research* (1996)—and the entry on "Music" in the *Oxford Illustrated Companion to Medicine* (2001).

Jeremy Holmes, MD FRCPsych UKCP, is Consultant Psychiatrist/ psychotherapist in North Devon, visiting Professor at the Psychoanalysis Unit University College London and at the Psychology

Department, University of Essex, and honorary Consultant Psycho-therapist at the Tavistock Clinic. He first consulted CR in 1973 and saw him as a patient for the next six years. CR recontacted him some time later after seeing a review JH had written on *Psychoanalysis and Beyond*, and thereafter they met up from time to time. As a psychiatrist, he has tried to combine psychiatric and psychotherapeutic approaches in his work within the NHS and was recently chair of the psychotherapy faculty at the Royal College of Psychiatrists. He is a member of Severnside Insitute for Psychotherapy. His main clinical and academic interest and publications have been in attachment theory and its relationship to psychoanalysis. Publications include: *John Bowlby and Attachment Theory* (Routledge, 1993), *The Search for the Secure Base: Attachment Theory and Psychotherapy* (Bruner-Routledge, 2001), *Introduction to Psychoanalysis* (with A. Bateman, Routledge, 1995), *Narcissism and Depression* (Icon Books, 2001 and 2003), and *Integration in Psychotherapy: Models and Methods* (edited with A. Bateman, Oxford, 2002). He is currently co-editing the comprehensive *Oxford Textbook of Psychotherapy* (due 2004/5). He has been married (*en deuxième noce*) to Ros for the past 25 years and he has four children, three grandchildren, and four step-children. He has recently partially retired (working roughly one day per week NHS, one day private psychotherapy practice) and is trying to spend more time with his family, dog, tennis raquet, garden, and thoughts.

Edgar Jones is Reader in the History of Medicine and Psychiatry at Guy's, King's, and St Thomas's School of Medicine. He originally trained as a historian, completing a doctorate at Nuffield College, Oxford. Having decided to train as an analytical psychotherapist, he then joined the department of psychiatry at Guy's Hospital, was awarded a doctorate in clinical psychopathology (an investigation into the form of belief in schizophrenia and anorexia) and studied for a diploma in clinical psychotherapy. Charles Rycroft was his analyst throughout his various trainings. He moved to King's College Hospital/Institute of Psychiatry in 1998, where his research has focused on the nature and treatment of war syndromes, including post-traumatic stress disorder and the history of military psychiatry. He is an associate member of the London Centre for Psychotherapy.

R. D. Laing (Ronnie to his friends and colleagues) was born and educated in Glasgow, where he qualified as a doctor and psychiatrist in 1956 before moving to London to join the staff of the Tavistock Clinic and train at the Institute of Psychoanalysis. Charles Rycroft was his training analyst, and his supervisors were D. W. Winnicott and Marion Milner. After qualifying as a psychoanalyst in 1960, he went into private practice, at the same time continuing to work as a psychiatrist in the public sector. He was director of the Langham Clinic (1962–65) and was involved in research into psychiatric disturbance in families with the Tavistock Institute for Human Relations (1961–67). In 1964 he founded the Philadelphia Association, a registered charity concerned with establishing a network of households where people in extreme mental distress could spend some time without having to undergo orthodox forms of psychiatric treatment.

His first book, *The Divided Self*, exploring the role of the schizophrenic patient as "outsider", estranged from self and society, was published in 1960. In it he sought to demystify madness, to break down the divide between the sane and the insane, and to provide an understanding of "mad" communication and behaviour— themes he continued to develop through further writings and clinical work. Subsequent books include *The Self and Others* (1961), *Sanity, Madness and the Family* (1964) with Aaron Esterson, and *The Politics of Experience/The Bird of Paradise* (1967). Anthony Clare, in his entry on Laing in the 1981 *Makers of Modern Culture: A Biographical Dictionary*, edited by Justin Wintle, writes that "The overall impact of Laing's writings on psychiatry seems likely to be judged in terms of the emphasis he placed on the *experience* of madness at a time when psychiatry was more preoccupied with its *form.*" Laing was born in 1927 and died in 1989.

Peter Lomas worked in neurosurgery and general practice for several years before training at the Institute of Psychoanalysis. He held positions in various branches of child psychiatry, during which time he wrote a number of papers on postnatal depression. He now lives in Cambridge with his wife Diana; they have three children. He practises as a psychotherapist and is a Founder Member of the Cambridge Society for Psychotherapy, a learning community in which those who aim to acquire the art of psychotherapy do so in a non-hierarchical set-up. He is the author of five books on psychotherapy, the most recent of which is *Doing Good? Psychotherapy out of Its Depth*. A second edition of *Cultivating Intuition* is due to be published in 2004. The main theme of Peter Lomas's work is the belief that psychotherapy is essentially a moral undertaking and is more rooted in ordinary living than contemporary theories and techniques would suggest.

John Padel (1913–1999) was a close long-standing friend of Charles. He got a first in Mods and Greats at Oxford, and he was an accomplished cellist. He taught classics in schools for ten years before marrying and then, two years later, decided to study medicine and train in psychoanalysis (simultaneously). Charles had already trained in medicine, begun practising clinical psychoanalysis, and published works on psychoanalysis, which John much respected, before they met. After training John lectured at the Tavistock Institute and abroad on the history of psychoanalysis and published papers on theoretical aspects of the history. He took groups of GPs and social workers and did joint marital therapy as well as clinical psychoanalysis, psychotherapy, and supervision. In 1988 John published an edition of the Shakespeare sonnets in a revised order, having become convinced after several years of research that this was the order in which Shakespeare actually produced them. John and Charles had much in common and met regularly for lunch for about twenty years, and Charles sometimes stayed with John's family in the Lake District. John and Charles admired each other's talents and tactful use of clinical experience and shared a strong sense of history, a love of literature, and a deep moral and humane respect for other people. They also shared a mistrust of the internal politics of the British Psychoanalytical Society. John was always glad to acknowledge his admiration for Charles's work.

Jenny Pearson read English at Bristol University and worked as a journalist on *The Times* in the 1960s, after which she became a freelance journalist, writer, and editor. Her first book, co-written with Jack Lambert, was *Adventure Playgrounds* (1974). She helped her friend Diana Rigg to collect and edit her anthology of unfavourable theatre reviews, *No Turn Unstoned* (1982), and helped two other friends, the composer/conductor Sir Andrzej Panufnik and the singer Frankie Armstrong, with their autobiographies, *Composing Myself* (1987) and *As Far As The Eye Can Sing* (1992). She was part of the revival of traditional storytelling in the mid-1980s, which led to training as a Sesame drama and movement therapist, working with myth and story. She was contributing editor of *Discovering the Self through Drama and Movement: The Sesame Approach* (1996). She has trained as a counsellor with WPF and as a psychoanalytic psychotherapist with AIP. Her most recent book, co-edited with Frankie Armstrong, is about voice work and its effect on women's attitudes, entitled *Well-Tuned Women: Growing Strong Through Voice Work* (2000). She was married to Charles Rycroft from 1978 until his death in 1998. She has two children from previous partnerships and two grandchildren.

Paul Roazen studied at Harvard, The University of Chicago, and Magdalen College, Oxford, and taught full-time in the Department of Government at Harvard and as Professor of Social and Political Science at York University in Toronto, from which he has now retired back to Cambridge, Massachusetts. He is the author of *Freud: Political and Social Thought, Brother Animal: The Story of Freud and Tausk, Freud and His Followers, Erik H. Erikson: The Power and Limits of a Vision, Helene Deutsch: A Psychoanalyst's Life, Encountering Freud: The Politics and Histories of Psychoanalysis, Meeting Freud's Family, How Freud Worked: First Hand Accounts of Patients, Canada's King: An Essay in Political Psychology, The Historiography of Psychoanalysis, The Trauma of Freud: Controversies in Psychoanalysis, Oedipus in Britain: Edward Glover and the Struggle Over Klein, Cultural Foundations of Political Psychology,* and *On the Freud Watch: Public Memoirs.*

Anthony Storr (1920–2001) psychiatrist and writer, was notable for his eclectic and humane approach to the problems of the human condition. In his relationship with patients, his approach to teaching, his broadcasts, reviews and articles, and above all through the books which brought him a global readership, his influence was widespread. He said of the first of his books, *The Integrity of the Personality* (1960), that he wrote it to clarify his own mind about the practice of psychotherapy. The books that followed included *The*

Dynamics of Creation (1972), a study of creativity; *The Art of Psychotherapy* (1979), written for his students and still widely used; *Solitude* (1988), which argued that solitude, as well as human relationships, was essential for individual psychic well-being. Music was his life-long passion, and he was finally persuaded to write about it. He was reluctant at first, feeling he did not have enough technical knowledge, but *Music and the Mind* (1992) was very well received by professional musicians and amateur music-lovers alike. His final book, *Feet of Clay* (1996), a study of gurus and the reasons for their hold over their followers, still has obvious relevance today.

John Turner is Senior Lecturer in English at the University of Wales Swansea. He is the author of *Wordsworth: Play and Politics* (1986), co-author of *Shakespeare: The Play of History* (1988) and of *Shakespeare: Out of Court* (1990), all published by Macmillan, and author of a book on Macbeth for the Open University Press (1992). He has written a dozen articles on D. H. Lawrence and is now engaged in writing a book on Lawrence and the history of the psychoanalytic movement. During the course of this work he has translated the love-letters of Otto Gross and Frieda Weekley (1990) and written on David Eder (1997/98), both for *The D. H. Lawrence Review*. He has given a number of lectures to psychoanalytic audiences, and the text of his essay was originally given as a workshop paper at the Winnicott 2000 International Congress in Milan.

Maryon Tysoe is a Chartered Psychologist and a Fellow of the British Psychological Society. She gained her first degree and PhD at Nottingham University, before holding research and teaching posts at the universities of Surrey, Sussex, and Kent. She then decided to write full-time about psychology for the public. She worked as a freelancer and then on staff as psychology correspondent for the weekly magazine *New Society*. While there she wrote the profile of Charles Rycroft at Editor Paul Barker's behest. In the same year she won the Periodical Publishers Association award for Technical Writer of the Year, regarded as the "Oscar" for specialist writing in British magazines. Since then she has written several books, including *Love Isn't Quite Enough: The Psychology of Male–Female Relationships*, broadcast often on radio and television, and contributed numerous articles to magazines and to newspapers such as the *Guardian* and the *Independent*. She has been Editor of *The Psychologist*, the monthly magazine of the British Psychological Society, and is currently writing her first novel.

Dudley Young was born in Chicago and apparently had a happy childhood. In adolescence he probably met the Devil, but nonetheless went on to become The Canada Scholar at Cambridge, where his first meal at High Table nearly put him off the academic life "for good", as they say. A compromise was found, in the shape of Essex University, where he has taught Literature since 1968 and counted the seasons on a little farm nearby. He was at least once sorely tempted by marriage, but Fate kindly intervened, not long before Barbara Cartland gravely announced that "A man would have to be seriously barking to marry these days". Of his *Origins of the Sacred* (1991), Charles wrote: "This is a book to be lived with and meditated upon", and for some years now he has been wrestling with Greek Tragedy, the results of which even his friends think overdue.

ANALYST
OF THE IMAGINATION

Introduction

Jenny Pearson

This book was first conceived in a conversation with Paul Roazen when he was over from Cambridge, Massachusetts, just a few months after my husband died. Paul and Charles had been friends for many years, corresponding regularly and exchanging papers in manuscript. Whenever Paul had visited, I was always aware of a zest and brightness in the way they shared and enjoyed one another's company, so his visit at this time was poignant in a particular way. As we reminisced about Charles, I mentioned that I had a vague idea of putting together some sort of book, inviting contributions from people who had known and worked with him. Paul was very encouraging, urging me to gather biographical material from friends and relatives as well as papers from colleagues, and he agreed to contribute a chapter. By the time he left, we had a project.

The journey from that point to this has proved more challenging than any book I have worked on. A large part of this has been the personal challenge involved in producing a book about someone so close to me. It has involved distancing myself in order to grasp the subject, a process that became quite painful as it created a kind of split in my remembering. On the one hand, there was the

1

old Charles I knew and loved—on the other, the stylish public figure of Rycroft, striding across the stage of psychoanalytic history. I have thought a lot about this split, and I have come to realize that it is only partly me defending myself, wanting to protect that area of mind that is able to keep those who have been close to us alive in a timeless place where we can still encounter them in memory and dreams. As the work progressed, I also came to recognize that the split in my remembering bears some relation to a split that Charles created between an impressive public performance and a private self that had suffered and learnt to keep quiet about it. He had his ways of bridging this divide when he chose to, ranging from irony to a completely disarming informality and humour. He approved of and occasionally quoted W. H. Auden's (1932) dedication: "Private faces in public places / Are wiser and nicer / Than public faces in private places."

It was impossible to know Charles, or indeed talk to him for any length of time, without becoming aware of complexity and depth. He revealed different aspects of himself according to where, when, and in what circumstances he encountered people. In twenty years of marriage, I got to know him and his life story from numerous conversations and visits to people and places that mattered to him. Nevertheless, work on the book has drawn me into a process rather like unravelling the plot of a detective story. In their different contributions, people have described very different versions of him. I have been reminded of the degree to which he could, if he chose, control how people saw him according to whether he liked and trusted them or preferred to keep them at a distance!

The Rycroft some saw as aloof, remote, and hard to know could suddenly be revealed as a rather shy, informal, self-deprecating man who invited laughter and even a degree of protectiveness. Not so many people encountered this aspect of him: for those who did, it became obvious that his aloofness was something of a mask. He understood the value, even the necessity, of masks. I remember him explaining to me how the "false self" described by Winnicott was also a guardian self: if it was snatched away, there was a strong risk that the person so revealed might disintegrate completely. On a lecture platform or at a book launch, Charles could be sharp, ironic, formidable, successfully concealing a fundamental shyness and vulnerability. However, he would usually respond if he felt that someone was inviting him to come out and play. A nice example of this playfulness is an interview he gave to the social psychologist and writer Maryon Tysoe for an article in *New Society* in 1985, marking the publication of *Psychoanalysis and Beyond*. I have included her description of their meeting in the biographical section: it is an endearing verbal portrait and conjures up his presence beautifully.

The book gathered a lot of momentum from a conference on "The Contribution of Charles Rycroft", set up by the *British Journal of Psychotherapy* and the Freud Museum in June 2001. This was essentially a line-up of papers delivered by friendly colleagues, but, like his famous 1968 dictionary of psychoanalysis, it turned out to be a "critical" discussion, looking for truth in a manner that would surely have met with his approval. It felt fitting that the conference was hosted by the *British Journal of Psychotherapy*, the journal that published his last writings under the editorship of Jean Arundale, and the Freud Museum, where he both gave and attended talks in the latter years. Papers were read by Margaret Arden, Jeremy Holmes, Paul Roazen, and Susan Budd, who kindly gave permission for them to appear in this book. Charles's great friend, Anthony Storr, was scheduled to present a paper, but he died only two months before the conference took place. He was sadly missed, and so was his unwritten paper, which would have been of great interest, reflecting a long friendship between two very cultured and articulate men, one who began as a Freudian and the other as a Jungian. I am grateful to Catherine Storr for permission to include Anthony's thoughts about Charles from a talk that he gave at the memorial meeting at Burgh House, Hampstead, in November 1998. Charles's other great friend and fellow analyst, John Padel, died in 1999 and is represented here with his own kind permission by the obituary he wrote for *The Times*, 5 June 1998.

Reading the obituaries in the days after he died, I was reminded of Charles's very prolific writing in the 1960s and 1970s, when I first got to know him. At that time his books and articles seemed to be everywhere, translated into many languages: his first gift to me was a copy of *Reich* in Japanese! I remember a younger analyst I met at a dinner party telling me that Rycroft was "the most famous psychoanalyst in Europe". At that time he often gave public lectures, not only to audiences within psychoanalysis and psychotherapy, including several at the Institute of Contemporary Arts and one to a huge audience at All Souls College, Oxford. An obituary in *The New York Times* described him as the British psychoanalyst who "offered a new generation of therapists new ways to interpret not just dreams but Freud's entire legacy" (Burkhart, 1998).

I remember my own excitement on first encountering Charles's books in the 1970s. I had previously read little about psychoanalysis and had a fairly crazy impression of it from literary sources like Iris Murdoch's novel *A Severed Head* (1961). I had made some slight attempt to look at Freudian theory, being interested in dreams, but what I read of Freud's dream symbolism felt wrong in ways I could not begin to analyse. I was delighted to discover someone with a strong grasp of Freud who was able to write about him in language that I could understand and, even better, to disagree where his own experience, professional and personal, convinced him that Freud had got it wrong. There was something reassuringly grounded about the way Charles connected his subject with recognizable human experience. I am told that a number of people were drawn towards the profession of psychoanalysis from my generation as a result of reading him.

Looking back on his achievements in the late 1990s, I came face to face with a startling question: Why is it, I asked myself, that in eight years of training, first in psychodynamic counselling and then in psychotherapy, I was never once required to read a book or a paper by Rycroft? In fact, I had read all his books long before I entered training, but that is not the point. My question is about the curious fact that a writer who informed and inspired a whole generation—my generation—with his insights and interpretations of the more indecipherable and questionable aspects of Freud's message is no longer handed out to people who are training in the field. After asking around and reading the contributions to this book, a number of answers or possible answers to this question suggest themselves. It becomes clear that the question of who is currently read and who is not has as much to do with professional politics, and even fashion, as with deeper questions about the workings of the human mind. I realize that I am asking a big question that leads on to further questions and speculations. What sort of a thing would psychoanalysis be, at this point, if those aspects of it opened up by Charles had been followed through rather than pushed aside? Further still, what are the forces at work in society at large that are surely reflected in the current state of psychoanalysis? Where does Charles stand in relation to other battles, lost and won? This part of the story is taken up by his friend Dudley Young, with whom Charles spent time and talked much during the transitional years.

I remember making a decision to put my husband's books aside when I began training as a therapist in 1989. I knew them well and felt that I should immerse myself thoroughly in the recommended literature, so that I would have the required thinking base from which to communicate with fellow trainees and colleagues. Training is a lengthy business, and the field of study is enormous. Having come to the end of my training a while back, I have recently returned to reading Charles's books, intrigued to discover how they would strike me now that I have worked out an orientation of my own within his field. To my delight, I still find his ideas and his writing fresh as daisies! Asking myself what is so enjoyable about him, the quick answer that comes to mind is a connection to Hans Christian Andersen and "The Emperor's New Clothes" (1959). There is a refusal to go along with the accepted view, an insistence on a terminology that does not involve bowing to authority, that shifts the weight of received thinking and makes room for openness and clarity. Several of my colleagues, having stumbled on his works, have remarked upon his virtues.

Looking at his books in the context of the received canon, I find myself wondering whether it is his very independence of mind that gets him left off reading lists. His sharp, clear thinking takes him along a route of his own. Where other writers seem to feel a pressure to line up their ideas with authority and precedent, he insists on thinking things through for himself. He is steeped in Freud, but also draws inspiration from wider fields outside psychoanalysis, such as ethology, linguistics, communications theory, history, and literature, for insights into what is going on in his consulting-room. In terms of psychoanalytic schools of thought, he is unclubbable. While agreeing in many respects with Winnicott's view of object relations, he had too many thoughts of his own to be labelled Winnicottian. He was supervised by Melanie Klein and admired her contribution, but he was most definitely and vocally not a Kleinian. By the same token he always resisted attempts by his admirers to form a Rycroftian school, objecting that such a move would be anti-creative and would discourage people from thinking for themselves. This insistence on keeping a mind clear to think runs counter to much that goes on in training, where people enter the bewildering, unprovable labyrinths of psychic life and often feel a desperate need for solid landmarks and demarcated inner places around which to organize themselves. The vivid landmarks of Kleinian thinking, in particular, offer a strong base from which to map the territory: it is a small step from here to treating her concepts and inner landscape as concrete and real. Charles became very impatient with people who lined up their ideas with received thinking and would not let the work of analysis engage their own imaginative processes. His sense of humour got him into trouble in a field where loyalties are passionately held. There were Kleinians who didn't speak to him for years after *The Observer* published his clerihew:

It would be fine
To be Melanie Klein
If the pleasure weren't cloyed
By having come after Freud.

The same insistence on thinking for himself led him to discover very early in his career that it was possible to write about psychoanalytical ideas and practice without using jargon: he realized this half way through the papers that are published in his early book, *Imagination and Reality* (1968b). He would sometimes advise people who thought of reading it to start in the middle, read to the end, and then go back to the early chapters if they found they were sufficiently interested. It gave him intense pleasure to work through complex ideas to a point where they could be expressed in ordinary English. *A Critical Dictionary of Psychoanalysis* (1968a) was created around a collection of definitions of psychoanalytic terminology that he built up during his own training. Every time he encountered a new term, he would attack it with a definition honed by the question he learnt to ask as an undergraduate at Trinity College, Cambridge: "What exactly do you mean by that?" The *Critical Dictionary* is still in print and doing well, 35 years on. From time to time I meet psychiatrists, therapists, historians, and even novelists who confess they could not manage without it.

Charles was an independent thinker and something of a loner in a professional world riven by factions and passionate allegiances. His confident assumption of the independent position at the beginning of his career was initially welcomed and encouraged within the British Psychoanalytical Society. In 1954, eight years after qualifying, he became a training analyst and a member of the Training Committee, where for a while he took over Winnicott's position representing the Middle Group. In 1956 he became a consultant in psychotherapy at the Tavistock Clinic and became R. D. Laing's training analyst under a scheme that allowed promising young psychiatrists of train at the Institute of Psychoanalysis. In the same year, he was chosen to represent the British Society by reading a paper at the big international gathering in London to mark the Freud Centenary in 1956: Melanie Klein left the meeting early, saying that she was tired! At this point Charles was a rising star of the psychoanalytic establishment. But he soon began to react against time spent on committees and administrative work, which was often boring (see his account of training committee meetings in "Reminiscences of a Survivor"—chapter 15) and took up energy that he was eager to direct towards thinking and writing. Pearl King, a contemporary of Charles's who holds the history and documentation of the Society at that time, recalls his analyst Sylvia Payne saying that too much responsibility was heaped on Rycroft too early in his career. Feeling overburdened and impatient with the strife between factions in the Society, which, in his view, got in the way of intelligent discussion, it was not long before he began the "strategic withdrawal" that culminated many years later in quietly allowing his subscription to lapse.

These, briefly, are the facts behind the story of Charles's defection from the psychoanalytic establishment, which, in the words of Susan Budd, has turned into "what the anthropologists would call a myth". The themes "Why did he leave the Society?" and "He shouldn't have left!" were still alive and highly charged at the conference three years after his death. They echo through the chapters that follow, including "Rebel Rycroft" by his friend Dudley Young and "The Innocence of Charles Rycroft" by Harold Bourne, a friend and colleague from way back, when they were both psychiatrists at the Maudsley. In talking with some of his former colleagues, I have recently come to recognize some of the hurt and disappointment felt when he allowed his membership to lapse in 1978, the year we were married. However, I remain convinced that it was something he needed to do at that point in his life. Charles was, for better for worse, a brilliant and creative thinker who chafed under the impact of noise, distraction, interruption, and repetition—aspects of ordinary living that he felt as invasive, to a point where he was impelled to get away. Sadly, this was often at great personal cost to himself and to those who lived close to him. He had a low boredom threshold and limited patience for discussing familiar ideas—even his own, once he had thought them through. He could be entertaining, lively, and very good company in short bursts, but for the most of the time he needed space and quietness. By the time I got to know him, he had learnt to manage his surroundings in such a way that he did not have to suffer too much impingement. His daily life was somewhat hermit-like: taking frequent walks and spending a lot of time on his own, with occasional, fairly brief forays into the social world. Living this way gave him the peace he needed, enabling him to stay focused on his work as a practising psychotherapist and a writer, up to five days before he died at the age of 83. He never ceased to find patients interesting and was probably at his happiest seated at his desk with his small portable typewriter, communing with his thoughts.

It was characteristic of him to have been publicly inscrutable on the subject of leaving the British Psychoanalytical Society, partly from a very English sense of tact about his negative feelings (which were largely historic) and partly for these other, private reasons that he did not choose to talk about. After thirty years of living near central London and working hard at two parallel careers, he felt an urgent need to make big changes if he was to survive creatively. Our move, shortly after we married, from Hampstead to Kew was literally as well as symbolically a move away from the centre in search of peace and quiet, more time for writing and fresh subjects to write about. Time that might have been spent at Hampstead parties and analytical meetings was now spent walking in Kew Gardens, along the river, and around the wharves of Brentford, from which he would sometimes return with descriptions of locations where he might set a novel or a detective story. These didn't materialize, but in the back room overlooking our garden at Kew he did write *The Innocence of Dreams* (1979), the book he was most pleased with to the end of his days. He also took up gardening and read more literature and history and a lot less about psychoanalysis. While keeping well away from the Institute, he stayed in touch with colleagues through the 1952 Club, an independent group of which he was a founder member and whose meetings he often attended. I was kindly invited to a meeting of the "52 Club" three years after he died, when they were talking about his life and work. Again, there was talk about his departure from the Society, and in this context I spoke briefly about the move to Kew. There was a sudden movement of understanding, and someone remarked, "He did what we are all supposed to do. He grew out of psychoanalysis!"

Charles's move away from the psychoanalytic establishment had serious repercussions for him in the long run. The reaction stirred up by his departure seems to have turned into the central "Rycroft story", to the extent of pushing his contribution to psychoanalytic thinking into the background. There is irony here: his creative contribution seems to have been driven into exile, in retaliation for the fact that he moved away in order to be more creative. Putting this book together, I have done my best to redress the balance by including a fair representation of his analytic ideas, including and especially around his central theme of imagination and dreams.

If Charles's relations with the Freudian establishment were troubled, his relations with the Jungians were quite paradoxical. While his thinking was rooted in a thorough study of Freud and the post-Freudians, he parted from Freud in his emphasis on the importance of imagination to the healthy working of the mind. This was the theme of his famous early paper "Beyond the Reality Principle" (1962) and it remained crucial to his work, including "Freud and the Imagination" (1975), a paper that has been a source of inspiration and insight to writers, and *The Innocence of Dreams* (1979). His emphasis on the importance of imagination and what Freud called "primary process" brings him into an area that was of central importance to Jung, though Charles's conclusions were reached independently from Jung. As a result, Jungians became increas-

ingly friendly towards his ideas, reviewing his books in their
journals and occasionally inviting him to give talks and debate with
them. Some Jungians have expressed irritation at his slightly face-
tious claim in the introduction to the *Critical Dictionary* that he
suffered from "the not uncommon constitutional defect of being
incapable of understanding Jung's writings". Again, this is his
sense of humour at work, slightly disguising the fact that Charles
was simply not drawn to Jung—partly, I suspect, because he preferred to work his own way through the territory of imagination
and partly because of Jung's habit of working from basic assumptions, which Charles was "constitutionally" unable to share. However, he did encounter Jung's thinking in many conversations with
his friend Anthony Storr and in reviewing books by Jungian writers. By the time he came to write *The Innocence of Dreams*, he had
abandoned his earlier, wilful ignorance of Jung to a point where he
was able to write a full chapter about him. *The Innocence of Dreams*
was reviewed enthusiastically in Jungian journals and is now required reading for the MA course on Jung and the post-Jungians at
the University of Essex.

Charles's interest in dreams and their interpretation was an
important feature in his consulting-room, in contrast to recent
trends in Freudian practice, which often seems to more or less
ignore dreams while focusing on transference and work "in the
here and now". Jungians, however, continue to work with their
patients' dreams, and many seem to find the Rycroft dream book a
help in doing so. It seems to be making a real contribution towards
Jungian thinking, reciprocating the contribution that Charles eventually allowed Jung to make towards his.

Another place where his ideas seem to be coming into their own
is the relatively new arena of the university literary departments,
where psychoanalytical thinking has become a regular part of the
syllabus. Obviously an analyst who understands something about
the workings of the imagination will be of interest to students of
literature. And so it turns out in a relatively new paper, published
in 2002 in the *International Journal of Psycho-Analysis* and written by
John Turner, a member of the English department of the University
of Swansea. Its title is "A Brief History of Illusion: Milner, Winnicott and Rycroft", and I am happy to be able to include it in this

collection. The author tells me that he once met Charles and was greatly encouraged by their conversation.

The grouping of Milner, Winnicott, and Rycroft is an interesting example of benign mutual influences taking place outside the framework of recognized schools of analysis. In fact, they knew one another and talked quite a lot at one stage. There are letters from Winnicott to Charles commenting on his early papers and arranging informal meetings between the two of them. Marion Milner, originally under the pseudonym "Johanna Field", wrote a book *On Not Being Able To Paint* (1950), which Charles valued for the light it throws on the creative process. She was one of his supervisors in training, and she was his chosen analyst when he went back into analysis in search of the roots of his creativity in the 1970s. Looking back on Charles's early days as a practising analyst, it is almost possible to see these three as an informal, loosely knit group, drawn together by a shared interest, exchanging ideas, and all writing independently on the theme of imagination. This quiet communion of three like-minded people stands out in very English contrast to the grouping around Melanie Klein, a much more vocal and territorial alliance from which Winnicott gradually and firmly detached himself. It is worth noting that R. D. Laing, a controversial figure but one of the most articulate and creative voices of the counter-culture and the anti-psychiatry movement, was simultaneously in a training analysis with Charles and in supervision with Milner and Winnicott.

Charles's involvement in the theme of imagination made him an encouraging witness of my own first venture into the therapeutic world. This was 1989, when an interest in traditional storytelling led me on to a training in drama and movement therapy (the Sesame Course at Central School of Speech and Drama). Though not too enthusiastic about the inroads this made into my time, Charles was generous enough to follow my progress and listen to my accounts of the experiential work I was doing in the studios at Central. When I came to edit and partially write a book about drama and movement therapy some years later, he read everything I wrote and was a helpful critic. I gradually came to recognize that he was not merely being supportive but actually understood and approved of what goes on in the arts therapies. It was characteristic of him to be open-minded about a therapeutic approach that was different and relatively new. His own way of being with patients was open and free from psychoanalytic dogma, allowing the dialogue and communion of the session to emerge in a shared language and at great depth. Robin Higgins, a psychiatrist with a deep interest in music, has written about this from his own experience in Charles's consulting-room, picking up on an idea Charles once expressed in writing that "One cannot . . . help regretting that none of the pioneers of the unconscious thought naturally in auditory terms. If they had, we would perhaps have a psychology in which thoughts are conceived of as themes, which can occur in different modes and keys . . ."

With his belief in the value of imagination, it is not surprising that Charles warmed to the idea of working with patients through direct engagement in the arts. This openness to change and new developments was something he kept as he grew older: in his last years he welcomed a trend that he described succinctly with the words "Psychoanalysis is out. Psychotherapy is in!" To this he would add, with a spark of his old wickedness, "I am a psychotherapist, not a psychoanalyst. To be a psychoanalyst you have to be a member of the British Psychoanalytical Society!"

Trends are difficult to pin down, but I have heard many reports in recent years that in the United States psychotherapy has been moving away from Freud and taking more of its inspiration from Jung. Coupled with more solid evidence in Britain of a steady increase in working with the arts in therapy, this suggests to me that the *Zeitgeist* may be moving towards much stronger recognition of the link between mental health and imagination. If this is the case, the moment may have arrived for a new generation of psychotherapists to wake up to the message and inspiration of Rycroft.

My hope is that this book will help to open up a new readership for him—not a following, which is the last thing he would want, but an open-minded readership of people who want encouragement to go on thinking their own way through the deeply liberating experience of psychotherapy. There are plenty of people around who are willing to tell us what psychotherapy is, what happens or should happen between therapist and patient, what happens between mothers and babies, and so on. There are not so many who encourage therapists to be in "uncertainties, mysteries, doubts, without any irritable reaching after fact and reason", in the words Charles liked to quote from the poet John Keats. This is the creative position, the one in which it is possible to go on asking the question, "What is psychotherapy?" without necessarily finding an answer to it. To hold this position involves keeping a mind open and free, being fully in the moment, and thinking for ourselves about what is happening there. If enough of us can achieve this, we could even find ourselves in the position of the audience at the end of Shakespeare's *The Tempest*, allowing the old man to return to the country from which he became an exile, our applause setting him free.

References

Andersen, H. C. (1959). The emperor's new clothes. In: *Hans Andersen's Fairy Tales*, trans. L. W. Kingsland. London: Oxford University Press.

Auden, W. H. (1932). Dedication (to Stephen Spender). *The Orators*. London: Faber.

Burkhart, F. (1998). Obituary: "Dr. Charles Rycroft, 83, Post-Freudian Interpreter of Dreams." *New York Times*, June.

Milner, M. (1950). *On Not Being Able To Paint*. London: Heinemann, 1973.

Murdoch, I. (1961). *A Severed Head*. London: Vintage, 2001.

Rycroft, C. (1962). Beyond the reality principle. In: *Imagination and Reality*. London: Hogarth Press.

Rycroft, C. (1968a). *A Critical Dictionary of Psychoanalysis*. London: Nelson/Penguin, 1970.

Rycroft, C. (1968b). *Imagination and Reality*. London: Hogarth Press.

Rycroft, C. (1975). Freud and the Imagination. *New York Review of Books*. Reprinted as: "Freud and the Literary Imagination." In: *Psychoanalysis and Beyond*. London: Hogarth Press, 1985.

Rycroft, C. (1979). *The Innocence of Dreams*. London: Hogarth Press.

CHAPTER ONE

Charles Rycroft: a memoir

Anthony Storr

It is just about thirty years ago that Charles Rycroft and I became friends. For a while, he almost became part of our extended family: for he used to come and stay in our Welsh cottage during family holidays. I remember that, on the first occasion, he feared the cold of Snowdonia and came equipped with an electric blanket. One night this caught fire, which filled the room with smoke and was very alarming: but Charles adroitly threw the blackened remnant out of the window, so no great harm was done. It seemed out of character for Charles to have such a modern device as an electric blanket. Gadgets were not his scene. He regarded our dishwasher with the utmost suspicion, and I completely failed to persuade him that using a word processor was preferable to doing everything by hand.

It was on these holidays that I learned how good he was with children. He seemed to have a natural sympathy with the young, which he retained even into old age, so that one had no qualms

---

An address given at a the Memorial Meeting organized by the family and held at Burgh House, Hampstead, on 7 November 1998.

about referring quite young patients to him, even when he was in his seventies. He was never in the least patronizing and so did not talk down to the young, who consequently felt at home with him.

I admired many things about Charles. First, the sharpness of his intellect. He had a highly critical mind, which manifested itself early in his life, when he got a first in Economics Part I at Cambridge. I don't think economics played a great part in his later life, but he retained a strong interest in history, which he also read at Cambridge, and in which he continued to read for pleasure into his old age. His critical intelligence manifested itself in an intolerance of slipshod thinking and writing, and greatly contributed to his independence of mind.

Second, I enormously admired him as a writer. Analysts are not always noted for the clarity of their writing—think of Lacan. But Charles's writings are crystal clear. He was, rightly, uneasy about Freud's ambivalent attitude to phantasy; and many of Charles's best writings are concerned with the positive aspects of the creative imagination, which he refused to dismiss as escapist, as Freud tends to do. His paper of 1962, "Beyond the Reality Principle", has become a classic. In it, he criticises Freud's division of mental functioning into the two varieties that Freud named "primary" and "secondary" process. Charles objected to Freud's dismissal of primary processes as "archaic, unrealistic and inherently non-adaptive" and pointed out that the healthy person integrates phantasy with abstract, rational thought in such a way that "phantasy continues to engage external reality (objects), enriches it and enables the imaginative elaborations of personal relationships to be understood and appreciated".

Charles had a keen appreciation of literature, which is reflected in the elegance of his writings. He was widely read and had a lively interest in both prose and poetry. I think it was Charles's appreciation of literature that made him dissatisfied with Freud's interpretation of the writer's art, and which led Charles to write: "The aim of psycho-analytical treatment is not primarily to make the unconscious conscious, nor to widen and strengthen the ego, but to reestablish the connexion between dissociated psychic functions, so that the patient ceases to feel that there is an inherent antagonism between his imaginative and adaptive capacities." He goes on to quote the famous passage of E. M. Forster, which begins "Only connect the prose and the passion . . .", which, I am sure, is familiar to you all.

Charles's book *Anxiety and Neurosis* was first published in 1968. It is a pioneer interpretation of anxiety in terms of biology and, as such, was ahead of its time. Charles regards anxiety as a heightened sense of vigilance, which is originally protective in function as a response to threat but becomes distorted in neurotic behaviour, giving rise to defensive manoeuvres of an hysterical, obsessional, or schizoid kind. Re-reading this book recently demonstrated to me the depth of Charles's understanding of defence mechanisms. It is a brilliant book, perhaps still not sufficiently appreciated. As he wrote himself, the book shows "that anxiety and the neuroses are phenomena which can be understood imaginatively as exaggerations of tendencies that are present in all of us and intellectually as manifestations of well-known biological principles".

In his book *The Innocence of Dreams* (1979), Charles reverts to one of his main preoccupations: Freud's distinction between primary and secondary mental processes. Once again, he is at pains to point out that, unlike Freud, he does not regard these two forms of mental functioning as antagonistic. He compares dreaming with waking imaginative activity and concludes that they have in common the fact that they both create images independently of the will. But dreaming is also a communication from the dreamer to himself and is thus too private to be universally comprehensible. Charles's treatment of dreams, as is the case with his other writings, is both imaginative and rational: a perfect example of that fusion between primary and secondary process that he admired in others.

None of us can be sure that our writings will survive our deaths for very long: but Charles's *Critical Dictionary of Psychoanalysis* (1968b) is likely to last as long as interest in Freud and his writings continues. His definitions of what are often extremely difficult concepts to formulate are impeccable and will be found invaluable by anyone writing on psychoanalysis, whether or not the writer is an analyst.

Now, it is not often that one turns to the writings of psychoanalysts in search of a good laugh; but if you are in need of cheering up, please read or re-read Charles's essay in his book *Psychoanalysis and Beyond* titled "Memoirs of an Old Bolshevik" (1985). This gives a hilarious account of Charles's recruitment into and membership of the Communist Party, which lasted all of two years while he was an undergraduate at Trinity College, Cambridge. A short passage from it will illustrate what I mean:

I should explain that the university Communist Party was at that time divided into two schools of thought, which were widely known as the gospels of St Matthew and St Mark, Mark being an intellectual Jesuit, Matthew a romantic puritan. Matthew believed that the bourgeoisie were damned, but that individual bourgeois could be saved if they were prepared to give up everything for the Party and throw in their lot with the working class. Ideally they should renounce their private incomes or give their capital to the Party, but failing that they should at least change their accents and their clothes and sound and look like proletarians. Matthew, who came from an upper-middle-class family well known for its high culture and intelligence, had made this sacrifice himself, but he never quite believed that anyone else had done so sincerely; in which he was perhaps right, since the romantic appeal of undergoing a class metamorphosis attracted imitators whose motives were affected rather than sincere. Among his converts there were both true and false Matthewians; the latter were camp-followers and "camp-communists".

Mark, on the other hand, believed that communism was the heir to all that was best in liberalism, socialism, conservatism, rationalism, catholicism, and anglicanism. It was "Forward from Everything", and he encouraged his recruits to continue to live exactly as they had before their conversion. It was, he believed, their revolutionary duty and destiny to spread the gospel from whatever station it had pleased the dialectic of history to call them to. He also held that culture was a weapon in the class struggle and that even research in aesthetics was a legitimate form of revolutionary activity. Prolonged meditation on the foot of a Chippendale chair would, I once heard him say, bring a Marxist to a closer understanding of the class structure of eighteenth-century England.

Mark's view of communism suited me down to the ground. I continued to hunt during the vacation and justified doing so by displaying in my rooms in college a poster issued by the Society of Cultural Relations with the USSR advertising the facilities for fox-hunting offered by the Georgian Soviet Republic. Nor was I alone in being attracted by Mark's all-embracing interpretation of the nature of revolutionary pastoral activity—which was, I now realize, the Marxist equivalent of St Augustine's "Love God and do what you will." Such an opportunity for having everything both ways was too good to be missed, and it became fashionable in my college to join the Party. Doing so became, indeed, a recognized form of social climbing.

Some of Charles contemporaries were afterwards unmasked as traitors, of whom the most notable was Antony Blunt. The security services continued to take an interest in Charles for many years after he had left the Party; and he was more than once interviewed in case he could throw any light upon who might have been the fourth, fifth, or sixth man in the array of spies.

Charles sometimes gave the impression of being diffident, but he possessed an unusual degree of intellectual self-confidence. This accounted for the characteristic that I most admired in him: his independence of mind. Wittgenstein once wrote: "It is good that I did not let myself be influenced." Charles might justly have written the same about himself. Psychoanalysts are usually profoundly influenced by their training and seldom entirely succeed in resolving the transferences they develop towards their training analyst. Not so Charles. He was analysed by Ella Sharpe and Sylvia Payne, but I doubt if either lady deeply affected him. His supervisor, Marion Milner, was, I think, much more important to him. He always spoke warmly of her insight and continued to seek her advice on difficult problems throughout his life.

He always retained complete intellectual independence. He acknowledged a debt to both Winnicott and Milner, but he had little patience with those who idolized one or other of the leading members of the psychoanalytic establishment. He was especially critical of Melanie Klein, whom he regarded as both narcissistic and dogmatic. He had a soft spot for brilliant eccentrics like Masud Khan—perhaps because he identified himself with their rebelliousness. This may also have accounted for his acceptance of R. D. Laing as a trainee. The analysis may not have been a total success, as Laing's subsequent career indicates; but Charles, in the face of considerable opposition, firmly supported Laing's candidacy as a psychoanalyst and wrote warmly of his intelligence and independence of mind.

Another example of his sympathy with rebels is his Fontana Modern Master on Wilhelm Reich (1971). As you may remember, Reich had the distinction—probably the unique distinction—of being expelled both from the International Institute of Psychoanalysts and from the Communist Party. Towards the end of his life he was prosecuted and imprisoned by the American authorities because he refused to recognize their dismissal of his so-called "orgone boxes" as fraudulent. Reich was later moved to a mental hospital, where he died. Charles regarded Reich's life as "tormented, persecuted, and futile" but, at the same time, extended a quite remarkable degree of understanding and sympathy towards him. In fact, Charles had a striking capacity for empathy with psychotics, which is also demonstrated in his paper "On the Defensive Function of Schizophrenic Thinking and Delusion-Formation" (1960). Most of us have difficulty in entering the distorted world of the schizophrenic patient, but Charles was able to appreciate and explain delusional thinking in such a way that it becomes comprehensible.

In recent years, since I moved from London to Oxford, I saw much less of Charles. But if I had to go to London, I would telephone him, and we would have dinner at the Savile Club, of which we are both members. I notice I am not so keen to go there any more because Charles won't be there to meet me. He was a very dear friend, and I greatly miss him. Everyone here will join me in extending our deepest sympathy to his son and his daughters, and especially to his wife, Jenny, who did so much for him.

References

Rycroft, C. (1960). On the defensive function of schizophrenic thinking and delusion-formation. *International Journal of Psycho-Analysis, 43.*

Rycroft, C. (1962). Beyond the reality principle. In: *Imagination and Reality.* London: Hogarth Press.

Rycroft, C. (1968a). *Anxiety and Neurosis.* London: Allen Lane/Penguin, 1971: London: Karnac, 1988.

Rycroft, C. (1968b). *A Critical Dictionary of Psychoanalysis.* London: Nelson/Penguin, 1970.

Rycroft, C. (1971). *Reich.* London: Fontana.

Rycroft, C. (1979). *The Innocence of Dreams.* London: Hogarth Press.

Rycroft, C. (1985). Memoirs of an old Bolshevik. In: *Psychoanalysis and Beyond.* London: Hogarth Press.

CHAPTER TWO

Outstanding within the "impossible" profession

John Padel

Within the "impossible" profession of psychoanalysis, Charles Rycroft was an outstanding, if mercurial, figure. Born into the heart of the English Establishment, he was by nature a radical who in the 1930s saw the menace of Fascism long before most members of his class paid it any heed. At Cambridge he briefly joined the Communist Party (although he claimed it took little moral courage, since it was the fashionable thing to do at the time), visited the Soviet Union, and then, as part of a Bloomsbury milieu, which included Virginia Woolf's brother Adrian Stephen, became interested in the subversive discipline of psychoanalysis.

Rycroft's father was Sir Richard Nelson Rycroft Bt. Charles Rycroft was the second son of his second marriage. Although intended for the Army, he chose Cambridge, where he took a first in Economics in Part I and was awarded an Exhibition. In Part II he

---

This obituary of Charles Rycroft appeared in *The Times* of 5 June 1998. It was unsigned but is reproduced here with the kind permission of its author, who died in October 1999.

read History and was then awarded a research studentship. In his postgraduate year he applied for psychoanalytic training.

Ernest Jones, the leading figure in British psychoanalysis at the time, suspected him of being a dilettante but told him that he might be accepted if he qualified in medicine. Rycroft applied to University College Hospital and, at the age of 23, he began a double training in medicine and psychoanalysis.

Once he was doubly qualified, he both practised psychoanalysis and did a variety of administrative jobs for the British Psychoanalytical Society until 1961, acting as scientific secretary for three years. His lucidity was a blessing to more than one of his audience, who often felt that they had understood a paper only after Charles had contributed to the discussion.

Through the 1950s he gradually became disillusioned with the infighting and rivalry between Kleinian and Freudian factions that characterized the British Psychoanalytical Society at that time—despite valiant efforts on the part of his second analyst, Sylvia Payne, to heal the rifts. He began, well before his time, to question the scientific basis of psychoanalysis and its intellectual isolation. He therefore made what he called a "strategic withdrawal" from the society and concentrated instead on writing reviews and articles for the wider public. Some felt that he did his cause (and that of psychoanalysis) a disservice by this, but Rycroft, a sensitive and shy man, preferred guerrilla warfare to full-scale confrontation. The idea of "Rycroftism" and forming yet another faction was anathema to him.

As a psychoanalyst he avoided jargon, and in his theoretical writing he always simplified Freud's technical terms and discarded whatever seemed to him inappropriately brought in from sciences such as physics. He related human behaviour to biology and insisted that psychoanalytic thinking was a linguistic discipline, being clinically a search for meaning; he pointed out that Freud's greatest book was entitled *The Interpretation of Dreams*, not *The Explanation of Dreams*.

Rycroft's best-known book, *A Critical Dictionary of Psychoanalysis* (1968b), was written before it was planned. During his psychoanalytical training he kept a list of definitions of technical terms as he met them. So, for the book, he had little more to do than put them in alphabetical order. He readily apprehended the need for structure and could write in clear and elegant English. It made him an excellent book reviewer and respondent to other people's papers and lectures. The short article was his ideal medium. The bibliography of his works consists of more than 160 such pieces and seven books, three of them selections of his short articles.

Rycroft's writings, both his two longer books, *Anxiety and Neurosis* (1968a) and *The Innocence of Dreams* (1979), and his collections of essays, have the double function of introducing psychoanalytic ideas to the general public and of re-examining those concepts and modifying them so as to make them less "scientific" and more semantic. Of Rycroft's three volumes of essays, perhaps the finest is *Psychoanalysis and Beyond* (1985). It is an excellent account of recent analytic thought, and all its pieces repay rereading. It typifies Rycroft's originality and clarity.

He believed that Freud's greatest contribution was his pointing to two levels in human consciousness—"primary" and "secondary"—the latter being rational and the former characterized by metaphor, most vividly seen in dreams. Rycroft argued that the "primary" processes were not primitive, as Freud had thought, but underlay all thinking, especially creativity. Imagination was a concept missing from psychoanalytic theory but was required to bridge the two modes of thinking. Bridges between normal and pathological, between conscious and unconscious, are a recurring theme in Rycroft's writings.

Despite his reticence and awesome erudition, he was, when suitably stimulated, a sociable man who enjoyed fun, gossip, and intense friendships. As an analyst he helped a large number of distinguished men and women. He was empathic and humane and never retreated behind a Freudian mantle. He had great tolerance of human frailty, while being quick to point out where his patients were deceiving themselves. He strongly believed that people should be allowed to make their own choices and never imposed a rigid number of sessions, length of treatment, or couch rather than chair. Unlike many analysts, he did not insist that his patients took their holidays at the same time as himself.

His intellectual fastidiousness, and the fact that he was by temperament a loner, meant that he eschewed religious or political organizations. However, he had strong beliefs in the possibility of amelioration of suffering at both personal and social level. He had a great respect for the past and for authentic choice. E. M. Forster's "only connect" was his motto. His ability to bring together the inner world of psychoanalysis with the wider sphere of psychotherapy, to trace links between the Establishment of his origins and the dissent of his adulthood, are qualities that will be sorely missed.

References

Rycroft, C. (1968a). *Anxiety and Neurosis*. London: Allen Lane/Penguin, 1971: London: Karnac, 1988.

Rycroft, C. (1968b). *A Critical Dictionary of Psychoanalysis*. London: Penguin. Second edition: London: Penguin, 1995.

Rycroft, C. (1979). *The Innocence of Dreams*. London: Hogarth Press.

Rycroft, C. (1985). *Psychoanalysis and Beyond*. London: Chatto Tigerstripe.

CHAPTER THREE

Charles Rycroft's contribution to contemporary psychoanalytic psychotherapy

Jeremy Holmes

To write about one's analyst, even after an interval of more than twenty years, is far from straightforward. The pitfalls of idealization, denigration, sibling rivalry with fellow patients, collusion, and narcissistic identification all militate against objectivity. On the other hand, to have been in a position to test a particular analytic approach *in vivo* must count for something, and being a patient can stimulate curiosity and a fascination with the analyst's ideas, which, with the passage of time, may reflect mature internalization that goes beyond acting out or oedipal intrusion. But if this piece strays outside the bounds of balanced exposition, perhaps due allowances will be made.

My chapter falls into three parts. First, I summarize Rycroft's critique of psychoanalysis as he encountered it in the period between 1940 and 1960 while training and working within the British Psychoanalytical Society. Second, I try to elaborate the theoretical perspective and psychotherapeutic methods that he developed in opposition to the conventional psychoanalysis of his day. Third, I link these with themes in contemporary psychoanalytic psychotherapy in an attempt to show how, even though he never formed a distinct school or movement or acquired overt followers, many of his ideas have passed into common currency.

First I must say something about Rycroft's style. To say that *le style c'est l'homme* would certainly be true of him, in both his literary and therapeutic personas. Clarity of thought, preciseness of phrase, freshness, wit, avoidance of cliché and jargon, a fondness for parentheses, an ability to stack one clause neatly upon another as each sentence wends its way to a satisfying conclusion—to read Rycroft is to be taken on a journey through intellectual territory with which he is so utterly at home that he can point out interesting anomalies and geographical curiosities without straying beyond the modest limits that he usually sets himself. There was something quintessentially *dapper* in Rycroft's whole approach—an lightness of touch, an ironic seriousness—that permeated his dress, his gait, his writing, his tentative yet authoritative interpretive stance, and his well-modulated tenor of voice and manner. He was, in short, a gentleman—in the Confucian sense of someone who is both true to himself and utterly respectful of others, polite but not conformist, caring but never controlling.

Peter Fuller, in his introduction to *Psychoanalysis and Beyond* (Rycroft, 1985b) emphasizes the *Englishness* of Rycroft in his response to a psychoanalysis that had sprung up on European soil, had transplanted to America with such apparent ease, but had never quite caught on in the mainstream of medical of intellectual life in Britain. For someone of Rycroft's intelligence and breath of vision, the oeuvre is modest, consisting mainly of essays and short pieces. Many of his best insights come as asides or throw-away lines. He displays all the virtues, and some of the limitations, of this English intellectual tradition: he is no system-builder; suspicious of grand theories and catch-all explanations, sensitive to illogicalities and paradox, he espouses common sense and abhors grandiosity and pretension.

To repeat, Rycroft's "Englishness" is both a strength and a weakness. In cricketing terms, now obsolete, one was either a gentleman or a player. Although after qualification in 1948 Rycroft rapidly established himself as a significant figure on the psycho-analytic scene, it was not long before he became increasingly reluctant to play psychoanalytic politics. He beat a "strategic retreat" (his phrase), which meant that he never, in my view, fully developed his central ideas within an atmosphere in which they could be challenged and extended. Although for a while an insider—he was scientific secretary of the Institute of Psychoanalysis in the 1950s and his admirable *Critical Dictionary*, never out of print since its publication in 1968, would be on the bookshelves of most practising psychoanalysts—he always felt somewhat excluded from the psychoanalytic inner circle and eventually ploughed a rather lonely furrow as psychoanalysis's psychoanalyst. As he put it, he took up "a stance external to both psychoanalysis as a theoretical system and the psychoanalytical movement as a socio-historical phenomenon; one which would, hopefully, enable me to be objective about both" (Rycroft, 1985b, p. 121).

This book is devoted to the idea of *legacy*—which at its most general can be understood as that which is handed down from one generation to the next. So it is perhaps legitimate to speculate how Rycroft's own legacy was cruelly interrupted by the death of his father when he was around 12. This had a significant material effect—he was never particularly well off—and it made him highly sensitive to the impact of loss and bereavement (one of several connections with his fellow psychoanalytic renegade, John Bowlby). To continue with this unwarranted psychobiographical speculation, when the process of identification with the father is interrupted, boys may then veer between slavish imitation, in the guise of "parentification", or "negative identification"—that is, unmodulated rebellion. Perhaps *The Critical Dictionary*, and Rycroft's mature stance *vis-à-vis* psychoanalysis, could be seen in part as a healthy transcendence of these two tendencies, born out of his response to his father's untimely death and an attempt to breathe fresh life into a psychoanalytic tradition that, he felt, had become ossified and infertile.

Rycroft's critique of psychoanalysis

Rycroft's central critique of classical psychoanalysis is that it presents itself as a *causal* theory of human behaviour rather than, as he chose to view it, as a theory of *meaning*. Psychoanalysis purports to find the causal or etiological origin of neurotic behaviour, and, armed with this knowledge, the patient is then supposedly liberated from its thrall. With his highly developed critical and sceptical sensitivity Rycroft understood that *causes* in the strictly scientific sense are highly unlikely to be unravelled in the consulting-room. His creative self saw the psychotherapeutic enterprise as an attempt to understand the patient's communications, direct and indirect. In this view psychoanalytic expertise consists in unravelling confused, disguised, or unwitting communication and in transmitting that understanding to patients, so that they may be better able to communicate with themselves. Most of Rycroft's major criticisms of psychoanalysis flow from this basic position.

He did not claim originality in this shift to a meaning-based metapsychology, merely associating himself with a number of authors such as Home, Shafer, and Erikson, who had come to similar conclusions. Jaspers, not as far as I know cited by Rycroft, similarly distinguished between understanding (i.e. an empathic and ultimately semantic account of human experience) and explanation (a causal theory about the origins of mental states), albeit from a psychiatric rather than a psychoanalytic tradition.

Rycroft's history-of-ideas angle on this is that Freud and subsequent psychoanalysts were keen to claim intellectual respectability for their new discipline and so dressed up their theories in pseudo-scientific garb, presenting psychoanalytic concepts such as ego, or the unconscious, or libido as though they had similar philosophical status to gravity or valency or genes. He questions the existence of these reified hypothesized psychological entities. For him there is no such thing as "an Unconscious"—a ghost in the machine that manipulates our waking consciousness—but, rather, unconscious *processes,* which need to be taken into account when trying to understand the complexities of human behaviour: "the unconscious is only a metaphor and . . . mental processes do not really take place inside anything and do not have spatial relations to one another" (Rycroft, 1985b, p. 115). From a Rycroftian perspective a dream or slip of the tongue is not "caused" by the workings of the unconscious or by repressed drives seeking discharge, but it can be unravelled (or interpreted—Rycroft points out that Freud's most famous work was not called "The Causes of Dreams") in terms of its personal meaning for the dreamer or malapropist.

Whether this radical espousal of hermeneutics and narrative really solves the problem of psychoanalysis's epistemological status is a question beyond the scope of this chapter. Psychoanalytic concepts can undoubtedly be subjected to scientific enquiry, although the consulting-room is perhaps not the best arena for such investigation. Nevertheless, Rycroft's perspective has the huge advantage of liberating dreams and slips of the tongue, and psychoanalysis generally, from the tyranny of psychic determinism. Perhaps dreams sometimes have a personal meaning, sometimes not; perhaps the meanings we attribute to dreams are post-hoc, imposed on them, as Wittgenstein suggested, by a meaning-making part of the mind that is distinct from the dream-forming process. This position is also compatible with Timpanaro's (1976; Rycroft, 1985b) famous critique of the Freudian theory of verbal slips of the tongue. Like Rycroft, Timpanaro is impressed by, but sceptical of, the virtuosity of Freud's explanations. As a Marxist social commentator who made his living as a proof-reader, he prefers to see most slips as resulting from compression and "banalization"—that is, the automatic elision of words and intrusion of standard phrases into complex text. Here, too, one can argue that sometimes a slip is of psychic significance, sometimes not, providing a more balanced and tentative perspective than the classical standard psychoanalytic approach.

This constructive tentativeness, coupled with rigorous logical criticism, coloured Rycroft's approach to therapy as well as theory. Although capable of being extremely tough, he would offer his interpretations in a questioning, provisional-seeming, way, allowing the patient to disagree, to elaborate, to correct minor details on his own behalf. Thus the whole process became open-ended and dialogic (to use an Americanism Rycroft would probably have disliked) rather than dogmatic or persecutory.

Although Rycroft saw psychoanalysis as a theory of meaning rather than causation, he sensed the danger of divorcing the discipline from its roots in medicine and evolutionary theory. Hence his description of psychoanalysis as a "*biological* theory of meaning" (his italics): that is, as rooted in the body and its destiny, with sex, birth, illness, and death as central themes. He saw the pseudo-scientific position of psychoanalysis as a trap that cut it off both from semantics and from the emerging new sciences of cybernetics and ethology. He was impressed with Bateson's ideas about communication deviance and double binds and with Bowlby's introduction of attachment theory as an evidence-based ethological angle on psychoanalysis. This espousal of the biological became an at one point an *ad hominem* (or rather *ad feminam*) assault: he viewed many psychoanalysts as essentially cerebral urban creatures who combined in a paradoxical way intense personal fastidiousness with a theoretical espousal of such primitive emotions as envy and hatred and greed:

> Most analysts . . . had quite uncanny ideas about nature and animals. They had just no idea how animals or bodies work. They would be aghast if a cat brought in a bird it had killed in the garden. Absolutely appalled! . . . Lots of analysts seemed to be determined to perform the sexual act by the use of intellect rather than instinct. [Rycroft, 1985b, p. 28]

(I don't entirely agree with this—it seems, rather, that some highly cerebral people are attracted to psychoanalysis because it provides an entrée for the body into their intellect-dominated world while at the same time providing a theoretical framework for this disturbing process of embodiment).

A third consequence of the shift of psychoanalytic emphasis from causes to meaning, from the expression of drives to communication, was that it enabled Rycroft to dispense with the presumed conflict between the "reality principle" and the "pleasure principle" and the consequent muddle that psychoanalysis tended to get itself into in relation to creativity and the imagination.

In classical Freudian metapsychology maturation and psychic health is seen as a shift from domination by the pleasure principle towards that of the reality principle, whereas in neurosis, so the argument goes, the opposite is true. Since much imaginative activity and artistic creation is clearly pleasurable and not based in reality, and yet is only tendentiously "neurotic", this creates serious theoretical difficulties. Here Rycroft, drawing heavily on Winnicott, but also on Coleridge and the romantic poets, argues that effective communication is both pleasurable *and* informative, and that there is a third zone—neither pure pleasure nor pure reality—where interpersonal exchange, playfulness, humour, and imagination hold sway. For him, psychic health is associated with a species of *poise*: being able to hold a balance between primary and secondary processes, being in touch with both reality and imagination. Neurosis, from this perspective, arises when there is an imbalance, or excess of one or the other. Here again we see the return of the notion of the Confucian gentleman, able to render (to change the religious metaphor) unto Caesar and to God in equal measure.

Rycroft's critique of the pseudo-scientific stance of psychoanalysis extended to the politics of psychoanalysis and to clinical practice itself. Real science is open to refutation: pseudo-science retreats into a closed self-referential system. Real science tests its ideas against reality: pseudo-science depends on unsubstantiated opinion and special pleading. Psychoanalysis at its worst is guilty of all such sins, and more. Rycroft was critical of what he saw as psychoanalytic over-valuation of interpretations, and especially transference interpretations, as the curative factor in therapy. Like Winnicott, he thought that "being there", holding, humanity, attention, and interest were as important as any special insights into the human psyche that psychoanalysis might claim. This position was not likely to endear him to those psychoanalysts who wanted to see their unique skills as the essential curative factors in neurosis and to devalue features that psychoanalysis might have in common with other psychotherapies.

> Transference interpretations do indeed indicate that the therapist possesses some theoretical ideas that enable him to elucidate matters that would otherwise be obscure; but . . . they also indicate that the therapist has been listening attentively, has remembered what the patient said during previous sessions and has been sufficiently interested to listen . . . therefore [they] are not merely ideas generated by a conceptual framework possessed by the therapist and fed by him to the patient's psychic apparatus, but also sentences uttered by a real live person who is devoting time and attention to another real live person. [Rycroft, 1985b, p. 63]

"Rycroftian" theory?

Given his fairly comprehensive, albeit piecemeal, critique of psychoanalysis, what did Rycroft, as a thinker and therapist who would not have been content with a purely atheoretical stance, find to put in place of the psychoanalytic ideas he rejected?

Here, I think, three influences can be detected: First, as already implied, there is the tradition of British empiricism and sceptical inquiry, which in a late essay he himself put under the heading of "Cambridge" (Rycroft, 1991). An offshoot of this was his capacity to locate both individual patients and psychoanalysis in a social and historical context, and thus to go beyond purely intrapsychic explanations and interpretations: "we are creatures of biological and *historical* destiny" (Rycroft, 1985b, p. 84, my italics).

This notion of historical determinism, with its flavour of the Marxism he imbibed at Cambridge in the 1930s, is balanced by a second major influence: the existential tradition, which can be summarized in the early Marxist idea that *man makes himself, on the basis of prior conditions*. I am not sure how intellectually enamoured Rycroft was with the sometimes obscure and rambling writings of "continental" philosophy, but he refers frequently to existentialism, and Rollo May, and, of course, his analysand Laing, get major entries in the *Critical Dictionary*. He cites John Macmurray, who could be described as a Scottish Christian existentialist. Macmurray was, in turn, one of Fairbairn's mentors, with whom Rycroft also clearly felt an intellectual affinity. The existentialist tenet that the essential humanness of man cannot be reduced to objective descriptors is consistent with Rycroft's critique of what he saw as psychoanalysis's reification and pseudo-objectification of the mind.

The notions of freedom, agency, and authenticity crop up frequently in Rycroft's writings, all of which can be linked to the existentialist tradition. Therapy's job, as he saw it, was to help patients liberate themselves from the constraints of upbringing, social expectation, and self-deception. He became a psychoanalyst at a time when to do so was slightly socially disreputable, and, although he claimed not to be able to understand one word of Lacan (personal communication), he would, I think, have been sympathetic to the radical edge to psychoanalysis that contemporary Lacanians have tried to revive. He was impressed by Shafer's (1976) "action language" for psychoanalysis, which views individuals as making and "choosing" their own lives. I place "choosing" in parentheses because clearly the idea of unconscious choice is problematic, and we certainly do not choose our biological and historical destiny. Nevertheless the idea of a person, or a Self, ultimately responsible for his or her own life, able to live with and overcome "Angst" (another favourite existential concept), is implicit in much of Rycroft's writing. Paul Tillich's (1952) famous title *The Courage to Be* was be a phrase of which Rycroft would have approved.

Similarly, Rycroft's emphasis on self-deception, false-self existence, or defendedness generally centres on the existentialist notion of *authenticity*. This can perhaps be linked with the idea of the "gentleman" as someone free from pretension and self-deception, who knows himself, accepts himself and others as they are, who retains his independence of mind without trying to impose it on others, who cannot be crushed, and who avoids all unnecessary violence. To live authentically is to be true to oneself, to have integrity in the literal sense, to be all of a piece, to be the "real thing", not some fake or simulacrum of a person, not conforming to expectations, inflating or adapting oneself for the sake of survival or self-aggrandisement or advancement.

Indeed, Rycroft is not above accusing Freud of moments of inauthenticity:

> I ... have often felt that there was something less than straightforward, something disingenuous, about his selection of which details about himself or his patients he should disclose or withhold on grounds of discretion, about his capacity to pass over obvious weaknesses in his arguments as though he himself had not noticed them, and about his tendency to have it both ways by offering incompatible interpretations simultaneously. [Rycroft, 1985b, p. 90]

Perhaps there is an element of an English gentleman's revenge here, from someone who had been accused of being an "upperclass dilettante" (Fuller, in Rycroft, 1985b) when he first applied for training at the Institute of Psychoanalysis and, once he did join, felt that non-Jews were treated as outsiders.

Authentic living is coherent living and is the antithesis of the "splitting of the ego" (Freud, 1938), which came into prominence with Kleinian authors like Rosenfeld and Segal. Like Klein, Rycroft saw Freud's late discovery of splitting as a defence mechanism (to use language he disliked) more profound than repression. It linked with such cultural notions as T. S. Eliot's "dissociation of sensibility" and the existentialist idea of alienation, and it was clinically relevant to the kind of patient he describes in "the analysis of a paranoid personality" (Rycroft, 1985a), who today would more likely be seen as borderline. While focusing on splitting as the primary source of inauthenticity, Rycroft also saw the need for benign dissociation in the sense of fostering through therapy a reflective self that is simultaneously actor and observer.

The third strand in Rycroft's non-analytic influences is, as I have mentioned, the Romantic tradition, and especially the writings of Keats and Coleridge. Without ever being quite explicit about it, I believe he saw psychotherapy at its best as an imaginative activity, akin to poetic responsiveness, and he would have seen the contemporary notion of countertransference, in which the analyst uses the feelings engendered in her by the patient to gain access to the patient's inner world, as a far more subtle and less automatic process than is often implied in psychoanalytic discourse. He was acutely aware of the implicit paradox in trying to legislate for spontaneity and creativity.

His paper "Psychoanalysis and the Literary Imagination", published both in *Psychoanalysis and Beyond* (1985b) and *The Innocence of Dreams* (1979), of which he was justly proud, tries to spell out the conditions under which imaginative activity is likely to flourish. These include "negative capability", the capacity to tolerate uncertainty without "irritably reaching after fact and reason"; the capacity to "play" with ideas and feelings without knowing in advance what their outcome might be; being able to encompass both "feminine" receptivity and "masculine" penetrativeness without too much anxiety; and having permeable ego-boundaries, thus being able to bring a wide variety of emotional and intellectual responses together without worrying about their sanity, respectability, or credentials. This benign splitting is the end-result of a developmental process that includes both the therapist's parental handling in childhood and the training therapy. For the therapeutic imagination to flourish, the therapist has the capacity to be receptive to herself, to be able to "hold" herself, to allow herself to be playful, and to tolerate awkward, embarrassing, or unacceptable aspects of herself. Here Rycroft's "biological theory of meaning" begins to come alive. Discovering meaning in therapy is no longer a scholastic exercise akin to code-breaking or dry lexicography, but an interpersonal activity that arises out of the sensitivities and subtleties of emotional communication, the prototype of which is, of course, mother–baby interaction. In their observational work with parents and infants, Trevarthen (1984) and others have shown these processes can be subjected to rigorous scientific enquiry without violating their essence.

There are links here too with Bion's (1970) notion of "maternal reverie", Winnicott's idea of transitional space as the "place where we live"(1971), Bollas's (1987) advocacy of freedom and spontaneity in the analyst's responses to the patient, Ogden's (1979) "analytic third". Rycroft's unique contribution comes not so much from the ideas he puts forward as, once again, from a particular *style* of thought and expression that exemplifies the very stance he advocates. He is less subjective than, say, Bollas and Ogden, less idiosyncratic that Winnicott, less theory-driven and obscure than Bion. For example:

> If the self tries to observe itself while creating it inevitably fails, since the self-as-agent must, willy nilly, become located in the observing, introspecting self and not in the part of itself it is trying to observe . . . the self that dreams, imagines, and creates is intrinsically nominative and can only be the subject of verbs, can only be "I" and never "me", and . . . it does a disappearing trick if one tries to push it into the objective, accusative position. [Rycroft, 1985b, p. 266]

This "subjective–objective", experiential–philosophical narrative style typifies Rycroft's analytic stance. It is highly sensitive to logical inconsistencies, concerned with the fundamentals of language and how people communicate not just with each other but also themselves, mixes clarity of thought with colloquialism and metaphor—"willy nilly", "disappearing trick"—in a way that is illuminating and memorable, is driven by ethical conviction and commitment—in this case to the fragility and importance of the imagination, and contains an implicit "accusation" that psychoanalysis has got it wrong if it tries to objectify creativity.

To conclude: how might Rycroft have viewed the contemporary psychotherapeutic and psychoanalytic scene? First, I think he would have welcomed the pluralistic world in which psychoanalysis, even if still in its own eyes *primum inter pares*, is but one among many psychotherapies, all of which are needed if the variety of human needs is to be met. (I once tried to explain to him the workings of psychodrama, which I had been pursuing in tandem with my psychoanalytic therapy. "Oh", he said, "you mean, it's a bit like playing charades at Christmas".) It is interesting, in thinking about Rycroft, to consider one of these new therapies, Hobson's Conversational Model—or Psychodynamic-Interpersonal therapy (PIT), as it is now called (Hobson, 1985; Margison, 2001). Hobson worked in public sector psychotherapy in Manchester, rather than the somewhat rarefied atmosphere of Wimpole Street. Hobson, like Rycroft, combined an interest in psychoanalysis, existentialism, and the romantic poetic tradition, was critical of persecutory tendencies within therapy, advocated a tentative negotiating style, and valued metaphor and meaning. Had Rycroft chosen to work in the NHS or had there been a University tradition of psychoanalysis in Britain, one could imagine the development of a similar Rycroftian therapy, called perhaps Psychodynamic Existential Therapy (PET) or even, given his interest in dreams, the Rycroftian–Existential Method (REM)!

Second, he would have been reassured to find that psychotherapy research has confirmed the importance of "common factors" in therapy (i.e. that non-specific conditions such as reliability, regularity, concerned interest, and so on, are as important in producing change as specific interventions such as transference interpretations) and the significance of the therapeutic alliance as the most reliable predictor of favourable outcome in the psychotherapy of whatever persuasion.

Third, he would have been interested to see how psychoanalysis is once more gradually opening itself up to "real" science—via attachment theory, child development studies, and neurobiology (Schore, 1994). For example, the distinction between "episodic" (*what* happened) and "semantic" (*how* it happened) memory in cognitive science is akin to Freud's distinction between secondary and primary processes as explicated by Rycroft, and this, in turn, can be linked with neural network theory that has come from computing science to neuroscience and now into psychoanalysis. Always an evolutionist, Rycroft would also have been interested in the applications of neo-Darwinism to psychotherapy (Holmes, 2001).

A final point concerns Rycroft's attitude towards "support" in psychotherapy. Some authors (e.g. Caper, 1998), including Freud, have tried to define the difference between psychoanalysis and other psychotherapies in terms of its neutrality and militant avoidance of persuasion or support. Caper argues that patients are continuously trying to manoeuvre therapists into superegoish condemnation or praise, and that therapists unconsciously collude with this and have continuously, via scrutiny of their countertransference, to bring themselves back to neutrality. Rycroft would, I think, have demurred here, arguing that Caper's project is inherently impossible, since there can never be a neutral Archimedean point from which to observe human nature, and that there is an inherent paradox at the heart of psychoanalysis, which simply has to be lived with. First, however well analysed and in touch with his countertransference, the therapist is always affected by the phenomena he is trying to observe: there are always two unconsciousnesses in the consulting-room communicating with one another, however "well analysed" one of them purports to be. Second, at a theoretical level, psychoanalysis cannot escape from the conundrum that "since psychoanalysis aims at being a scientific psychology, psychoanalytic observations and theorizing is involved in the paradoxical activity of using secondary process thinking to observe, analyse and conceptualize precisely that form of mental activity, the primary processes, which scientific thinking has always been at pains to exclude" (Rycroft, 1985b, p. 23).

Rycroft would, I think, argue that it is inevitable that the therapist will be, to a degree, supportive simply by virtue of her commitment to the therapeutic process, and that therapy is unlikely to be helpful if it is not supportive. What is necessary—I think he might have said (more elegantly than this of course)—is simultaneously to be supportive and to be able to reflect on the meaning and nature of that support and its impact on the patient. For instance, he would often allow sessions to proceed in quite a light, chatty way (in contrast to the uncompromising rigour of a Kleinian approach, at least as it tends to be caricatured) but then use this seemingly irrelevant conversation to open up deeper themes, rather as one might a dream or a Rorschach test.

This is actually a more psychologically holistic approach than classical psychic determinism, since it assumes that whatever interaction is set up between therapist and patient—describing a dream, a slip of the tongue, an apparently irrelevant conversation, or a supportive stance of the therapist—it will in one way or another reveal the key meanings and preoccupations of the patient. The therapist's skill lies in maintaining her benign split, or "double vision", between support and understanding meaning, and at the same time being able to communicate this to the patient.

Conclusion

Rycroft had a keen sense of history. When asked to describe "the God I want", he chose *Continuity*—the capacity simultaneously to look both forwards and backwards. He saw how some people who are attracted to psychoanalysis wish to become, literally, self-made men and women and to deny, destroy, or "ablate" their past and their parents in favour of their new psychoanalytic family. He is implicitly critical of this project, which denies the reality of the historical forces of which we are a product. At the same time he acknowledged, possibly with a touch of philosophical exasperation, that psychoanalysis is, *"sui generis"*, innovative, unclassifiable: "a psychological theory . . . which conforms to the cannons of neither the natural sciences, the humanities nor the arts" (Rycroft, 1985b, p. 230).

Kohon makes a similar point in his account of hysteria when he says that "psychoanalysis is like a nomadic tribe, never settling one place . . . it makes sense to talk about the double vision that the analyst needs to have" (Kohon, 1986, pp. 374–375). Rycroft possessed this double vision to the highest degree and used it with extreme tact. He was something of an intellectual nomad, but in this perhaps he was being more true to the paradox at the heart of psychoanalysis than his critics would like to think. He himself was certainly *sui generis*: highly individuated, deeply authentic, his own man, doing his own thing. He also embodied the spirit of continuity, both personally in his combination of conventionality and subversiveness, and professionally in his ability to mine the intellectual tradition of psychoanalysis while embracing new ideas from cybernetics and attachment theory. In sum, he was an agent of change and, quintessentially, a "gent".

References

Bion, W. (1970). *Attention and Interpretation*. London: Heinemann.

Bollas, C. (1987). *The Shadow of the Object: Psychoanalysis of the Unthought Known*. London: Free Association Books.

Caper, R. (1998). *A Mind of One's Own*. London: Routledge.

Freud, S. (1938). Splitting of the ego in the defensive process. *Standard Edition, 23*. London: Hogarth.

Hobson, R. (1985). *Forms of Feeling*. London: Routledge.

Holmes, J. (2001). *The Search for the Secure Base: Attachment Theory and Psychotherapy*. London: Routledge.

Kohon, G. (1986). *The British School of Psychoanalysis—The Independent Tradition*. London: Free Association Books.

Margison, F. (2001). Psychodynamic interpersonal therapy. In: J. Holmes & A. Bateman (Eds.), *Integration in Psychotherapy: Models and Metaphors*. Oxford: Oxford University Press.

Ogden, T. (1979). On projective identification. *International Journal of Psycho-Analysis, 60*: 357–373.

Rycroft, C. (1968). *A Critical Dictionary of Psychoanalysis*. London: Nelson/Penguin, 1970.

Rycroft, C. (1979). Psychoanalysis and the literary imagination. In: *The Innocence of Dreams*. London: Hogarth Press, 1991. [Also in: *Psychoanalysis and Beyond*. London: Chatto & Windus, 1985.]

Rycroft, C. (1985a). Miss Y—The analysis of a paranoid personality. In: *Psychoanalysis and Beyond*. London: Chatto Tigerstripe.

Rycroft, C. (1985b). *Psychoanalysis and Beyond*. London: Chatto & Windus.

Rycroft, C. (1991). Cambridge. In: *Viewpoints*. London: Hogarth Press.

Schore, A. (1994). *Affect Regulation and the Origin of the Self: The Neurobiology of Emotional Development*. Hove: Erlbaum.

Shafer, R. (1976). *A New Language for Psychoanalysis*. New Haven, CT: Yale University Press.

Timpanaro, S. (1976). *The Freudian Slip: Psychoanalysis and Textual Criticism*. London: Verso.

Tillich, P. (1952). *The Courage to Be*. London: Nisbet.

Trevarthen, C. (1984). Emotions in infancy. In: K. Scherer & P. Ekman (Eds.), *Approaches to Emotion*. Hove: Erlbaum.

Winnicott, D. (1971). *Playing and Reality*. London: Penguin.

CHAPTER FOUR

Charles Rycroft and ablation

Paul Roazen

A lthough it is a pleasure for me to try to pay tribute to Charles's originality within psychoanalysis, it is, of course, sad that he could not be present to listen to the kind of heartfelt tributes that he fully deserved to hear while still alive. I knew him from 1965 until 1998, and I would guess that he was shy enough not to have appreciated his success as an independent thinker. We fell into a pattern of usually seeing each other at dinner when I happened to come over to London, but I have checked my files and there are also approximately eighty letters from Charles there. On one of our last evenings together, he did remark that he felt that his career as an analyst had been "ruined" by the respective power of two women: Melanie Klein and Anna Freud. It is no doubt true that Charles's reputation and standing temporarily suffered from the complex politics of British psychoanalysis then, when ideological contests made it difficult for independent-minded people to win recognition. Although his *A Critical Dictionary of Psychoanalysis* (1968b) has become influential and widely sold, a book like *The Innocence of Dreams* (1979), even though admired by someone like Graham Greene, did not do as well in terms of sales as one might expect.

At the same time, I think that it would be understandable if Charles underestimated his own achievement; although books of essays and reviews (Rycroft, 1966, 1968a, 1968c, 1991; see also Rycroft, 1971) cannot be expected to prosper commercially, his work was, if only because of the impact of his publishing in *The New York Review of Books*, capable of being widely influential. Charles was like other early psychoanalytic pioneers in being broadly well-educated and cultured. It seems to me that in the face of the transitory fads and bureaucratic lethargy that afflict all fields, Charles did succeed in being a distinctive and original voice. Even though we no longer have the personal pleasure of Charles's intellect and person, I find that there is no problem in bringing to mind some of his most characteristic ways of thinking.

Psychoanalysis has had its distinctive manner of proceeding, and British analysts worked out their own special ways of conceptualizing things. Although a hundred years of Freud's school may not seem historically long, it has been enough to establish certain notable traditions of thought. Custom exerts its deleterious ways of inhibiting us, yet Donald Winnicott has been notably quoted on how impossible it would be to become creative apart from any received ways of thinking. In some sense Charles was curiously restricted by past ideas: like for most of us, his background did constrict how far he was able to go intellectually. And still, I think, he managed to break through independently on a variety of fronts.

I have chosen to discuss Charles's paper "On Ablation of the Parental Images, or The Illusion of Having Created Oneself" (1985). According to the *Oxford English Dictionary*, the word "ablation", dating back to the sixteenth century, means "removal", and ablation has come to signify cessation or remission within surgical, medical, and geological contexts. For a good while I did think that "ablation" had religious connotations, which a Catholic friend of mine assures me is, in fact, the case, but I now realize I had mainly mixed up the term with that of "oblation". It seems to me important that Charles implicitly was distinguishing ablation from either repression or denial, both of which he dealt with in his critical dictionary. I have picked this particular essay on ablation, which first came out in 1985, because it seems to me Charles at his best, and at the same time the most relevant to my own special concerns connected with the history of psychoanalysis.

I first met Charles in the summer of 1965, when I was in England interviewing early analysts about Freud. I also happened to be working on Jones's unsorted papers in the basement of the British Psychoanalytical Society; I came across Charles's name primarily because of his regularly reviewing then for the *Observer*, and I saw him once at his office. (He showed me then a scrap-book he had kept of the various newspaper reviews he had published; and I also have a distinct memory of his helpfully tutoring me in which order I should read various chapters of Winnicott's *Collected Papers*, 1968.) One time I saw Charles that summer, I took notes; he had just got back from Italy on a Sunday before a bank holiday, and he rang me up when his car was not ready. Our talk that day lasted, according to my records, nine-and-a-half hours; but the first subject I marked down—and this was the only occasion with Charles on which I made any such written report—concerned the issue of "self-created fantasies", the obliterating of the parent of the same sex, which could be "destructive" and also "creative". I understood Charles to be proposing an interesting variation on the familiar story of Oedipus.

I noted for myself, probably thinking of Freud, Charles's point that if one is both ego and father, then opposition to oneself becomes *lèse majesté*—the gods themselves have been offended. (That would help account, Charles thought, for one of the sources of Freud's intolerances about other people's ideas.) In my first book (1968), I cited Charles on how Freud's long-standing desire to get to Rome could be interpreted, symbolically, as the wish to transcend the religion of obedience to the father by the religion of love (Roazen, 1968, p. 176n). In this connection I had recommended to Charles the early biography of Freud by Helen Walker Puner (1992), and he read it; this point of Charles's about Freud and Christianity came up in a letter to me as part of his response to Puner's work. But Charles's more general idea was that if someone is to become his own father, then he has to create himself—which imposes quite a task, which can only be accomplished by a life-work. Genealogy of analysts is important, and what any father did for a living matters. But if one has obliterated one's biological parents, there is a lot to atone for—one must make up for it somehow.

It turns out that the original version of the Ablation essay had been written in 1965, but it was rejected both by the editors of the *International Journal of Psycho-Analysis* and by the editors of the International Psychoanalytic Library, which brought out Charles's *Imagination and Reality* (1968c). It was, Charles later wrote, thought "impolitic to publish an essay which discussed some of the psychopathological reasons which may lead people to become psychoanalysts" (Rycroft, 1985). After I had published a book on Erik H. Erikson (Roazen, 1976), Charles wrote to me as follows:

> A propos Erikson's name change: Some years ago I wrote a paper called On Ablation of the Parental Images or The Illusion of Having Created Oneself in which I described a group of patients who attempted to disown their pasts entirely, who denied that their parents had had any effect on them whatsoever, and who, if they were drawn to analysis as they often seemed to be, dated their lives from the moment they started analysis and regarded their true parent [sic] as having been their analyst and their true ancestry his or her analytical lineage. Such people, I said, aspired to be self-made in the most literal sense of the word or, if they couldn't achieve that, to have parents whom they themselves chose. When I read this paper to a group of analysts, I was embarrassed to discover that my thesis applied too well to too many analysts; most of the examples I had chosen were people who had aspired unsuccessfully to become analysts, but my paper gave the impression of being a roman à clef about actual analysts. It sounds as though Erikson exemplifies my thesis up to a point though I certainly didn't have him in mind when I wrote it. [10 November 1976]

Charles, then, evidently in response to what I wrote him, sent me (on 29 November 1976) a manuscript of his "On Ablation" paper, which did not appear in print for almost another decade. Incidentally, Charles commented in sending me that typescript: "If you ever think of having another go at my collected papers, read them in reverse order of printing. About half-way through I started eliminating technical terms from my style, and the later papers are quite readable."

As I once again re-read Charles's Ablation essay for purposes of this writing, I was struck at the outset by his referring to "the ahistorical tendency characteristic of ablators of parental images" (1985, p. 215). I should perhaps interject my conviction now that history-writing is inherently a subversive activity: students of history necessarily undermine generally received wisdom. Authoritarian regimes all through time have not been friendly to genuine historical activity. I am putting aside purely celebratory work—what in the States we would call flag-waving—in favour of the objective of history to expand our imaginations. Condescension about the past can be expressed in a variety of ways, such as righteous present-mindedness.

A typical lack of respect for historical sequences has, I think, bedevilled the writing about psychoanalysis to an exceptional extent. In my recent book (Roazen, 2000) about Edward Glover (someone whom Charles admired as a clinician—for a time they both practiced as part of the same suite at 18 Wimpole Street), I was essentially trying to introduce a complicating element into the generally received Family Romance among British analysts. Any simple line from Freud to Abraham or Ferenczi to Klein needs, I believe, to be seriously complicated. And Charles was, in general, also putting his finger on another typical feature of the literature about analysis when he commented on how ablators "seek out 'ideal' intellectual ancestors to replace the actual ones they have dismissed" (Roazen, 2000, p. 216).

The issue for the intellectual historian of establishing continuities as well as discontinuities within psychoanalysis, which I have found to be an essential problem with the literature, would appear to be entirely consistent with Charles's thesis about ablation. When Charles refers to patients who do not attend the funerals of their parents or "feel relief rather than grief afterwards", he might well have cited the example of Freud's own reaction to the death of his mother (see Roazen, 1975, p. 41). Charles intended to suggest that "the creativeness, the falsity and the dishonesty all derive from the same source": ablation. And he also had in mind that "persons of this kind may be drawn to psychoanalysis and the psychoanalytic movement in a way that may, perhaps, be beneficial to them but is harmful to psychoanalysis" (Rycroft, 1985, p. 220). The process of re-creating the self "can be regarded as imaginative and creative", but "it is also false, since it can only be squared with the dreary truth by suppression of some facts, by distortion of others and by subordination of memory to mythopoesis" (pp. 220–221).

In the erasing of the past and starting afresh, "the original parental values continue to operate unconsciously in an unmodified form":

> This unconscious survival of the consciously ablated parental images is responsible for the paradoxical picture such people often present to the world; messianic in their advocacy of their own self-created ideas, but shifty and ill at ease in their way of presenting them. If they write scientific papers their acknowledgements are either scanty or obscure, or, contrariwise, so extensive that their real indebtedness is hidden as successfully as a needle in a haystack. They are uniformly anti-historical, or rather ahistorical.... [Rycroft, 1985, p. 222]

Charles was arguing that their "denial of indebtedness ... makes them creative" (p. 223). And he used a passage from Sartre's autobiography *Words* in order show how "despair evoked by the absence of a living paternal image and by alienation from the body can be warded off by self-idealization" (p. 224). Charles also thought that his series of patients who were "ablators" were characteristically "incapable of grief" (p. 225).

Although ablators come to psychoanalysis for "genuine" reasons, "corrupt" ones also intrude: "there are certain aspects of the psychoanalytic situation which appeal to ablators because they seem to them to be designed to enhance the myth of self-creation and to provide opportunities for strengthening, not dissolving, their defensive system" (p. 227).

> Patients and student analysands who do in fact succeed in being analysed by the analyst of their own choice often, it seems to me, become proselytizers of their analyst's theories as much out of personal vanity as out of genuine appreciation and gratitude for his understanding and skill ... .reversing the humiliating biological fact that he did not choose his own parents. [p. 227]

Psychoanalysis is still recent enough for ablators "to argue, while remaining this side of madness, that nothing was known about human nature before Freud" (p. 228).

Charles was explicitly linking his argument to the state of British psychoanalysis. He pointed to

> the mere existence within the British Psycho-analytic Society of three—or it is more?—different schools of theory and technique, all of which claim to have better therapeutic results than the others. For such a bizarre situation to have arisen and to be still existing, some people must be deceiving themselves, some people must be idealizing their own ideas and work or that of their analysts, and objective criteria for deciding what kinds of patients are suitable for treatment and what sorts of results should be deemed successes must be entirely lacking. [p. 229]

Charles sounded concerned lest it be "unduly cynical" for him to propose that "in such a nebulous, ill-defined field, inauthentic, spurious characters can survive and flourish" (p. 229).

Charles was, importantly, proposing that psychoanalysis "has a special attraction for people whose own relationship to their bodies and their past is ambiguous and whose own inner frames of reference are ill-defined" (p. 230).

Charles pointed out that such ablators could be led "to idealization of the training analysis and of the so-called "apostolic succession" and to a tendency to believe that an analyst's competence derives solely from his personal analysis" (p. 230). (The problem of training analyses, and possible drawbacks or even its history, has been, I think, a curiously neglected subject—see Roazen, 2003a, pp. 51–57.) He was also alluding to a factor leading to "the social isolation of psychoanalysts", who could pursue their work "not as a profession but as a calling" (Rycroft, 1985, p. 231). And he was calling attention to the possible neglect of the significance of both biology and genetics. He concluded his paper, in his re-written 1973 form, by citing Winnicott's distinction between the "true self" and the "false self": "the 'true self' . . . is the depository of what the individual inherits from his parents, and can elaborate into something which is truly and uniquely himself, whereas it is the false self which harbours the defences, the disguises and the pretensions" (p. 232).

Now why does this paper of Charles's, entirely aside from the merits of its theses, seem so important to me? First of all, his argument has antecedents within my own psychoanalytic upbringing. One of the early people who inspired me, in the course of my interviewing her, was Helene Deutsch; and she had published an early paper on pathological lying, and she wrote some famous articles on the absence of grief, impostors, and what she called the "as-if" personality (Deutsch, 1965a, 1965b, 1965c, 1992a, 1992b, 1992c, 1992d; see also Roazen, 1985). She was also interested in "parthenogenesis" as an aspect of female psychology (Deutsch, 1965d, pp. 193 ff., 1991). While in no way denying Freud's stature in intellectual history, Helene had been trying to point to other aspects of human psychology that lay beyond the strict Oedipus complex.

Neurosis implies the presence of structured inner conflicts, whereas Helene Deutsch—and Charles also on ablators—was going beyond classical psychoanalytic thought. I remember her teaching me, in her nineties, that "the absence of affect is a feeling too". It is here, I think, that great literature, including even Shakespeare, can easily be misleading: Macbeth, Hamlet, Lear, and Othello are all examples of tragic heroes whose rich emotional responses are apt to seem prototypical. Yet in reality many of us often fall into the category of what Freud more than once dismissed as "riff-raff": people incapable of fulfilling the demanding example of the greatest literary models. In real life people do not live up to the psychological glamour of Tolstoy's Anna Karenina or Flaubert's Emma Bovary. It would be a romantic fallacy to think that Conrad's Lord Jim or any other great literary character were anything other than exceptional; in treating a self-destruction or suicide as a sign of the presence of character, Conrad was promoting a special idealistic view of human nature.

But comparatively little attention is apt to get paid to the issue of the relative absence of character. If I illustrate this with the example of Erik Erikson, I hope it should be taken for granted that I consider him one of the most creative analysts in the whole history of the field. But his name change was part and parcel of the new identity that early psychoanalysis could offer people: I am thinking of Otto Rank's also inventing his own last name. Although genuine ancestry took a distinct backseat in Erikson's efforts at autobiographical self-presentation, at the same time he exaggerated his own direct lineage to Freud. According to Erikson's most thorough biographer, when the Eriksons left Vienna in 1933,

"Freud came to the railroad station to see his family off, urging Erik to have a kind and loving heart" (Friedman, 1999, p. 97).

Now the truth is that by 1933 Freud was a sick old man who had had his jaw cancer for ten years; Erikson had only recently been accepted as a member of the Vienna Psychoanalytic Society and was of no notable standing either among the analysts or to Freud personally. Leaving Vienna was in general hardly favoured by Freud, even if Erikson had been jumped from associate membership to being a full member for the sake of being possible "export ware". For me it seems preposterous to believe that Freud actually came to that railroad station, whatever Erikson may have told the one source that his biographer later relied on. To me Erikson was engaged in fabricating a family romance of his own. (Perhaps Erikson was unconsciously competing with his later rival, Heinz Kohut, who reportedly had gone to the railroad station in Vienna to see Freud off in 1938.)

Erikson's own tortured relation to his parents got him into public trouble when he appeared to be guilty of autobiographical bad faith in connection with disguising his wholly Jewish ancestry. Yet this heavily ambivalent family background had not only helped stimulate his professional fantasies about his origins within the family of psychoanalysts but later interfered with his own parenting. Not only was Erikson less than ideal in fulfilling his own standard of "generativity" when it came to helping his own students (Erikson did not notably assist them), but his daughter has been publicly campaigning against Erikson as having been a disappointingly poor father to her. Remember, biological families are full of natural injustices—discrepancies of talent, birth order, emotional preference—from which any intelligent person can need to escape.

With all the psychoanalytic piety that has been associated with the figure of Freud himself, it seems to me that analysts themselves have had a striking lack of natural filial allegiance. A Paris analyst I know had a mother who was a professional painter, and when the Hartmanns were passing through on their way eventually to the States, she painted a portrait of Dora Hartmann. When my friend mentioned that she still had the painting, implying that it belonged elsewhere, I suggested that perhaps one of the Hartmann sons would want it. But when I asked them about it, not only was there no special eagerness for it, but I was asked: "Was it a good painting?" At the same time it seems to me worth pointing out how young grandchildren of Ernst and Marianne Kris wrote to Anna Freud as if she were a realistic family member.

Charles's concept of ablation helps to highlight something missing in many of the early analysts. To take an instance that has become notable: Anna Freud's analysis by her father (Roazen, 2003a, pp. 41–50). It could be asked to what extent the psychoanalytic parentage overtook the familial one. And subsequently Anna Freud proposed, within the context of dealing with legal custody problems for children, the notion of psychological parenthood as opposed to biological parenthood. (She accorded the psychological caretaker special preferential standing.) The analysis of Anna by her father remained a secret for many years, thanks to people like Marianne Kris and others: one has to ask for what purposes of family devotion these people were being defensive.

Charles's notion of the significance of ablation can help us to understand elements of phoniness and creativity. Inauthenticity can involve more subtle problems than one might imagine, and these help to account for the way the scholarship associated with so much in the professional literature strikes someone like me as a Potemkin village of artificial constructs. When in the course of my once interviewing Helene Deutsch I asked her whether she would like me to bring in to her the autobiography of her early mentor Julius Wagner-Jauregg, the first psychiatrist to win a Nobel Prize, she really had no interest in the subject. Although Wagner had once been a great figure in her life, after she became an analyst he was in a sense gone—almost as if he had ceased to exist for her. It might go almost without saying that Helene Deutsch, like so many of the other early analysts, had successfully escaped from her own Polish origins into the psychoanalytic family. Lest I needlessly leave others out of this ablation story, Melanie Klein's attempt to hold on to Abraham as the legitimizing source of her work really amounted to a hollow attempt to sustain her own psychoanalytic lineage. One would think it obvious that Freud's own extremely harsh private judgement about her contribution was, after his death, partly being enacted by Anna Freud and Edward Glover in the course of the struggle known as the Controversial Discussions.

The establishing of credentials becomes a key to often spurious, recurrent aspects of important thinkers throughout the history of psychoanalysis. Bruno Bettelheim was as inventive about his past as anybody in this regard (see Pollak, 1997; Sutton, 1996); and Masud Khan's first biographer must have been surprised to find that, despite Khan's earlier claims, there was no record at Balliol College, Oxford, of his ever having attended there (Cooper, 1993). The examples that one might assemble to illustrate the significance of ablation within psychoanalysis are almost too numerous to mention. How any of us deals with the past is partly a cultural matter and differs from country to country; the Japanese, for example, have thoroughly ablated General MacArthur's old offices in Tokyo, and Italians can be curiously blank about Mussolini. But Charles was pointing to ablation being a psychological question as well.

The students that any prominent analyst acquires become part of the legend within the family. Although Charles and I never discussed those he had trained, perhaps now would be the time to mention that among his analysands were such distinguished people as Alan Tyson, R. D. Laing, and Peter Lomas, to list only a few of those talented people who sought Charles out.

As much attention has been given in the field to constructing an informal family tree of who was whose analyst, everybody has steered clear of the emotionally charged issue of the real children of analysts and what they might have to report. Melanie Klein's daughter, Melitta Schmideberg, would be at the extreme end of the spectrum of those who relished hatred of their mothers but, alas, not alone in her bitterness towards analytic parenting.

It has to be curious how little attention has also been given to the gratifications and frustrations of being a training analyst. For Charles, though, the difficulties between Melanie Klein and Anna Freud made for a family row that he wanted to stand back from. Sylvia Payne was, I think, right in considering it unfortunate for Charles that so soon after the Second World War he was pushed into official office-holding within the British Psychoanalytical Society. Although his stepping outside traditionalist lines came to be one of his sources of originality, this reward was balanced by how easy it could be for others to ignore his contributions. The peril of ostracism for having betrayed the psychoanalytic family can be harsh; although heresy can be attractive to some, unconscious conformism can be even more inhibiting to many. Charles's security, stemming from his integrity as well as partly from his aristocratic social position, may have made him sensitive to the false pretensions of others. (My own American ignorance of proper British social rules might have helped Charles relax with me.)

In his writing about the significance of ablation within psychoanalysis, Charles had succeeded in highlighting a central aspect of my own interest in this field. For me what has counted more than anything was the history of psychoanalysis; and it was precisely because of the anti-historical or ahistorical bias within the field, which Charles had been trying to explain, that intellectual historians like myself could find so much of enduring interest. Even now, with all that has been published, I think there is a relative dearth of real historical scholarship in this whole area. Which theorist came before which other thinker still remains largely unexplored: as much as Winnicott admired Erik Erikson, for example, at least one book about Winnicott makes no mention of Erikson. Then, although I have already made the point in print, Peter Gay's biography of Freud proceeded without once raising the name of Wilhelm Reich (Roazen, 2001). Heinz Kohut skipped over the work of Franz Alexander, just as Alexander had dodged Jung. I have long been convinced that the early analysts were a fascinating group of pioneers whose lives and ideas will continue to be of historical interest. As a matter of fact, I would want to contend that the people involved in early analysis, and the fascinating stories that surround them, may be much the most important part of what the future needs to be reminded of. These analysts can be models of the problems that creative individuals have to deal with.

At least this is the historiographic side of things that I mainly talked about with Charles; and I regularly sent him examples of what I had most recently written. It is my impression that as the years passed, he grew bolder and more emancipated. And I am not alluding here to his allowing his membership in the British Psychoanalytical Society to lapse. When my *Brother Animal*, exploring Freud's relationship to Victor Tausk, first came out in 1969, Charles must have had difficulties with it; his introverted review (Rycroft, 1970), which I do not think we ever discussed and he failed to reprint, was, I think, hobbled by the constraints of traditionalist thinking. Charles's published view of my book might have lacked anything easily quotable for publicity purposes, but what he wrote was enough for Kurt Eissler to include Charles as part of Eissler's wholesale denunciation of *Brother Animal*; Charles was resentful enough to write to Eissler in protest. Anthony Storr, although I had only met him long after I was first in contact with Charles, had come from such a different intellectual tradition that he had no difficulty welcoming the book in an enthusiastic review. Peter Lomas—who, I only later found out, had been trained by Charles— was also unambivalent about *Brother Animal*. When Charles later reviewed the Freud–Jung letters for *The New York Review of Books*, he was so startled that he wondered whether they should ever have been published. The more time passed, the freer Charles could be in his thinking.

I cannot help wondering now what he would have thought of recent findings of mine in connection with how Freud, Anna Freud, and Jones dealt with the problem posed for the International Psychoanalytical Association by the rise to power of the Nazis (Roazen, 2003b, pp. 1–34). The main culprit of the tale, Ernest Jones, threw a retrospective smokescreen over what happened. (I felt so badly about the unfortunate role Jones played in my Glover book that I put in a particularly sympathetic photograph of Jones in his last days.) Charles had personal familiarity with Jones, who had interviewed him as an analytic candidate and then later, when Jones was travelling in America to take part in celebrating Freud's hundredth birthday, temporarily transferred to Charles a long-standing patient of Jones's from one of Britain's most prominent families. Does the concept of ablation help make comprehensible Jones's many idealizations of Freud? I am inclined to be less chari-table about Jones than Charles's concept might imply; for when it came to Jones's own behaviour on behalf of the IPA, and how he later tried to cover it up in his biography of Freud, it is hard for me not to think that Jones was deliberating lying about what had happened. To compress the story into a nutshell: the IPA reacted to the Nazis organizationally very much the way Jung had, in that there was created a category of direct international membership for those Jewish analysts in Germany who would otherwise not have had psychoanalytic legitimacy. But Charles's concept of ablation does help to understand why legitimate psychoanalytic credentials have always mattered so much.

As an intellectual I think Charles would have been intrigued by the story of post–Second-World-War psychoanalysis in Germany. An analyst (Carl Müller-Braunschweig)—who, we now know, gave away the names of Jewish Italian analysts to the German authorities—later became, following the collapse of the Nazi regime, along with a tiny handful of others—including one former Nazi Party member—the leader of what became a huge group of IPA German analysts. Collaboration with Adler and Jung was deemed more objectionable to the IPA authorities than whatever had happened with Hitler, and "revisionist" German analysts were excluded from the IPA. The German analysts have had to deal with their own questionable past, and ablation has not proven wholly successful. But Charles, I think, had managed to raise a key aspect of their psychological need for legitimate succession.

I suppose that with this small contribution I am trying to fit my own work into some sort of historical lineage. If my sort of thinking was O.K. with Charles, then perhaps Anna Freud might have been wrong when she once declared in a letter to Eva Rosenfeld: "All I can say is that Roazen is a menace whatever he writes" (in Roazen, 1993, p. 201). (The fact that in England Eva Rosenfeld successfully disguised her own prior analysis with Felix Boehm in Berlin could also be interpreted within Charles's concept of ablation: Roazen, 2001, p. 87. In 1965 Charles had encouraged me to see Eva as someone likely to be uninhibited, and he seemed pleased later to have been proved right.) When I presented some of my ideas about Edward Glover at the Portman Clinic in 2000, I was a bit bewildered to be told by one member of the audience that I ought to be presenting them at the Anna Freud Centre. I like to think that what is valuable about my work on Glover is that I succeeded in showing that the controversy about him fits none of the standard stereotypes. Myth-making about "heretics" like Adler and Jung, who remain even today psychoanalysis's "usual suspects", is part of the mythopoesis about which Charles wrote. When I had evidently in reviewing Charles's *Psycho-Analysis and Beyond* for *The New Statesman* twitted him about ignoring one of his own analysts, Sylvia

Payne, Charles wrote me (20 September 1985): "So far from mind-ing about your reservations I am pleased to receive constructive criticism—your implication that I am a bit of an ablator myself must, I think, be right." I was, of course, pleased when Charles quoted me in 1990 while reviewing a book of Peter Gay's in the *Times Literary Supplement* (Rycroft, 1990).

Peter Ackroyd's biography of Dickens contains a passage that reminds me of the general significance of Charles's notion of abla-tion. Ackroyd is referring to a "kind of filial betrayal" on Dickens's part:

> in a sense he had rejected both of his parents when he recreated himself in language. In that self-engendering which takes place in the act of composition he was in a sense divesting himself of origins and claiming a kind of imaginative orphanhood. Partly out of ambition, partly out of egoism. [Ackroyd, 1990, p. 830]

(Dickens, who carefully assembled the outlines and corrections for each of his books, ideal children, could be appallingly poor with his natural offspring—Roazen, 2003a, pp. 81–93) However central an issue in artistic creativity ablation may be, I think it has special relevance for psychoanalysis. Recently in Paris an analyst took me aside to show me that he had acquired at auction the ring that Freud had once bestowed on Marie Bonaparte. And I remember how struck I once was by Erik Erikson's having dedicated a book to Anna Freud at a time when she was keeping her distance from his work. Above all, perhaps, ablation as a concept can help one to understand why it has been so often a case of *lèse majesté* to talk about Freud within the regular categories of intellectual history.

The illusion of having created oneself played a role in Freud's biography even at the time of his death. For in deciding to have himself cremated, at odds with Jewish custom, and the arrange-ment by which his ashes were placed in an ancient Greek urn given him by Marie Bonaparte, meant that Freud was being self-creative one final time. (His more traditionally Jewish wife, at whose later funeral there was a rabbi, nevertheless asked to have her own ashes added to Freud's. Since there was not enough room, some of her remains were scattered.) The concept of ablation also helps one to understand the complexities of Freud's relationship with his intellectual predecessors, as well as how he could be throughout his career so preoccupied with the theme of plagiarism.

I hope that my paying tribute to the memory of Charles reflects the conviction that he succeeded in making himself into a genuinely original thinker within the tradition in which he matured. The spiritual daring I found in Charles was in a sense an extension of Freud's own historic independence, even though that common trait had inevitably to lead in different directions, and I found his brilliance fully matched by his broad humanity.

References

Ackroyd, P. (1990). *Dickens.* New York: Harper Collins.

Cooper, J. (1993). *Speak of Me As I Am: The Life and Work of Masud Khan.* London: Karnac.

Deutsch, H. (1965a). Absence of grief. In: *Neuroses and Character Types: Clinical Psychoanalytic Studies* (pp. 226–236). New York: International Universities Press.

Deutsch, H. (1965a). The imposter. In: *Neuroses and Character Types: Clinical Psychoanalytic Studies* (pp. 319–338). New York: International Universities Press.

Deutsch, H. (1965a). Some forms of emotional disturbances and their relationship to schizophrenia. In: *Neuroses and Character Types: Clinical Psychoanalytic Studies* (pp. 262–281). New York: International Universities Press.

Deutsch, H. (1965d). Motherhood and Sexuality. In: *Neuroses and Character Types: Clinical Psychoanalytic Studies.* New York: International Universities Press.

Deutsch, H. (1991). *Psychoanalysis of the Sexual Functions of Women,* ed. Paul Roazen. London: Karnac.

Deutsch, H. (1992a). Clinical and theoretical aspects of "as if" characters. In: *The Therapeutic Process, The Self, and Female Psychology: Collected Psychoanalytic Papers* (pp. 215–220), ed. Paul Roazen. New Brunswick, NJ: Transaction.

Deutsch, H. (1992b). On the pathological lie. In: *The Therapeutic Process, The Self, and Female Psychology: Collected Psychoanalytic Papers* (pp. 109–121), ed. Paul Roazen. New Brunswick, NJ: Transaction.

Deutsch, H. (1992c). On a type of pseudo-affectivity (the "as if" type) In: *The Therapeutic Process, The Self, and Female Psychology: Collected*

Psychoanalytic Papers (pp. 193–207), ed. Paul Roazen. New Brunswick, NJ: Transaction.

Deutsch, H. (1992d). Two cases of induced insanity. In: *The Therapeutic Process, The Self, and Female Psychology: Collected Psychoanalytic Papers* (pp. 91–100), ed. Paul Roazen. New Brunswick, NJ: Transaction.

Friedman, L. J. (1999). *Identity's Architect: A Biography of Erik H. Erikson* New York: Scribner.

Pollak, R. (1997) *The Creation of Dr. B.: A Biography of Bruno Bettelheim.* New York: Simon & Schuster.

Puner, H. W. (1992). *Sigmund Freud: His Life and Work* (with a new Introduction by Paul Roazen). New Brunswick, NJ: Transaction.

Roazen, P. (1968). *Freud: Political and Social Thought.* New York: Knopf; London: Hogarth Press, 1969; New Brunswick, NJ: Transaction, 1999 (3rd edition).

Roazen, P. (1969). *Brother Animal.* New York: Knopf.

Roazen, P. (1975). *Freud and His Followers.* New York: Knopf; New York, Da Capo, 1992.

Roazen, P. (1976). *Erik Erikson: The Power and Limits of Vision.* New York: Free Press; Northvale, NJ: Jason Aronson, 1997.

Roazen, P. (1985). *Helene Deutsch: A Psychoanalyst's Life.* New York, Doubleday; New Brunswick, NJ: Transaction, 1992 (2nd edition, with new Introduction).

Roazen, P. (1993). *Meeting Freud's Family.* Amherst, MA: University of Massachusetts Press.

Roazen, P. (2000). *Oedipus in Britain: Edward Glover and the Struggle Over Klein.* New York: Other Press.

Roazen, P. (2001). *The Historiography of Psychoanalysis* (pp. 246–247). New Brunswick, NJ: Transaction.

Roazen, P. (2003a). *On the Freud Watch: Public Memoirs.* London: Free Association Books.

Roazen, P. (2003b). *Cultural Foundations of Political Psychology.* New Brunswick, NJ: Transaction.

Rycroft, C. (1966). *Psychoanalysis Observed.* London: Constable.

Rycroft, C. (1968a). *Anxiety and Neurosis.* London: Allen Lane.

Rycroft, C. (1968b). *A Critical Dictionary of Psychoanalysis.* London: Penguin Books. Second edition: London: Penguin Books, 1995.

Rycroft, C. (1968c). *Imagination and Reality.* London: Hogarth Press.

Rycroft, C. (1970). Freudian triangles: Book review of *Brother Animal. The Observer,* 26 April.

Rycroft, C. (1971). *Reich.* London: Fontana.

Rycroft, C. (1979). *The Innocence of Dreams.* London: Hogarth Press.

Rycroft, C. (1985). On ablation of the parental images, or The illusion of having created oneself. In: *Psycho-Analysis and Beyond* (pp. 214–232), ed. Peter Fuller. London: Chatto & Windus.

Rycroft, C. (1990). Freud's best face. *Times Literary Supplement*, 6–12 July.

Rycroft, C. (1991). *Viewpoints*. London: Hogarth Press.

Sutton, N. (1996). *Bettelheim: A Life and Legacy*. New York: Basic Books.

Winnicott, D. W. (1968). *Collected Papers: Through Paediatrics to Psycho-Analysis*. London: Tavistock Publications.

CHAPTER FIVE

The development of Charles Rycroft's thought

Margaret Arden

C harles Rycroft began his private practice in 1947, before completing his psychoanalytic training. He was still practising a week before his death in 1998, just over half a century later. I shall try to give some idea of the development of his thinking from his early writing, when he was within the mainstream of the British Society, to his late development as an independent thinker and writer. I shall be using two sources of information: his own published work and my personal recollections of him. Rycroft was my training analyst until 1962, and I read all his papers soon after they were published. I had always been in the habit of thinking for myself, and he never made any attempt to influence me. Through reading his work, I was able to continue on my own path. Many years later I had a second analysis with him, during which I began to write papers of my own. He always made it clear to me which of my ideas he accepted and where he disagreed with me. He never made any value judgements about what I wrote but always made me feel that I had his support in my exploration of ideas. He approved in general of the way in which I built on his work in my own writing, but sometimes he thought I was trying to describe things that, he felt, were better left unsaid.

From the early 1980s we met as fellow members of the 1952 Club, where psychoanalytical ideas are discussed in a non-political atmosphere.

I shall begin with a brief account of his background and education. Rycroft was born in 1914 and spent his early years in the secure environment of an upper-class country house. His mother was the second wife of Sir Richard Rycroft the Fifth Baronet, whom Charles described as the most important man in the village. His father died when Charles was 11, and his mother had to return with her four children to her own family, as her stepson inherited the title. The death of his father and his mother's subsequent depression greatly affected Charles's future. His father had expected Charles to have an Army career. This was also the expectation at his school, Wellington College, which had been founded for the sons of officers killed in the First World War. Charles wrote that he was left very much to make his own decisions about his career, and it was a relief when there was no opposition at home or at school.

Rycroft read economics and history at Cambridge and then spent a year as a research student in modern history. He was briefly a member of the Communist Party, which he later described as a fashionable thing to do, but he was soon disillusioned. After Cambridge, he spent a year in Germany, where his independence of mind made him among the first to recognize the inevitability of war. This sharply differentiated him from his class, many of whom were in favour of appeasement until it was too late. If being a Communist did not require much courage, his interest in psychoanalysis certainly did. In the 1930s psychoanalysis was socially unacceptable—a disreputable foreign theory. When Rycroft first applied for psychoanalytic training in 1936, Ernest Jones rejected him as a dilettante and suggested that he would be more likely to be accepted if he studied medicine. In the event, Rycroft began medical and psychoanalytic training at the same time in 1937, and both trainings were disrupted by the war. His first analyst was Ella Sharpe, and after she died, he continued with Sylvia Payne. After graduating in medicine, he worked as a junior psychiatrist at the Maudsley Hospital.

These details are important because they show that by the time Rycroft qualified as an analyst, he was able to view its theory from many points of view. He had two primary perspectives: from science and the humanities. Because of his education and experience, he treated all the ideas he came across with the same healthy scepticism. He was unwilling to abandon any of his own identity or allegiances in favour of psychoanalysis. He was never able to embrace psychoanalytic theory (or any other idea) as a be-all and end-all. During his training he was puzzled by some of the teaching and made notes for his own use to explain the technical terms being used. Many years later these notes formed the basis of his *Critical Dictionary of Psychoanalysis* (Rycroft, 1968b).

The British Psychoanalytical Society was a very different organization in the late 1940s from what it is now. It was small enough for all the active members to know each other. The society had been severely traumatized by the Controversial Discussions during the war. The Kleinians and the Freudians were numerically small groups, and the majority or Middle Group had no recognizable leader. It was much later that the need for political organization led to the adoption of the name Group of Independent Analysts and the setting up of a committee. Psychoanalysis had yet to gain public recognition the United Kingdom, where there was still a strong feeling of social unity. There was hope for building a new society, particularly through the NHS, and a willingness to accept austerity for the sake of a better life ahead. Moral values were still firmly in place. This hope for the future was also strong within the psychoanalytic community—stronger than the differences between the groups. Analysts who had been raised on English empiricism did not feel at home with the dialectical thinking based on Hegel, which came naturally to Freud. Before the war this difference was tacitly ignored, because devotion to the common cause of psychoanalysis made the identification of such differences seem inappropriate. Rycroft was influenced by all the original thinkers of the time, particularly Brierley, Fairbairn, Milner, Payne, Rickman, and Winnicott, with all of whom he shared a common educational and cultural background. Although he never proclaimed a theory of his own, the theorists with whom he had most in common are Winnicott and Fairbairn.

When he qualified as an Associate Member, Rycroft's talents were immediately recognized, and he began to take part in the running of the Society. He was joint librarian with Masud Khan from 1952 to 1954 and also served on the Editorial Board of the

International Journal of Psycho-Analysis. His most important contribution in office was as Scientific Secretary. In those days, before photocopying, only a brief summary of the paper to be read was circulated before a Scientific Meeting. It was the task of the Scientific Secretary to open the discussion, and Rycroft was valued for his ability to understand and explain what the paper was about. In 1951, before he was eligible to become a training analyst, Rycroft was appointed a member of the Training Committee and its Acting Secretary. He has written that this appointment had little to do with merit but was partly due to the vacuum created by the war when very few analysts qualified. It was also due to the fact that Winnicott had just had a heart attack.

At that time committee members were unofficial nominees of the leaders of the three groups, so that Rycroft found himself representing Winnicott and his own analyst, Sylvia Payne. She had played a major role in establishing the Gentlemen's Agreement that brought about the cooperation of the various factions within the British Society after the war. Rycroft wrote that Payne's broadmindedness did him a disservice, because he qualified without appreciating the passionate intensity with which many analysts held their views:

> Too many did not have opinions that were open to discussion and possible modification but, instead, had unalterable convictions—including the conviction that anyone who disagreed with them had not had a sufficiently deep analysis. As a result the so-called scientific meetings were all too often not discussions but collisions. I once read a paper to the Society about a woman who had dreamed that the moon fell out of the sky into a dustbin. During the discussion Melanie Klein expressed her regret that I had not had a sufficiently deep analysis; at the time I took this as an insult to Dr Payne. I heard later than some of the audience had construed my paper as a conscious, deliberate allegory about Klein; it wasn't, but it's a pleasing idea. [chapter 15 herein]

It was Rycroft's dislike of being a pawn in a political battle that began his disillusionment with the Society. In the late 1950s and early 1960s, exasperated by the perpetual bickering, which made him feel he was sitting in on a family quarrel, he engaged in a strategic retreat. His wish to clarify psychoanalytic thought and communicate it to a wider public led him to develop a parallel career as an essayist and book reviewer. The last straw in his break with the Society was the Scientific Meeting in April 1964 when James Home read his paper "The Concept of Mind" (Home, 1966). In this paper Home argued that psychoanalysis is not a causal theory, but a semantic one, and one of the humanities or moral sciences—an idea that has since been widely accepted and was not exactly new at the time. Of this occasion Rycroft wrote: "speaker after speaker got up to assert his belief in psychic determinism, in the natural-scientific basis of psychoanalysis, each eager to make a declaration of faith and loyalty and dissociating himself from the heresy being propounded by Home. The only two speakers to support Home were Peter Lomas and myself."

It was an absolute requirement at that time that authors declared their debt to Freud and traced the connection between Freud's work and their own. It was unacceptable to disagree with Freud, which was why Home's paper caused such a furore. Ironically, long before the need for public relations was recognized by the Society, Rycroft became by far the best-known psychoanalyst in Britain through his newspaper articles. He started writing regularly for *The Observer* in 1959, *New Society* in 1963, *The New Statesman* in 1967, and *The New York Review of Books* in 1974.

My knowledge of Rycroft as a person cannot be separated from what I have read. Whenever I read something by him, it evokes the person I knew with a high degree of consistency. Rycroft disliked the idealization and proselytizing that went on in the society, and he refused to have followers. My relationship with him was never a social one. However, one can get to know one's analyst extremely well during an analysis. When I went back to him many years later, we were able to discuss how his thoughts about analytic technique and practice had changed over the years, which was a great help to me. He had kept his identification with the Freud who listened and found meaning in the patient's communications. He had grown away from the rigid and authoritarian aspects of psychoanalytic practice. The personal relationship between analyst and patient was always his primary concern. I think he must have shared some of my feelings about Freud. When I read Freud nowadays, it is always with mixed feelings. It is fascinating to follow his train of thought and the exploration of his patient's inner world, but at the same time there is a feeling of exasperation about the propaganda element, of his ideas being forced into a rigid frame.

Rycroft was a prolific writer of papers from the start, and his collected papers were published as *Imagination and Reality* (Rycroft, 1968c). In their introduction, the editors, Masud Khan and Jock Sutherland, stressed the importance of the empirical and catholic British tradition in which Rycroft was nurtured and found his own distinctive style. Rycroft's first paper, "A Contribution to the Study of the Dream Screen" (Rycroft, 1951) enlarged on two papers by Bertram Lewin on this subject (Lewin, 1946, 1948). Lewin described the dream screen as a blank sheet, like a cinema screen, onto which dream images are superimposed. The recognition of this element in a dream indicated, according to Lewin, both oral dependency and manic denial. Rycroft's elegant literary style is already present in this first paper. He gives an interesting clinical description of his own patient and makes several theoretical suggestions about the psychopathology. His language is that of orthodox psychoanalysis, but the individuality of his response to his patient is the most striking quality. It seems prophetic that his first paper should be about dreams. He described the same man from a different viewpoint in his second paper, "Some Observations on a Case of Vertigo" (Rycroft, 1953). Then he published "On Idealization, Illusion and Catastrophic Disillusion" (Rycroft, 1955), about a woman patient who dreamed that the moon fell into a dustbin. Rycroft used a similar dream by the Italian poet, Giacomo Leopardi, in the early nineteenth century, to illuminate his theme. He describes and differentiates between pathological idealization with its attendant risk of pathological disillusionment on the one hand, with, on the other hand, the normal process of idealization. Some experience of idealization is necessary in order for an infant to feel that the world is a good place to be, and disillusionment from it results merely in loss of omnipotence. This paper is an elaboration of Winnicott's work on the role of illusion in infancy.

Rycroft's next paper was "Symbolism and Its Relationship to the Primary and Secondary Processes" (Rycroft, 1956b). He acknowledged a debt to Ernest Jones classic paper "The Theory of Symbolism" (Jones, 1916), but far from building on Jones ideas, Rycroft demolished them completely. Following Freud, Jones had made a distinction between true symbolism, which is predominantly sexual, and "symbolism in the widest sense". The cardinal characteristics of true symbolization were, for Jones, that the process is unconscious and the affect invested in the symbolized idea has not, as far as the symbolism is concerned, proved capable of sublimation. In other words, true symbolism was of repressed unconscious material that could not otherwise be thought about. He wrote that "words, badges, gestures are not true symbols even though they represent some other idea from which they derive a significance not inherent in themselves" (Rycroft, 1958). For Jones and Freud, symbolism was always regressive. Although this theory was mistaken, it made sense when psychoanalysis was in its infancy. Rycroft rejected this attempt at an appropriation of symbolism by psychoanalysis as both arrogant and parochial. He challenged the view that symbolism is a function of the primary process, seeing symbol formation as a general capacity of mind. He also rejected Freud's idea that primary and secondary process are in opposition. Rycroft was influenced in this by Ella Sharpe's work on metaphor and also by Marjorie Brierley's idea of psychoanalysis as process theory. Brierley had adopted the term "holism", which was first used by the philosopher Jan Smuts. She described "a movement away from analysing into things into analysing into processes". This holistic approach has always been present in the Independent tradition. Although it may appear that the analysts I have mentioned conformed to the principles of Freud's mechanistic theory, it was not their basic means of expressing their ideas. It is my impression that Rycroft's ideas about symbolism and dreams have been silently incorporated into the thinking of many analysts without Jones' errors ever being acknowledged. Jones was still alive when this paper was published, and he wrote to Rycroft, expressing his general agreement; Jones wrote that in 1916 his ideas had been presented as a reaction to Jung's flight into mysticism.

Rycroft's next paper, "The Nature and Function of the Analyst's Communication to the Patient" (Rycroft, 1956a) was his response to Suzanne Langer's book *Philosophy in a New Key* (Langer, 1942). Langer was a student of Ernst Cassirer, who first established the then unfamiliar truth that both intellect and intuition use symbols. Following Cassirer, Langer wrote: "The great contribution of Freud to the study of mind has been the realization that human behaviour is not only a food-getting strategy, but a language; that every move is also a gesture." Rycroft wrote: "The various impractical, apparently unbiological activities of man, religion, magic, art, dreaming and symptom formation ... arise from a basic human need to communicate, and are really languages." Langer named the two modes of thinking discursive and non-discursive symbolism, and Rycroft preferred her terms to Freud's. This short paper was developed further in his next, "The Function of Words in the Analytic Situation" (Rycroft, 1958), where he applied Langer's distinction between signs and symbols to the analytic situation. He saw the analytic setting and the analyst's behaviour as signs to the patient that a meaningful relationship can develop. The patient will recognize the signs, and make use of the setting, to the extent that object relations are already a possibility in his or her mind.

I was present in the audience as a student at a Scientific Meeting when Rycroft read his paper "On the Defensive Function of Schizophrenic Thinking and Delusion Formation" (Rycroft, 1960). This clinical paper has the second aim of considering the schizophrenic's search for an identity and a sense of significance. The patient was a young man who was confined to a mental hospital after thirteen years of all the treatments then available, the last four being analysis with Rycroft at his father's instigation. Rycroft compares his patient's illness with Freud's famous account of Schreber. Freud described Schreber's delusional system as an attempt at recovery, the construction of means by which the outside world would be recathected. The time scale was much shorter in Schreber's case. Rycroft describes a three-year period during which his patient, like Schreber, lived in a psychic limbo where nothing seemed real and people seemed to be cursorily improvised. Over the next year a delusional system developed, to some extent as a result of the treatment. The patient had the idea that everything was hypothetical: for example that his analyst was not really Dr Rycroft, or there might be several Dr Rycrofts. Freud interpreted Schreber's experience of people as cursorily improvised as the result of his having withdrawn interest from both internal and external reality. Rycroft took the view that this withdrawal had an actively defensive function; it ensured for the patient that no aspect of reality would be either frightening or tempting and also that none of his own thoughts could be considered delusional. Rycroft quotes Bateson, who put forward the theory that the loss of the capacity to distinguish between the different modes of communication constitutes the critical disturbance in schizophrenic thinking (Bateson, Jackson, Haley, & Weakland, 1956).

After three years of analysis the patient's defensive system began to break down with the emergence of paranoid fantasies that influenced his behaviour. When it became necessary to admit him to hospital, Rycroft undertook the arrangements. Before getting into the ambulance, the patient said goodbye and drew his analyst's attention to the fact that there were two moons in the sky. Despite the clarity of the arguments presented, Rycroft was asked during the discussion following his presentation why he had not continued to treat the patient after his admission to hospital. His reply was, "Because I did not think I was God." Rycroft gives an elegant explanation of the two realities, which goes beyond Freud's classic account. The idea of withdrawal of cathexis does not answer two questions: by whom people are being cursorily improvised? And why this is the same as "magically conjured up"? Rycroft shows how the history of the patient's relationship to his own thought processes provides an explanation. The withdrawal of interest in other people is part of the same process as the repression of his own instinctual life. People who were once significant for him were external evidence of his own emotional needs. The withdrawal that frees him from guilt and anxiety also renders him a nonentity in his own and other people's eyes. Freud showed that this state of total despair and futility leads to spontaneous attempts at recovery by some other means than insight into what is being repressed. Like Schreber, Rycroft's patient had two incompatible realities and eventually decided to keep the delusional one to himself.

Another paper presented in 1960, but not published till 1985, was "Miss Y—the Analysis of a Paranoid Personality" (Rycroft, 1985a). Miss Y had provided some of the material for Rycroft's papers on the significance of words in analysis. In this beautifully written case history Rycroft mentions that he is presenting his own emotional responses "in order to give a truer account of the dynamics of the analytic process than would be possible if he presented himself as a detached observer". This reminds us that in 1960 the importance of countertransference had yet to be explored. Although he does not write explicitly about psychic truth, it is implicit in Rycroft's accounts of work with patients that such a thing does exist, and that successful therapy depends on a truthful exchange between analyst and patient. Miss Y had constructed her own system of psychopathology on the basis of self-analysis, and Rycroft discusses her system seriously. He points out the limited value of a theory based on one case, and also that her theory is not true; but he subjects it to the same appraisal as the standard psychoanalytic theory and finds that many of her ideas are worthy of consideration. Because of his withdrawal from the Society, Rycroft did not write any more clinical papers. This can be seen as a great loss, because his clinical skills were recognized as on a par with his written work, and he was in great demand as a therapist throughout his career.

Rycroft was always part of the world of ideas outside psychoanalysis and more open than conventional analysts towards new ideas. He was interested in linguistic philosophy, existentialism, and new disciplines such as cybernetics and ethology. He was one of the first analysts to realize that many of the criticisms levelled at psychoanalysis needed to be taken seriously because the creation of systems that explain everything is the opposite of scientific. He wrote: "Freud used language which presupposes the split between the objective and subjective worlds to express ideas which annul it." There were very few analysts who understood this at the time. A major theme for him was the question of authenticity, closely connected to that of psychic truth. He was expert in understanding the ways in which people deceive themselves and their analysts and, long before family therapy appeared on the scene, he realized that interpersonal factors operate to keep patients ill. He was also aware of the limitations of Freud's one-person psychology and was an early admirer of Bowlby's work on attachment and loss. He once said to me that he and Bowlby were ploughing the same furrow from opposite ends. Bowlby was right to stress the importance of an intimate continuous relationship for the infant's well-being, but he was unconcerned about symbolism and imagination. They both understood that only satisfaction of instinctual needs in infancy can lead to a love of reality.

In *Anxiety and Neurosis* Rycroft set out a straightforward biological explanation of psychic phenomena (Rycroft, 1968a). His object was to explain the basic facts of mental life without the assumptions derived from nineteenth-century mechanical science, which, he felt, distorted Freud's theory. He saw Freud's death instinct as an unbiological and unnecessary part of Freud's determinism. The role of childhood trauma in neurosis was based on inference and could not be proved. Delving into the past was a journey in search of meaning, not facts. The patients of deterministically minded analysts could see their problems as being the result of what had happened to them and so evade responsibility for their own lives. Rycroft's view was that in such innate responses as the startle reflex or a baby's cry, anxiety had an adaptive function akin to vigilance. He thought that the basic facts of human existence were in danger of being overlooked by analysts who made unconscious fantasy their focus of attention. He pointed out that psychoanalysis was in danger of making consciousness an "epiphenomenon". If neurosis was due to forgotten childhood events, then the whole of the personality, and not just neurosis, was being explained causally, so that choice and decision-making were illusory. For Rycroft this is unbiological; it is also incompatible with the assumption that making the unconscious conscious will enable the patient to free himself from the repetition compulsion. He used the basic biological reactions to danger, "fight, flight, or submission", to classify the neuroses according to their modes of defence against anxiety. He saw change taking place in therapy as largely due to the patient becoming aware that defence mechanisms that had made sense in childhood were no longer necessary and could be abandoned.

In Rycroft's most prolific year, 1968, A Critical Dictionary of Psychoanalysis also appeared. The dictionary was an immediate success and has been in print ever since. He revised it with a new introduction in 1995. By contrast, Anxiety and Neurosis did not make much of an impression.

Rycroft refuted two common misconceptions about the nature of psychoanalysis. The first of these is Freud's intention that psychoanalysis should be a natural science, a science of mind on a par with physics and chemistry. Freud wrote about people as if they were psychic apparatuses, whereas in his behaviour towards patients he interacted with them as human beings. Freud's second misconception was to suppose that pathological phenomena could be used to construct a theory of normal behaviour. For example, although anxiety was frequently pathological, it was not necessarily so. This mistake led Freud to suppose that creativity could be explained in terms of neurotic fantasies; Freud knew that he had an unsolved problem in this area.

In his next book, *The Innocence of Dreams* Rycroft (1979) challenged some of Freud's most basic theories about dreams. He rejected the idea that dreams are wish-fulfilling in favour of a simple concept of primary and secondary process as complementary modes of thinking, so that dreams are just sleeping thoughts. They are not to be regarded as phenomena with causes but, rather, as experiences that are part of the continuum of the inner life of the individual. He rejected Freud's distinction between latent and manifest content, pointing out that Freud had made a category error in claiming that most of the symbols in dreams are sexual. Freud's theory does not explain why a person's sexual desires are disguised in some dreams and not in others. With hindsight it is clear that Rycroft was correct in his view that Freud's emphasis on repression was culture-bound. Rycroft saw dreams as messages to oneself about biological destiny, so that sexuality is not "something else besides" as Freud claimed, but basic to our understanding of ourselves. He disagreed with Freud's idea that the primary process is more primitive and needs to be replaced by rational secondary process. He thought the two processes need to be harmoniously combined for mental health. He reversed Freud's idea that dreams preserve sleep—his view being that we sleep in order to dream. This has been confirmed by studies of REM sleep that were not available to Freud. Rycroft exonerates Freud because in his time the only "real" truths were scientific truths. He wrote that the reason the majority of dreams are not understood or granted meaning is that we live in a society in which alienation and unconscious hypocrisy are endemic and in which it is difficult for adults to find cultural equivalents to the childhood experience of good enough mothering.

Rycroft published two more books, *Psychoanalysis and Beyond* (1985b) and *Viewpoints* (1991b). Both were collections of his essays and book reviews. *Psychoanalysis and Beyond* was selected and edited by the art critic Peter Fuller, and it contains two autobiographical pieces from which I have quoted. Fuller's introduction was the first general appreciation of Rycroft's work, and it provides a good summary of his thinking. Fuller described Rycroft's view of men and women as separate psychobiological entities who necessarily enter into relationships. There is also the historical dimension: Rycroft often referred to T. S. Eliot's concept of a dissociation of sensibility—"modern man, unlike mediaeval man, views reality from two unconnected and incompatible standpoints, one scientific and objective, the other imaginative and subjective." He warns that the solution of adhering consistently to one stance or the other involves "letting more than one baby out with the bath water". Rycroft's picture of modern man shifting uneasily between these two positions is a more sophisticated version of Winnicott's view of the continual struggle to reconcile the inner and outer world by means of transitional phenomena. Rycroft saw the aesthetic dimension as the essential means of accomplishing this task.

I shall conclude by trying to summarize the qualities that distinguish the late development of Rycroft's thought. He always valued common sense, and he deplored its absence in some of his colleagues. He also valued the old-fashioned virtues of courtesy and honesty. It distressed him that colleagues could suppress crucial information when referring a patient because it might affect his decision whether to accept the patient for treatment. He brought his breadth of vision to every subject he wrote about, and, whenever possible, he argued from first principles, not from a specifically psychoanalytic viewpoint.

For me, Rycroft's work on imagination and creativity is his most significant achievement. In "Psychoanalysis and the Literary Imagination" (Rycroft, 1985c) he makes a statement about the importance of dreams that was present throughout his writing from the very beginning: "The dreaming, creative, imaginative self is not open to inspection or introspection . . . it can only be 'I' and never 'me,' and it does a disappearing trick if one tries to push it into the objective position. It is somewhat similar to the concept of time, of which St. Augustine wrote that he knew what it was as long as no one asked him what it was, but if he was asked he did not know."

In his essay "On Selfhood and Self-awareness" (Rycroft, 1991a) he wrote: "It would, I conceive, be possible to emigrate, change one's name, one's profession, one's religion, one's political opinions and still be true to oneself; and to maintain the same position and opinions throughout life and be untrue to oneself. What is at stake is the maintenance of a consistent, continuous, unique pattern of growth in a changing world, and given the contingencies of history and life, internal and external consistency do not necessarily correspond."

Winnicott said that it takes ten years after qualifying to make a psychoanalyst. During that decade Rycroft made significant theoretical and clinical contributions. He then went through what must have been a very difficult period of transformation. In order to continue his own development, he had to dissociate himself from many aspects of the British Psychoanalytical Society. It was characteristic of him that he remained officially a member until long after this process was completed. Rycroft believed in the importance of self-development, and while learning all his life, he remained true to his own self. He kept his distance from ideas he could not accept while taking a keen interest in any new ones that seemed promising. He thought that *The Innocence of Dreams* was his best work. He never lost his interest in the practice of psychoanalysis, which he valued highly. I think the essence of his development over the years is that his theory and practice of analysis reflected his own maturing point of view.

As Rycroft was the only significant figure to leave the Society without proclaiming a theory of his own, I feel obliged to speculate about what his theory would have been if he had had to formulate it. He saw psychoanalysis as a biological theory of meaning, a unique phenomenon belonging neither to the natural sciences nor, since it is a clinical discipline, to the humanities. He saw it as having arisen in response to the needs of an alienated twentieth-century society. He would probably go further and say that the needs of the twenty-first century will turn out to be for something rather different. A central feature of his theory would be the role of symbolic transformation in the development of the individual towards maturity.

Not surprisingly, undertaking this exercise demonstrates why there is no school of Rycroft. He did not want to label ideas with his own name because he did not feel they belonged to him. Each train of thought that led to one of his insights contained elements of what he had learned from others, which could be identified. His aim was to be a well-informed and wise person whose opinions were worth reading, and not to assert his own identity.

He saw the resolution of tension between the inner and outer worlds as the wellspring of creative activity and creative living. His work is a symbol of the continuity that he saw as our greatest need in a changing world.

References

Bateson, G., Jackson, D., Haley, J., & Weakland, J. H. (1956). Towards a theory of schizophrenia. *Behavioural Sciences, 1* (4). Reprinted in: G. Bateson, *Steps to an Ecology of Mind*. London: Paladin, 1973.

Home, J. (1966). The concept of mind. *International Journal of Psycho-Analysis, 43*.

Jones, E. (1916). The theory of symbolism. In: *Papers on Psychoanalysis* (2nd edition). London: Baillière.

Langer, S. (1942). *Philosophy in a New Key*. London: Oxford University Press; Cambridge, MA: Harvard University Press, 1951.

Lewin, B. (1946). Sleep, the mouth and the dream screen. *Psychoanalytic Quarterly, 15*: 419–434.

Lewin, B. (1948). Inferences from the dream screen. *International Journal of Psycho-Analysis, 24* (4): 224.

Rycroft, C. (1951). A contribution to the study of the dream screen. *International Journal of Psycho-Analysis, 32*.

Rycroft, C. (1953). Some observations on a case of vertigo. *International Journal of Psycho-Analysis, 34*.

Rycroft, C. (1955). On idealization, illusion, and catastrophic disillusion. *International Journal of Psycho-Analysis, 36*.

Rycroft, C. (1956a). The nature and function of the analyst's communication to the patient. *International Journal of Psycho-Analysis, 37*.

Rycroft, C. (1956b). Symbolism and its relationship to the primary and secondary processes. *International Journal of Psycho-Analysis, 37*.

Rycroft, C. (1958). An enquiry into the function of words in the analytic situation. *International Journal of Psycho-Analysis, 39*.

Rycroft, C. (1960). On the defensive function of schizophrenic thinking and delusion formation. *International Journal of Psycho-Analysis, 43*.

Rycroft, C. (1968a). *Anxiety and Neurosis*. London: Hogarth Press.

Rycroft, C. (1968b). *A Critical Dictionary of Psychoanalysis*. London: Nelson; London: Penguin, 1995 (2nd revised edition).

Rycroft, C. (1968c). *Imagination and Reality*. London: Hogarth.

Rycroft, C. (1979). *The Innocence of Dreams*. London: Hogarth Press.

Rycroft, C. (1985a). Miss Y—The analysis of a paranoid personality. In: *Psychoanalysis and Beyond*. London: Chatto Tigerstripe.

Rycroft, C. (1985b). *Psychoanalysis and Beyond*. London: Chatto Tigerstripe.

Rycroft, C. (1985c). Freud and the literary imagination. In: *Psychoanalysis and Beyond*. London: Chatto Tigerstripe.

Rycroft, C. (1991a). On selfhood and self-awareness. In: *Viewpoints*. London: Hogarth Press.

Rycroft, C. (1991b). *Viewpoints*. London: Hogarth Press.

CHAPTER SIX

Insiders and outsiders

Susan Budd

It proved surprisingly difficult to write this paper. I have admired Dr Rycroft's writings for many years, but when I came to consider what his legacy to the psychoanalytic world has been—and therefore, what his place in that world had been and might have been—I had the sensation of stepping from a firm rock onto shifting sands. Partly, he had left the British Psychoanalytical Society before I began to train, and partly, the intellectual hegemony that he had reacted against was by that time in some disarray. The landscape against which he located himself looks quite different; but is that because I am of a different generation, or because I am standing in a different place ? I have no personal recollection of him in the Society to guide me, and the landmarks by which he steered are not all recognizable to me. I knew Charles Rycroft hardly at all; I only began to meet him at the very end of his life. In that sense, I am an outsider to those who did know him well, either as a friend or in that very odd and special way in which patients come to know their analysts.

The legacy of a psychoanalyst can have several aspects. For most analysts, their most important memorial is their work with their patients, and with their supervisees, if they have them. They may also be active members of their professional bodies, they may also work elsewhere, for example in the National Health Service, and they may write, either for insiders—that is, their fellow-professionals—or for the general public. Some may write for both. It is for his writings that Dr Rycroft will be chiefly remembered—his writings and for the fact that he resigned from the British Society but continued to work as a psychoanalyst. This affected the nature of his legacy in several ways, and I have chosen to focus on the issue of insiders and outsiders, and the ways in which they both repel and need each other.

After Dr Rycroft's resignation, his analysands could not formally become psychoanalysts. (This, incidentally, is an important hidden cost to the Society of the resignations of senior figures.) He chose to work in private practice, so that his work with analysands remains for the most part hidden and unknown. As Margaret Arden said, after he left the Society, very few of his papers described his clinical work in any detail, and so we have no knowledge as to how his views influenced his technique other than by hearing from his analysands. His influence and ideas were exerted through his writing, rather than through holding any organizational posts. I believe that the British Society lost a great deal, but so, perhaps, did he through the loss of a particular kind of sounding-board, that of his fellow-professionals.

The psychoanalysts who have gained a following among British psychoanalysts tend to be those who develop new insights into difficult patients or into ways of handling apparently intractable impasses in the analytic encounter. Winnicott, Klein, and Rosenfeld are examples of analysts' analysts; they gained influence not only because of their contributions to theory but also because of their new insights about clinical work. Rycroft did not write in detail about his clinical work, but about the basis of psychoanalytic knowledge, and after 1964 he wrote for the general public, and not for learned journals (Rycroft, 1985: "Where I Came From" p. 206).

(Since I first wrote the above, Jeremy Holmes has argued to me that some of Rycroft's papers do contain passing references to his technique. I think that insofar as they are distinctive, they are concerned with the careful and courteous attention to the "real" relationship between patient and analyst, as it might be continued beyond the boundaries of the session and its fixed roles, and how it coexists with the therapeutic relationship. This distinction, characteristic of classical ego-psychology, was largely obliterated in England by Melanie Klein's insistence, which is both correct and tautological, that all relationships are transference relationships. This, of course, raises another dilemma, of which Rycroft was well aware: if that is the case, on what grounds does the analyst's demonstrable claim to superior objectivity rest? But while he was critical of the attempts of the classical tradition to discount the importance of the personal relationship between analyst and patient, he was no existentialist: a point I return to later.)

Charles Rycroft was initially a very prolific writer; in 1968 he published three books. But after 1968, he published only two more books on specific topics, a brief biography of Reich and a book on dreams. His output was mostly composed of book-reviews, and these were published, together with various lectures to distinguished lay audiences, in two further volumes. Compared to most psychoanalysts, this is a large output, and, together with R. D. Laing, Donald Winnicott, and John Bowlby, he must have been one of the most widely known psychoanalysts in the latter half of the twentieth century. However, one may regret—I don't know if he himself regretted—that he did not go on to make any further contribution to psychoanalytic theory commensurate with his gifts and intelligence, and I wonder if this may have been because he felt that he had lost a professional audience.

To take an example, to which Margaret Arden has already referred. Rycroft's writings did not give the countertransference the significance that it was to assume in British psychoanalysis from the 1960s onward. The entry in the *Critical Dictionary* (Rycroft, 1968) runs as follows:

1. The analyst's transference on his patient. In this, the correct, sense, counter-transference is a disturbing, distorting element in treatment. [This was Freud's view. He thought that the analyst should strive to master his countertransference. S.B.]

2. By extension, the analyst's emotional attitude towards his patient, including his response to specific items of the patient's behaviour. According to Heimann, Little, Gitelson and others, the analyst can use this latter kind of counter-transference as

clinical evidence, i.e. he can assume that his own emotional response is based on a correct interpretation of the patient's true intentions or meaning. [p. 25]

In the 1973 edition, he added a quotation from Paula Heimann and pointed out that Melanie Klein disliked the over-use of the concept because it was too subjective.[1] But British psychoanalysts have used the analysis of the countertransference more and more, and a fruitful tradition of work has been based upon it. Charles Rycroft knew many analysts and kept up with current thinking, but perhaps the exploration of the countertransference seemed less central and important to him because he was outside the institutional context in which attention to it was expected. There is a sense in which continually thinking about or calling attention to yourself in a session—"you mean me"—is very un-English. But I also think that many of the phenomena that analysts now try to think about and describe are not really comprehensible if we stick to common sense.

(Perhaps Melanie Klein—dogmatic, uneducated, emotional European that she was—was because of that equipped to plunge in and try to describe what she saw. She was one of Tolstoy's hedgehogs; Rycroft was a fox. She was also, of course, the quintessential outsider: an uneducated woman who had been forced out of the Berlin Society, and gained her influence among British psychoanalysts because she seemed able to grasp some of the very odd aspects of interaction with some patients.) Rycroft, I think, was well aware of the potential for deceit and hypocrisy of this line of thought—the analyst who blames the patient for causing his own shortcomings. But work in this area engenders a very intense therapeutic encounter, which is both powerful, dangerous, and thoroughly ill-mannered.

If we think about the dog that didn't bark in the night—the role in the profession that Charles Rycroft didn't have—it is not because psychoanalysts ceased to read him. Thanks to the invaluable CD rom of the contents of the main psychoanalytic journals written in English from 1920 on, we can see that psychoanalysts did continue to refer to his writings until 1990 or so, but almost entirely to his writings on symbolism and dreams. Elegant and insightful though this work is, he did not put forward any theory of his own; rather, he argued that the commonsense view of symbolism and dreams is nearer the truth than the psychoanalytic one. Dreams are not necessarily based on repressed wishes but are night-time thinking; symbolism is not a way of representing the repressed but is part of imagination, a valuable mental capacity. He disagreed with Freud's view, as expressed in the "Formulations on the Two Principles of Mental Functioning" (1911b), that there are two different ways of thinking, dominated by conscious and unconscious processes, one of which is to be preferred because it is in touch with reality and more grown-up. Rycroft saw that this must imply that there is a knowable reality that is separate from thought-processes, and that someone can decide what that reality is. I think that Freud was more aware of the dilemma than he thought, and less dismissive of the importance of creativity and imagination. I shall return later on to the importance of the idea of common-sense.

Insiders and outsiders

I would like to have considered Dr Rycroft purely in terms of his ideas as reflected in his writing, but somehow the nature of his relationship with the British Society kept getting in the way. I think that this is partly because he himself frequently referred to it in his writings and partly because other people treated it as such a significant matter. It is an important part of his legacy. I have been given four completely different accounts of the reasons for his rift with the Society. So we must ask ourselves, I think, why it is that the story of his departure is told and re-told, and for what purposes the variants of the story are being used. In other words, we have here what anthropologists would call a myth; something happened, but the meaning of what happened has been reconstructed by various people for various purposes. You will remember that Lévi-Strauss told us that myths are good to think with: they establish various kinds of oppositions in the social and moral world. The particular set of oppositions that I would like to explore is that of the insider and the outsider.

Each profession, organization, each group, has to mark itself off from the rest of the world and, in doing so, it must decide who is an insider and who an outsider. It comes as no surprise to find that powerful feelings cluster around the boundary, and processes familiar to us all—projection, splitting, identifications, idealization, denigration—come into play to deal with fears of contamination and muddle. I think that it is difficult in all disciplines, but certainly in psychoanalysis, to live on the boundary; powerful forces tend to push us to being either inside or outside, and we have to carve out a special role to remain on the edge.

I would argue that after he left the British Society, Charles Rycroft's public role in psychoanalysis was essentially that of a popularizer.[2] As he said, when he realized that he did not want to remain a member of the Society, he was fortuitously offered an opportunity to write for the general educated public about psychoanalysis, and the nature of this audience conditioned what he was able to write. Insiders are often grudging and envious about popularizers; after all, they command wide audiences, social recognition, and possibly wealth and do not have to adhere to the shibboleths of the profession or work to support it. They often criticize popularizers for diluting or betraying the pure gold of the insider's world view. However, in the long term they have reason to be grateful to them, because they attract outsiders to the profession.

Psychoanalysis is a relatively closed world—especially if you live outside London, outside the therapeutic milieu, you are unlikely to meet one, and their company makes most people uneasy because of the sense of shame and pollution that is associated with mental illness and emotional distress. They deal with their anxiety in several ways, but mostly by making the psychoanalyst into something very strange and odd—in other words, an outsider. The popularizer is the person who tries to put this into reverse, who brings the news of what is going on within psychoanalysis and makes it all sound clear, easy, and common-sensical. In that sense, Freud's *Introductory Lectures* (1916–17) were masterpieces of popularization, but as time went by and a profession grew up around him, you can see a technical vocabulary begin to form and his writing begin to differentiate. What he wrote for the profession becomes increasingly unintelligible to outsiders; it uses a special vocabulary, which rests on shared assumptions and experience, whereas his easy, lucid style remains in those works addressed to a more general public.

The insiders exert pressure on writers to become more inside, to develop a vocabulary that enables them communicate quickly and easily with fellow professionals. As is well known, when Freud's works were translated into English, Ernest Jones wanted to gain them a position within medicine, and so simple, concrete German words such as the I, the Above I, the It, acquired a Latinate gloss—the ego, the superego, and the id. But the popularizer must be aware of how psychoanalysis is viewed from the outside: he has to keep his audience, and so he becomes, to some extent, a prisoner of their ideas and concerns. If he develops ideas of his own, they must be stated in terms his audience can understand, and so they become detached from the discourse of the insider.

The idea that insiders and outsiders understand things differently was to continue and gather speed throughout the second half of the twentieth century, as various dispossessed groups—women, the working-class, blacks, homosexuals—challenged the hegemony of the WASP and the DWEM and asserted that to claim certain kinds of knowledge requires having a certain identity, a certain kind of experience. Robert Merton, the great sociologist of science and a figure not unlike Charles Rycroft, contributed a paper to the debate from which I have borrowed my title (Merton, 1972), in which he pleaded the case that both kinds of knowledge could exist, strengthen each other, and be examined. Merton argued that there are two kinds of understanding—"acquaintance with" (relying on direct familiarity with something, depicting it) and "knowledge about" (abstract formulations that do not "resemble" what has been directly explained). He believed that we should constantly try to bring the two together without compromising either, and, as I shall go on to argue, Rycroft also thought that we had to try to combine causal and hermeneutic understandings.

Merton argued that the insider doctrine—you must be one in order to understand one—is logically fallacious, because our identities are never identical and are always shifting. Sometimes insiders concede that only the outsiders, the disinherited (he has American Blacks in mind) have special perspectives and insights. Their sufferings have sensitized them. In opposition to this view is a long tradition that believes that any kind of group loyalty is corrupting to human understanding—that knowledge is most accessible to outsiders.

We can see both tendencies operating in our field: the claim that you can only really understand if you have had a specific kind of experience or analysis, and the claim that, if you have had, you will have lost all objectivity and become a camp-follower. We can also see that as we move between aspects of our professional identities, our reference groups change. We may shift from defining ourselves as Kleinians or Lacanians to identifying ourselves as psychoanalysts or psychoanalytical psychotherapists, or as British analysts rather than French, or American, or as members of a particular generation, or as inside the power-structures of our various organizations or as relatively peripheral, or as people who work inside the NHS or people who don't, as medically trained or from a literary background, as working in London or outside it, as people who believe that there is an unconscious mind versus those who don't; and as we shift, so do our allegiances. Charles Rycroft cut across established allegiances: he was an orthodox analyst whose views were no more heterodox than those of many analysts, but he chose to work outside professional structures. Mary Douglas has shown us how these anomalous figures both define and assault our systems of boundaries, and they tend to be seen as both sacred and polluted. I think that it might have amused Dr Rycroft to be compared to the scaly-tailed pangolin (Douglas, 1966, pp. 168 ff.)

Common sense

Rycroft's legacy must be founded on his writing style; it was elegant and lucid, but it was also a very personal style. The authorial voice sounds very near to us, and implicitly appeals to us to accept what he says because it is merely common sense, so that it is harder to separate our feelings about the man from those about his writings than it is for other authors. And, indeed, he wrote more about his life and what had formed him than most psychoanalysts would do.

I was one of the people who first found out about psychoanalysis through reading about it, and among my earliest reading were various works by Charles Rycroft and R. D. Laing, his analysand. They were the bridge across which I travelled to a closer contact with psychoanalysis. It was therefore distressing to me when I became a student to find that very few analysts wrote as clearly and evocatively as they did. With the wisdom—or hardening of the arteries—that comes with moving into the profession, becoming an insider, I now think that the matter is more complicated.

In part, we can understand the growth of jargon, or technical terms, as part of the process of the formation of a discipline and a profession: that is, the creation of something that has an inside, where technical language is being used to convey a meaning quickly and accurately. Critics of psychoanalysis commonly fasten on its dense and impenetrable style, and are unwilling to concede that it needs a technical vocabulary. They find it especially distressing because it deals with the apparently personal, the familiar, but casts it in unfamiliar terms. We find it hard to 2accept that we are not experts on ourselves. I think that in reading psychoanalysis we can feel this sense of self-alienation, and it is partly why its heavy, term-laden style is so resented. Something that feels familiar, even charming—the little boy, say, who wants to marry Mummy when he is grown up—is given a serious, frightening gloss as it is grouped with other things that are much darker and more perverse.

When we look at reactions to the revelation of situations where perverse desires have been acted out—abuse in children's homes, say—we can see how hard it is for people to accept that these things really do happen, and how easy it is to blame the psychoanalytic messengers, to feel that they are deluded by their perverse imaginations, or contaminated by what they have to tell us. In such a situation, the psychoanalyst is always on the verge of being made an outsider, the possessor of unbearable knowledge. Analysts react to this in various ways. Our profession must be secretive for many reasons, and therefore it generates curiosity and gossip. It is tempting to try to avoid being stigmatized by separating ourselves from it, to imply that we, and the group we belong to, are reasonable beings, and the others are not. If, as was the case in the British Society during and immediately after the war, the factions come from different social groups, the tendency to locate everything we fear in the others is very hard to check. The opposite tendency is to claim that only we and our circle are really psychoanalysts; the rest have departed from a basic tenet and have become outsiders. The outsiders' dislike of psychoanalysis has a corrosive effect on the inside of the profession, and leads to fears of dilution and accusations of disloyalty.

We can see the insider–outsider theme being played out in many ways at this time. Charles Rycroft felt that for someone of his class—the English gentry—an interest in psychoanalysis made him an outsider. He happened to be an undergraduate at Cambridge in the 1930s, when it had briefly become something that educated people should know something about. The Bloomsbury group were interested in it, partly because it had interesting things to say about the arts, was felt to be more tolerant of deviant sexual behaviour, but perhaps above all because it seemed to be subversive of established authority. It was members of the Bloomsbury group who had persuaded Rycroft to apply for training. Peter Fuller, the art critic and his analysand, quotes him on his sense of divided loyalties:

> My attitude to analysis is really determined to a large extent by the fact that my intellectual loyalties and allegiances ... have been to a tradition other than that of the analytical one. Mine has been derived from my family background, education at Cambridge, and at University College Hospital. All the time, I have been in pursuit of a way of viewing human nature acceptable to that tradition. [Fuller, 1985, p. 6]

In other words, to become a psychoanalyst made him an outsider to his class and to English intellectual life, which, until recently, has not been prepared to engage with psychoanalysis. Yet his ties to that class, and his search for a theory of human nature that should be acceptable to them, made him feel that he was an outsider to both the Freudian group who came from Vienna just before the war and the group who gathered around Melanie Klein. I find myself wondering whether this situation felt familiar—he had, after all, been dispossessed of his home after his father's death, when primogeniture created a gap between him and his father's lineage. Many members of the Independent Group in the British Society—Bowlby, Winnicott, Brierley, Fairbairn—showed signs at times of having joined a family where they did not always feel at home, but they seem to have been able to continue as members.

(Perhaps the cohesive English establishment tradition that Rycroft was referring to was already assailed; and the second half of the twentieth century has not been kind to the gentleman-ideal.

It would always have been hard to have accommodated psycho-analysis within it. Freud knew how disruptive it was: why did the Americans greet him with open arms? "Don't they know we are bringing them the plague?")

Looking back on it now, with the aid of Pearl King and Riccardo Steiner's invaluable collection of documents dealing with the Controversies of 1941–45, the period during which Rycroft was training, I find myself feeling very uncomfortable (King & Steiner, 1981). The dogmatism of the quarrels is unappealing, and we can see why Rycroft was alienated, but perhaps the English were simply unable to understand the significance of what had happened to the refugees from continental Europe. The well-known Strachey grumble about the tendency of the Kleinians on the one hand and the Viennese Freudians on the other to claim a monopoly of scientific truth, as the foreigners who had invaded our peaceful compromising island, puts very clearly how many of the English analysts felt.

But why were both of these psychoanalytic camps so uncompromising and unable to rely on tolerance, compromise, and common sense? The answer must partly lie in what had been happening in Europe, where reason and common sense had been abandoned, leaving analysts either forced into exile or disavowing a great deal of psychoanalysis as a Jewish science. Those who left, full of loss and guilt about the various compromises that they had had to make and about those who had been left behind, must have felt that almost all they could bring with them was their identity as psychoanalysts. To find, on arriving in England, that it had been transformed and that even there they were seen as outsiders must have felt very painful, and the idea that common sense would resolve disputes ironic. Common sense was exactly what had been assailed. It is common sense to believe that a Jewish dentist or musician is no different from any other kind. But when a sense of commonality has broken down, so has the notion of common sense.

Psychoanalysis and the English

Psychoanalysis was not enthusiastically incorporated into English intellectual life. Perry Anderson could sum up the situation in 1968 as follows:

What has been the impact of psychoanalysis in British Society
in general? The irony is that it has been virtually nil. It has been
sealed off as a technical enclave: an esoteric and specialized
pursuit unrelated to any of the central concerns of mainstream
"humanistic" culture. There is no Western country where the
presence of psychoanalysis in general culture has been so
vestigial. [p. 42]

This is, of course, no longer the case. Psychoanalysis may not be
particularly flourishing as a therapy, but there is widespread and
growing interest in the contributions that it can make to general
intellectual life, and links between clinical trainings and university
courses in cultural studies are growing rapidly. This process started
in Europe and America but is by now widespread, and psychoanalysis is discussed and argued about beyond the clinical situation.
Rycroft's Freud was a positivist whose ambition was to create a
science of historical causes and psychic effects similar to chemistry.
More recently, Freud has been redescribed as a hermeneuticist,
alert to the ambiguities of memory and construction, who knew
that deferred action confounded any science of causes. As with
Marx, we can find evidence for both of these Freuds.

If we look at "The Concept of Mind" (1966), the paper by H. J.
Home whose reception at the British Society had been the final
straw for Rycroft, in it he drew a sharp distinction between science,
which deals with dead objects in terms of causes, of how things
happen, and the humanities, which deal with live objects and are
concerned with why things happen and therefore with the mind,
motives, and our capacity to understand other people by identifying with them. Home thought that the technique of psychoanalysis
implied that it is the study of meaning; but its theory attempted to
present it as a science. There was a confusion between the interpretation of behaviour and the description of behaviour; between
meaning and fact. He thought that instinct theory was invalid and
needed to be replaced by a theory of object relationships. This view
assumes that there is a radical disjunction between theories of
mind and brain.

Rycroft may have supported Home, but he does not seem to
have agreed with him. He was not arguing that we can understand
the psyche solely in terms of what is enacted between two people
in the session. Throughout his writings, we find repeated refer-

ences to the need to integrate biology, and bodily experience, with the study of meanings and psychic experience. In 1962 he published a critical review of Guntrip's "Personality Structure and Human Interaction" in the *International Journal of Psycho-Analysis*— the last time he was to write for it. I quote from him at length because he put the issue with his customary clarity. He pointed out that Guntrip was criticizing Freud

> for failing to produce a "personal" psychology, when it was precisely his achievement to recognize the extent to which human behaviour is determined by impersonal forces and to initiate a technique by which these impersonal tendencies could be personalized. Although there are, I believe, good reasons for dissatisfaction with Freud's id-ego-superego terminology, Guntrip's dismissal of the concept "id" on the grounds that it is impersonal reveals his failure to understand a whole area of Freud's work, since Freud chose this term (*das Es*, the It), precisely because repressed, unconscious mental processes operate impersonally, and only acquire humanity and individuality after they have become conscious and egotized.
>   At this point it becomes clear that the ideal of a truly personal psychology, owing nothing to the biological sciences, is a chimaera. ... Nowhere does Guntrip discuss symptom-formation, dream-work, symbolism, working-through, psychosomatic disease, or affects, and yet these are the areas of analytical enquiry which most strongly suggest that mental processes obey laws which have some relation to biological ones, and in which some of the "impersonal" concepts rejected by Guntrip have proved most useful. [p. 355]

This brings me to the only conversation I ever had with Charles Rycroft. I had written a critique of the object-relations tradition in Britain for its neglect of the role of instinctual behaviour, especially adult sexual behaviour, and Rycroft had got to hear of this and asked me to send him a copy (Budd, 2001). Several weeks later I drove him home, and we had a brief conversation about it. He said that he regretted that he had been so widely identified as purely an object-relations theorist, because he thought that the key question was how explanations in terms of meanings were to be integrated with biological explanations. He thought that he was too old to do it; in fact, he died a few months later.

Recently, there have been various developments in neuro-science and evolutionary biology that offer exciting possibilities that we may be able to integrate more closely our understanding of the mind, the brain, the body, emotions, and our experience of ourselves. Attachment theory has been developed to enable us to understand how attachment and non-verbal communication link brain and body, not just within individuals but between them (Pally, 1998). Methods of observing the brain in action can show us how traumatic experience restricts and distorts the way synapses form, and how psychotherapy can actually increase the number of neural connections. Works such as Antonio Damasio's *The Feeling of What Happens—Body, Emotion and the Making of Consciousness* (2000) begin to show us how we can understand both the biology of the mind and the nature of the sense of self as the same thing.

In integrating this new knowledge, it is important for psycho-analysts not to react to knowledge from the outside as if it will destroy what is good about the inside. Perhaps the memory of Charles Rycroft, who was a courageous man, can remind us that there are valuable ways of being a psychoanalyst and working for it outside its own establishment. Freud himself was well aware of this. Talking to Eva Rosenfeld several decades previously about the quarrels and defections within Viennese psychoanalysis, he had summed it up concisely: "The goody-goody ones are no good, and the naughty ones go away."

Notes

1. There is a nice story about a supervisee coming to see Melanie Klein and recounting a session, ending by saying, "so, you see, the patient put his confusion into me". "No, dear", said Mrs Klein, "*you* are confused".

2. Several people have objected to my use of this term. They seem to equate it with "vulgarizer". My own view is that it is an established term within the history of science—see the title of Richard Dawkins' Oxford chair, the important role of figures such as T. H. Huxley, Steven Pinker—indeed, of almost all scientists who are read outside a narrow group of colleagues. Popularization is of immense political and social importance, since it governs how a discipline is perceived; to do it well is a difficult and complex task. I think that anxiety about the term is partly anxiety about leakages across the insider/outsider boundary.

References

Anderson, P. (1968). Components of the national culture. *New Left Review*, *50*, p. 42.

Budd, S. (2001). No sex please—we're British: Sexuality in English and French psychoanalysis. In: Celia Harding (Ed.), *Sexuality: Psychoanalytic Perspectives* (Chapter 3). London: Brunner-Routledge.

Damasio, A. (2000). *The Feeling of What Happens—Body, Emotion and the Making of Consciousness*. New York: Vintage.

Douglas, M. (1966). *Purity and Danger: An Analysis of Concepts of Totem and Taboo*. London: Routledge & Kegan Paul.

Freud, S. (1911b). Formulations on the two principles of mental functioning. *S.E.*, *12*.

Freud, S. (1916–17). Introductory Lectures on Psycho-Analysis. *S.E.*, *15–16*.

Fuller, P. (1985). Introduction. In: Charles Rycroft, *Psychoanalysis and Beyond*. London: Hogarth Press.

Home, H. J. (1966). The concept of mind. *International Journal of Psycho-Analysis*, *47*: 42–49.

King, P., & Steiner, R. (1991). *The Freud–Klein Controversies 1941–1945*. London: Routledge.

Merton, R. (1972). Insiders and outsiders: A chapter in the sociology of knowledge. *American Journal of Sociology*, *78* (No. 1, July).

Pally, R. (1998). Emotional processing: The mind–body connection. *International Journal of Psycho-Analysis*, *79*: 349–362.

Rycroft, C. (1962). Review of Guntrip's "Personality Structure and Human Interaction". *International Journal of Psycho-Analysis*, *43*: 351–355.

Rycroft, C. (1968). *A Critical Dictionary of Psychoanalysis*. London: Nelson/Penguin.

Rycroft, C. (1985). Where I came from. In: P. Fuller (Ed.), *Psychoanalysis and Beyond*. London: Chatto & Windus.

CHAPTER SEVEN

The question of independence in psychotherapy

Peter Lomas

A large proportion of the diagnostic criteria and treatment procedures current in medicine find general acceptance. The reason for this is that such measures, however imperfect, rest on the authority of a scientific basis. The same cannot be said for psychotherapy, as its critics are quick to point out. In contrast, the justification of much psychotherapy relies much more on the sway of its most revered thinkers, the degree to which their pronouncements appear to match the practitioner's subjective experience, and the tenuous and often conflicting theories that are offered as a blue-print for key phenomena. It is little wonder that the therapist struggles to maintain intellectual confidence and that debate is so often angry and strident. Psychoanalysis, by far the most creative and influential approach to psychotherapy for the past century, has been beset by dogmas and intrigues despite the richness of Freud's vision. The sad story of the perennial feuding among psychoanalysts has been rigorously laid bare by Roazen (2001).

The atmosphere, for anyone training at an Institute of Psychoanalysis, has not been conducive to free thought. It required much courage and confidence to seriously assess the value of theories and techniques in which the students were surrounded. The lectures, the seminars, books, the supervisor and, above all, the training analyst combined to produce an almost closed system of thinking, almost as difficult to escape as it must have been for those in past centuries who took in Christianity as they breathed the air around them.

Although I consider myself to be a rather critical person, and although I read around the subject more, I think, than is usually expected, the theory took hold of me and the technique dominated the way I related to my first patients. I had one lucky break. I went, by chance, to Charles Rycroft for my training analysis. Rycroft did not indoctrinate me into theory, nor did he attempt to turn me against it. He gave me room to think for myself, and if he considered that I was really thinking my own thoughts, he supported and encouraged me. Although he adhered to orthodox technique, the deadening effect of pure psychoanalysis was lessened by the fact that he would at times chat about himself and openly convey his thoughts about life and analysis as he might to a colleague, and in this area I felt on an equal footing with him. He never pretended that the Institute was the only source of wisdom and that I was a mere novice with little to contribute. Indeed, when he saw signs in me that I was struggling to find new ground, he was delighted. There appeared to me, however, to be a curious split between the generosity with which he shared his thoughts and his reserved manner. For example, he called me "Dr Lomas", and when I pleaded with him to be more informal, he resorted to "Lomas" in the best public-school tradition—which, to my mind, was even worse. I wish he had allowed himself to show more vulnerability and thereby enable me to empathize with him more readily. I do not know whether this barrier to closeness was due to pride or shyness or was a consequence of psychoanalytic strategy.

Psychoanalytic technique, by its very nature, predisposes the patient to develop an idealized transference. In the privacy of the consulting-room, where the way that the analyst behaves in ordinary circumstances is largely unknown, the patient has a poor chance of making a realistic assessment of what makes him speak and act in the way he does—an assessment necessary to the development of independent thought. In a training analysis the student is in an even greater position of vulnerability. The possibility exists of healthy feedback from fellow students about the analyst's personality and behaviour, but there appears to be a taboo on sharing such information, often justified by a fear of interfering with the transference. This state of affairs still continues, as far as I know, in spite of the widely held belief that training analyses so often result in proselytizing—a fact that led Edward Glover to declare, many years ago, that they should be abolished.

I can now see, in retrospect, some of the effects of psychoanalytic training on my own autonomy. It was a mixed bag. The interpretation of those inner elements in me that restricted my freedom was a blessing. The fact that Rycroft talked more freely about his thoughts than was customary at the time and that he encouraged the rebel in me was a blessing. But the technique, which remained the mainstay of his practice and which, I suspect, suited a certain aloofness in his character, and the pervasive certainty voiced around me that psychoanalysis was the only true path to wisdom made it difficult to think my own thoughts.

It has taken me decades of hard and often painful thinking to emancipate myself sufficiently to arrive at what I now believe to be a recognition of values in healing that do not derive from psychoanalysis and are in some respects opposed to them. Assuming that students of psychotherapy retains their independence of mind throughout the training, the question then arises as to how they handle their critique of orthodoxy. In the early days of psychoanalysis the practitioner whose views departed sufficiently from those of Freud left or was manoeuvred to leave the group of loyal members. Such departures were usually acrimonious on both sides. In more recent times, with the notable exception of Freud–Klein–Glover controversies, the British Society has been less manifestly turbulent. But the question of independence remains.

How did Rycroft deal with his growing disaffection? Except in the context of my analysis and the limitations imposed by this, I never came close enough to him to really know him. I believe this to be a combination of elements of transference that were still with me and his own reserve. There are, therefore, many people who can give a more knowledgeable answer to the question. I will, however, try to convey my own impressions.

Rycroft's contributions to the Scientific Meetings, as they were called, were incomparable in their lucidity. If he wished to make a particular point, he would do so precisely, clearly, unfussily, and with good humour. He pulled no punches in his views, yet the subversiveness of some of them may often have passed unnoticed. It was as though he were to say, "If you can't understand that, I'm not going to shout." Brawling was not his style, and he found it demeaning, distasteful, and uncreative. In speaking to me about his criticisms of the Society's lack of capacity for useful debate, he used the words "perseveration" and "incantation". He must, I imagine, have felt anger about this state of affairs, and I think he sometimes found expression for this in a sharp and delicate irony. On one occasion, at an International Conference, he was given the task of summarizing a discussion. His précis was accurate enough, but it pared down the debate to its bare bones. Only those sitting nearby, able to spot the glint in his eye, realized that he was gently relieving the Emperor of his clothes.

Strident voices tended to carry the day. Rycroft, by maintaining his integrity, has not made as much impact on the Society as others less creative. To some extent this is true of his writing. He did not invent striking new names or new techniques. It may be, however, that the discerning psychoanalyst who now turns to his work will find that his subtle critique of orthodox thinking constitutes important advances.

The myths about those who leave the fold of psychoanalysis, either by a too-radical departure from theory or practice or by resigning from the Society, are interesting, to say the least. Unhappily, particularly in the early days, they are directed by angry defensiveness to a degree that is shameful to the profession. Usually the one who leaves is pathologized to a lesser or greater degree. A notable example was the denigration of Ferenczi, lead by the venomous attacks of Ernest Jones. More recently the viciousness of the early years appears to have abated. Nevertheless it is not easy, as I know from my own experience, to leave for genuine intellectual reasons without having to face interpretations that have little basis in reality. Rycroft left the Society, I think, because he came to believe that it was not a useful forum for constructive debate. He passionately believed in creativity and nourished his own and that of others as best he could. A narrow and dogmatic intellectual environment was anathema to him. The last straw, as he himself has said, came at a meeting in which James Home read a paper called "The Concept of Mind". It was a brave and ground-breaking address, but, with the exception of Rycroft and myself it was received with universal contempt. I remember a long and vitriolic speech by one member of the audience, which evoked an unprecedented ovation. It is hardly surprising that this event brought Rycroft's disenchantment to a head.

I find much to agree with in Susan Budd's illuminating essay, "Insiders and Outsiders". Her description, however, of Rycroft's later essays as popularization—as if their value rests simply on his unparalleled capacity to clarify psychoanalytic ideas for the general reader—implies an idealization of psychoanalytic theory. The subtlety of ordinary language is better able to convey the nuances of personal and interpersonal experience than any psychological theory. I do not wish to undervalue theory, which can stimulate and jolt us into new directions and serve as a shorthand among professionals, but it is an insecure basis for our work, which is essentially a practice. Rycroft's essays are a contribution to the discipline of psychotherapy—and it should not be forgotten that in later years he referred to himself as a psychotherapist. Moreover, nothing that Rycroft wrote was mere exposition: his reviews of the ideas of particular psychoanalysts always contained a critique. What is to be regretted is that in later years he stopped writing about his own experiences with patients. I do not myself know why this was so. Perhaps he could not find a publication that he considered suitable for the revelations of his patients that such an endeavour is likely to entail. Or it may be that he never found a way of incorporating the effect on his practice of his continued intellectual development. But, whatever the reason, it is a loss.

An independence of mind is absolutely necessary if Freud's work is not to be permitted to stagnate. Scientists must be allowed to have ideas that depart from accepted thinking, and artists need to be free to paint what they are inspired to paint. Psychotherapy is no different. Practitioners should be free to speak and act in whatever way they believe to be right, provided that they do so in ways that are morally acceptable. Currently, however, psychotherapists are required to belong to a certain school of thought within the profession. Consequently, being a psychotherapist is not equivalent to being a scientist or an artist. All schools of psychotherapy have this dilemma. Psychoanalysis is not an exception to this—it just happens to be by far the most important in the field. Given this situation, the psychoanalyst whose views depart uncomfortably from orthodoxy has the choice of trying to accommodate to mainstream theory and practice or leaving the Society.

R. G. Collingwood (1958) writes:

> I have already had occasion to criticize the view that artists can or should form a special order or caste, marked out by special genius or special training from the rest of the community. That view, we have seen, was a by-product of the technical theory of art. This criticism can now be reinforced by pointing out that a segregation of this kind is not only unnecessary but fatal to the artist's real function. If artists are really to express "what all have felt", they must share the emotions of all. Their experiences, the general attitude they express towards life, must be of the same kind as that of the persons among whom they hope to find an audience. If they form themselves into a special clique, the emotions they express will be the emotions of that clique; and the consequence will be that their work becomes intelligible only to their fellow artists. [p. 119]

Psychotherapy is, I believe, closer to art than it is usually thought to be, and Collingwood's assertions could well be applied to psychoanalysis. Unfortunately, practitioners do, in fact, tend towards a "special clique" and to think and feel in terms of the clique. Those of independent mind who wish to break out into a wider world inevitably face intellectual and professional conflicts. Rycroft faced this conflict in his own particular way with his characteristic integrity, but at a cost. If psychoanalysis is to grow and flourish, it needs to be taught, practised, and discussed in a way that reduces this cost. The greatest potential for psychoanalysis, to my mind, lies in bringing the discipline out into a wider world in which ordinary language, morality, and ways of being are central to the endeavour.

References

Collingwood, R. G. (1958). *The Principles of Art*. Oxford: Oxford University Paperbacks.

Roazen, P. (2001). *The Historiography of Psychoanalysis*. New Brunswick, NJ: Transaction.

CHAPTER EIGHT

Rebel Rycroft

Dudley Young

In the autumn of 1968, a busy year for my generation, I went mildly crazy, and found myself at 18 Wimpole Street. At the end of our third weekly session, which had been given over to a spirited argument about the concept of cure, the learned doctor, smiling owlishly, suggested that our professional relationship was obviously in tatters: the transference, which had taken about thirty seconds to establish, had vanished as magically as it had arisen; and since he was in any case only my "auxiliary therapist", as he put it (my ex-girlfriend being in the chair), the obvious thing was to continue the discussion over supper one evening.

And so we did. This led on to weekends *chez moi* in North Essex, which continued over the next ten years. The frequency of his visits varied, not least because we were both unmarried and some of our girl-friends meshed better than others; but for a couple of years he came so often that he thought it best to rent a room in my house. When Jenny arrived and succeeded in battening him into London domesticity, we continued to meet, usually for supper at the Savile, and this carried on until he died.

Thirty years, then: quite a long innings as the world goes, and much to be grateful for; and though as friend and sometime valet I may be supposed to have been privy to his non-heroic side, I propose to spill no beans—or, more precisely, such privileged information as I possess in no way tempts me to darken what I have to say. My subject is Rycroft, man and work, with only such warts as may deepen our understanding of his singular contribution to the culture and why it has been under-valued.

The road to Cambridge

Central to any sustained understanding of his place in the picture is some idea of his placelessness: the man was marginal through and through. This is more complex than it sounds, for I principally mean by it not that he was of marginal importance, a minor figure at the back of the picture, but that his marginal magic enabled him to be both insider and outsider, present and absent, member and non-member, gentleman and player. Some of you will be familiar with this notion from Mary Douglas (via Van Gennep) and its buzzword in the schools, "liminality"; for those of you who are not, a brief social narrative will I hope give it some body.

The Rycrofts were hard-riding country gents, fox-hunters and soldiers, with a tendency to marry up a little. Charles was the fourth son of Sir Richard by his second and much younger wife, and Charles was fully 28 years younger than the first son, which will already suggest that he both was and was not Rycroft. This suggestion becomes the more impressive when ageing Papa dies, first-born son inherits, and the 11-year-old Charles is banished with his depressed mother and siblings to a life of genteel poverty in deepest Essex. Thus Rycroft to no-Rycroft, rolling acres to country church mouse—and then, for good measure, the sensitive boy (his mother's, not his father's, son) is sent to Wellington, to become the soldier his dead but still potent father had in mind: altogether the wrong school, Charles was a born Wyckhamist.

Enough dis-placement here to put a young man off the rails, one might think, but Charles sorted it at Cambridge; by which I mean a mask was fashioned wherein the disparate and contradictory elements were unified into something rich and strange, irony of course being the keynote—as indeed it remained to the end. (I should perhaps emphasize that I am using the word "mask" in the honorific and ultimately thespian sense, as Nietzsche and Yeats did, referring to the *persona* modern man needs to construct, not pejoratively in the sense of a phoniness that dissembles.)

A glimpse of this self-fashioning can be gathered from his brief Cambridge account entitled "Memoirs of an Old Bolshevik" (1985). The virtue of this piece is its mordant wit, so reminiscent of his table talk on a good night. But in the end it is camp Rycroft rather than vintage Rycroft in my view, and hence misleading to strangers. Its problems are both formal and psychological—the first in that he disapproved of autobiography (ego ego) and the second in that it covers a period of acute turmoil and transition, sensitive material that drives the wit a little hard in places as it tries to "cover" what has not been sufficiently mediated (as the Marxists used to say). The upshot is some mildly snobbish stuff, uncharacteristic. Of course it was written playfully, in carnival mode, and shouldn't be taxed too soberly; but I want to look at it with some care, both in order to say "he was better than this" and also because it provides some important information that the scholar in me prefers to "As he said to me one night in his cups . . .".

The piece begins with his going up to Cambridge, whereupon he joined the Conservative Association—as a dis-placed Rycroft well might—but within a month he had moved right across the board to the Socialist Club—as a dis-placed Rycroft probably should (in the 1930s anyway). From there it wasn't perhaps a great deal further to the Communist Party; and thus were the outlines of Rebel firmly etched in the mask. I say "firmly", but the essay wobbles on this and other matters. Its tone is mostly one of mockery, and the reader is left with the impression that this lefty business was more of an undergraduate jape than anything serious, a fashionable affectation *au fond,* the thinking man's inversion of a silvered cigarette holder.

It was and it wasn't. Charles was at best only theoretically enthralled by the working classes: practically speaking, the juxtaposition of bodies in a pub, not to mention the embrace of brotherhood, was more than a little embarrassing to all concerned—as it still is for many, heaven knows, despite the significant dismantling of class-consciousness in the meantime. But this is not the real point. What moved Charles to the radical left, as he quietly states at the outset of the essay, was neither working-class oppression nor romantic primitivism (nor even revenge upon the father), but the fact that only the Left was taking fascism seriously, the total seriousness of which he had just witnessed first-hand in his German sojourn before going up.

Had he written the serious piece on being a Cambridge lefty, it would have focused on Germany, on the crypto-fascism of a decadent aristocracy toying with self-parody, on English upper-class collusion (take a bow, Diana Mosley) and the death of fathers— plus a few jokes on the comedy of class comedy. A shame he didn't, says I, but there you are: not only was he agin autobiography— excessively, in my view, see his intemperate piece on Rousseau— but I think we must suppose that the matters involved were just a little too hot to handle with ease. And so, in the comic piece he *did* write, the serious subject is duly noted in the second paragraph, and the rest is given over to a frolicsomeness that doesn't quite work.

Jungian wheeze: Little Orphan Charlie, upper-class Cinderella, thought he might get out of the ashes if he could figure out who he was. The golden city of Cambridge glowed on the horizon—that's where the answer was. One day out walking, a fairy chipmunk said "The way to Cambridge is via Germany"; and so it was, and so he went, and there he was admitted to some secret knowledge, that the dragon of History (yes, capital H) was even then giving birth to something monstrous, which an Auden poem (written some four years later) describes as "that new European air that makes England of minor importance". Armed with this knowledge, he proceeded to Cambridge and was inducted half-sleeping into the Company of Rebels, the price of admission being that he stand on his head in King's Parade from time to time over a period of two years.

Fairy-tales are occasionally useful. I am trying to get back to the question of Rycroft's mask, and it is taking longer than I thought it would. "Rebel" is easy: against and for what is the difficult part. My short answer, since time runs on, is "for truth and against denial", the cry of any proper radical; and that what chiefly constellated the radical Rycroft persona at Cambridge was the knowledge of monstrosity nearby, almost in the family, which was being systematically denied not only in the thoroughfares but by the *bien pensants* in Cambridge.

The obvious parallel is with Orwell: again the upper-middle displacement, again the uneasy fastidiousness (the workers smell), and again, as with Rycroft, the real enemy was fascism, and the ultimate commitment was to truth and the fear of its vanishing. (If you doubt this, look at the last pages of Orwell's *Homage to Catalonia*.) The crucial difference was that Orwell had an easier Oedipal hand to play, quite clearly declared his rebellion, went to Spain, down and out—properly heroic doing *and* writing; whereas Charles the ironist gave up his occasional headstands in 1935 (by which time the Russian bear was looking distinctly grim to all with eyes to see) and became a psychoanalyst in Wimpole Street.

For some sense of the strangeness here, consider the Russian bear for a moment. Bertrand Russell, major man, had seen his ugliness in 1920, Malcolm Muggeridge had seen it by 1930, and Orwell saw it soon after. Most thinking Englishmen were more or less "of the left" in the 1930s, but the CP?—only the hardliners and the homosexualists, for the most part, the Philbys and the Blunts. So what was Charles doing? My simple answer would be that he was going just a little far in the fashioning of his mask, into the foothills of ablation—daddy *delenda est*—and that this is registered in the slightly hysterical wit of the Cambridge memoir. (MI5 were less than wholly amused. He was last called in for interview over the Blunt affair, I think, and quite enjoyed it, wore his Bolshie with pride.)

In any case the next move was into psychoanalysis, and the enabling chipmunk in this instance was Karin Stephen & co, through whose affection and guidance he was inducted as "Last of the Bloomsberries". It is worth noting that Rycroft, though correctly cherished in the analytic world as avatar of the imagination, was not a natural for the arty-party: his early forte was mathematics, and he spent his first year at Cambridge reading economics. Even in later life, when his intuitive touch had become very fine, it was secondary to the abstract power, the amazing speed and clarity of mental movement. (These two talents were nicely combined in what was, I think, his greatest therapeutic asset: a remarkable sensitivity to the spoken word and all its subtexts. Though not very musical, his hearing was extremely acute, picking up a false note the moment it began to go off, and moving with alacrity to the cause—often our old friend the double-bind, whose tricksy moves never fuddled him.)

By the time he went down from Cambridge, Bloomsbury had made a significant contribution to the masking of Rycroft, though of course the work was not yet complete. A comic illustration of this came in 1936 when he was rejected for analytic training by Ernest Jones on the grounds of dilettantism. Jones, though in many respects an unattractive man, was no fool; and that he failed to see the core of seriousness embedded in the light touch of Bloomsbury manners may well be because Charles had not yet managed to mesh them convincingly.

So ends my little social narrative, though heaven knows it is barely begun. I hope I have said enough to indicate my belief that the major making of Charles was at Cambridge—often acknowledged by him as his spiritual home—where the strong but dangerously difficult hand he had been dealt by circumstance was shuffled, sorted, and disposed in the form it was to retain more or less for the rest of his life. Its magical centre, as I have already suggested, was a remarkably elastic identity, a passport imaginatively to enter more rooms in the House of England than most—than any?—of his generation. Of course, on a bad day the chameleon feels homeless and alone; but, as the man said, no free lunch in the psychic realm either.

The baronet's son who joins the CP without disavowing the Father is probably a Tory-Radical. We are a smallish band, but our most distinguished members include Jonathan Swift, Dr Johnson, Burke, Wordsworth, and Cobbett (arguably), Bertrand Russell, and Orwell. Such people tend to be raised conservatively and then bump into some significant occlusion either psychic or historical or both, the answer to which is some form of Rebellion. The obvious difficulty in this story is how to kill the father without killing him, and many aspiring rebels expire in banality while sitting on the fence trying to solve the riddle. Truly bold spirits, on the other hand, absolute for rebellion, erase the Tory side of the dilemma and end up outside the city gates, mad, bad, or otherwise translated. And truly *unbold* spirits, finally, *pretend* to kill the father and father themselves; and they end up as phonies, with all the problems of ablation that Charles has so helpfully identified in his essay thereon.

Which leaves the small band of winners: those who actually ride the paradox of Tory Radicalism and live to tell the tale. It is, of course, a messy as well as a magical business from which no one emerges unscarred or unscathed; but the proof of success, insofar as it can be adduced, is in the addition of certain apartments to one's household identity, a liberty of word and gesture, room for manoeuvre denied to merely mortal man. Though each one riddles the paradox in his own way, the magic lies in a certain relation to word and gesture, ideal and real, whereby the spirit can endure the body's defeat. Shelley is pointing to it when he has Prometheus "hope 'til hope creates from its own wreck the thing it contemplates", though this is a little feverish, dialectical, even Germanic, for the English mind.

In the case of both Orwell and Rycroft, I have suggested, the rebel was committed only contingently to the working class and essentially to Truth; and though such contingency could have led simply to *mauvaise foi*, in fact it helped both rebellions to survive their defeat with something like Hamlet's "readiness"—though one should note that Orwell's early death released him from the difficulties of ageing gracefully. In Charles's case I can say with some certainty that the primary allegiance was to Truth, for we discussed it at great length—unsurprisingly enough, for my rebellion in 1968, which is what took me to Wimpole St, was similarly skewed by contingent commitments: although *marxissant* enough to join in the festivities, my principal concern was not that the workers were deprived but that the bosses were looking and sounding a little deranged.

Just as there were mods and rockers a little earlier, so there were politicos and hippies in 1968, and our differences grew and grew until they split the movement and the party ended. We hippies could and did talk politics, but our first allegiance was to the music, which opened first our bodies and then our minds to what was going on, not only here but *way over there*, in South-East Asia. I was 1-A for the Draft, my beloved daddy was an upmarket John Wayne, and hence unsurprisingly my attention became fixed (even transfixed) upon the monstrous thing emerging from Vietnam. At a certain point political horror goes beyond itself, into what can only be called the religious; and in both Nazi Germany and Vietnam I think this point was reached. Although we survived the 1960s, as we survived the 1930s, I am sure the culture was significantly disabled in both periods.

At such times rebels could do worse than read the Greek tragedians—and I still do; but one could hardly do better, as I hope to have indicated by now, than consult Charles Rycroft. I was by no means the only one to do so: young academics were freaking out everywhere in 1968, a vintage year, and he was known to be the main man—who *else*, for heaven's sake? (You had to be seriously nuts to get to Ronnie). There was indeed a queue to Rycroft's door, and it continued well into the 1970s. Could it be coincidence that 1968 found him on top form, publishing no fewer than three books? It could not. He saw that something very like the process that had initiated him into man's estate was at work again—at once a vindication of the road he took (less travelled by) and also a call to arms: some kind of epidemic was breaking out, for which his skills were particularly well suited. In view of this, is it not strange he chose never to write about it? I call it strange; and though I still don't have an explanation, something must be said.

First of all, I believe that only a fraction of what he had to offer the world ever got into print, and my private response to much of it was, "Ok, but you did this far better at supper last week." There is more than diffidence and modesty and scientific scruple at work here, but since it has to do with his professional withdrawal, I shall defer comment until we reach that hoary old matter. Second, he was somewhat constricted by Freudian scientism, which claims that just as physics is the science of nature, so psychoanalysis is the science of human nature; and since nature in both cases is more or less immutable, neither science has much time for History. This is, of course, not true: psychoanalysis is not a science, as Charles knew, and human nature is always in dialogue with its culture, as he also abundantly knew. But he *was* a Freudian, however deviant, and his heretical energies were significantly hedged by the Frowning Father. (I often used to taunt him with being a closet Jungian, to which his comic reply was, "But he can't write", and his serious reply was, "I can be of more use playing the hand I was dealt".) Third, he was by no means the only gifted writer I have known who has under-achieved: the condition is widespread. And, finally, I would suggest we have already roughed out some sort of answer by looking at the silences and the noise in his Cambridge piece: in addition to his formal strictures on autobiography (many of which I share) is the probability that his rage against old Daddy Rycroft for dying so savagely into the act of Primogeniture was never sufficiently stewed in the lower intestine to take its place in the casual comedy. But as to that, who is to say Charles wasn't right to keep this pain alive in the dark, the better to mask his vigilance? There is still altogether too much cant in North London about the need to banish inhibition and let it all hang out. Writers have long known that they need secrets to write from, and people do too. Still, I find it strange.

Exile from the kingdom

Dealing with Cambridge has pulled me into the 1960s, so we must now reverse a little to follow his psychoanalytic rebellion. The challenge was issued in his first major paper, on "symbolism" (1956), and this was amplified and strengthened in "Beyond the Reality Principle" (1962). At issue was Freud's barbarous distinction between the primary and secondary processes; and since this matter has by now been thoroughly aired in several places, I can be brief. In a nutshell, Freud decreed early on (1911) that insofar as the arts are involved with symbolism, they must be classified along with other forms of neurotic behaviour—at the innocuous end, certainly, so that a very good poem, for example, might be said to cauterize, if not altogether exorcize, the neurotic impulse that generated it; but any suggestion that a poem, by inviting its reader to convert some object into a symbol (two sticks into a cross, for example) can further invite the reader to help *authorize* the meanings that then become attached thereto (such as "the daily death of our Lord"), is bunk.

That's it. I am deliberately being a little provocative in my example here, since most of you will be at least vaguely in favour of poetry and at least mildly against religion. My purpose, however, is not to muddy the water but to indicate quickly that much is at stake—not simply the poet's licence to offer interior decoration to the middle classes (which is all he's been doing for some time now) but ultimately the culture's right to authorize any values at all.

Let us assume for the purposes of argument and generosity that Freud issued his decree innocently enough—or at least in a fit of absentmindedness, which is usually not innocent at all—because he was defining symbols as they arise from disturbed patients in the consulting-room: that is, pathologies for deconstruction. The trouble arises only when this grammar of pathology is taken outside the consulting-room and applied as metapsychology to healthy man making and unmaking his culture; at which point it becomes *big trouble,* exacerbating the nihilist paralysis into which Western culture has been sinking for some time.

Enter Rycroft on a white horse, ready to take the case. He knew that much was at stake, and he knew that all civilized analysts were uneasy with art = neurosis; and he further believed that the thing could be mended, despite Jones having reinforced the Freudian decree in a paper of 1918. All he had to do was quietly suggest that the materialism of Freud's metapsychology was looking a little dated (even the physicists were loosening up on ideal entities), analysts might properly be concerned with helping their patients choose life-enhancing symbols as well as discarding life-denying ones, poets do "dream awake" after all, Chartres cathedral is fairly impressive as neurotic statements go, and so forth. He wouldn't even have to mention Jung. Having established this little beach-head, he could then get on with the important business of building a proper metapsychology, aided by Wordsworth and Coleridge, on "the grand elementary principle of pleasure" which constitutes "the naked and native dignity of man".[1]

In other words not a very big deal, if his fellow analysts had been even quasi-rational—which of course they weren't. They were far too busy tearing each other to pieces to give him a hearing. Moreover, not only was he Mr Lah-dee-dah, *and* a bit English, my dear, but he was tampering with the tablets, proposing that Father's statue be slightly modified. And so the paper on symbolism entered the pool with hardly a ripple; and very soon after this—on

5 May 1956, to be precise, Freud's centenary—he began his retreat from the Society. From this distance the decision appears to me entirely rational: not only had he already wasted quite enough of his precious time on the bickering (about which the less said, the better) but the issues raised in the symbolism paper were of signal importance. He had played his card, a very good one as it happens, and it was their move. On his part there was no slamming of doors, no noisy letters of resignation—simply a quiet retreat to the side-lines of private practice to await the return of sanity.

It never came. The nettle of symbolism was not to be grasped; and so, in the late 1970s, with nary a whimper, he allowed his membership in the Society to lapse. Although this alienation from his professional body-politick both saddened and angered him (not to mention his failure to induce a certain level of intellectual rigour into the discipline for which he still harboured at least quasi-scientific hopes), it must be emphasized that he was by no means alone. Indeed, he was strikingly un-alone: almost everyone any good in the 1960s was taking liberties with classic metapsychol-ogy—Winnicott's "transitional" realm is a significant and uncon-tentious example. Many of these deviants also withdrew from the temple; and yet, as Charles pointed out in a characteristically telling phrase, they "also failed to spell out in convincing detail the full implications of the criticisms of Freudian metapsychology that they had made" (1985, p. 21)—and he includes in this list of deviants both himself and Laing.

What on earth, the outsider may well ask, was going on? What was inhibiting even the best and the brightest from speaking out clearly? The question is ultimately a large one, and I will offer only a short and breezy view: in the foreground one sees the obvious socio-psychological difficulties about amending holy writ; and also that the classic position nicely expresses and condones our modern ambivalence about the imagination—not to mention the decon-structive tendency, still widespread in academia, to rubbish the arts. In the middle ground and beyond, however, the craggy moun-tain ranges loom: if imagination is to be recognized again as *the* symbol-making power whereby cultures are made and unmade, as it most assuredly *is*, it will soon enough demand restitution of its central position in the temple; and all hell may break loose, as it almost did in Paris 1968 when the graffiti proclaimed "*L'imagina-*

tion au pouvoir". Where, then, is the accredited priesthood that will regulate the flow of symbols as they emerge? Who, for starters, is to say "Mozart: yes, Wagner: no"?

And in intellectual terms, who is to supervise the orderly removal of the scientismic suppressers as science makes room for what Kant called "belief" [*Glaube*] and we might as well call religion?[2] Back to Kant and Coleridge, as Charles acutely knew; but he also knew that Coleridge's lucubrations have been gathering dust in the University Museum for some time now.

What I am suggesting, in short, is that rebel Rycroft had a big fish on the line, one that could indeed turn into something like Moby Dick; and that though the mild emendations he called for in the matter of symbolism could, in principle, have been readily granted, it is not so very surprising that in fact they were not. Along with other major figures of the 1960s (Laing and Erikson particularly) he pursued his quarrel with the metapsychological nonsense, though as he said, with less than "convincing detail" on the "full implications" thereof. I still call it brave and fine: after all, the culture wasn't listening, and performances in an empty theatre are tiring.

Sonnenuntergang

My theme has been rebel Rycroft, now more or less done, and what remains is a drift through late afternoon. I choose a German word, not only to draw the thing out but also to recall his quiet and quirky Germanic aspect—that important exercise in self-making in the year before Cambridge, and also his enduring love of Goethe, in whom the country gent on his walks could bed down innocently with science. Walking was what Charles and I principally *did,* and a walking stick (plus pretty parkland) were all we needed to exchange our twentieth-century mess for eighteenth-century *claritas,* through which we ordered the human condition with a simplicity still discernible in Wordsworth's voice and Constable's eye. Though English science was arguably less innocent than German—that wicked Hobbes, look you—we agreed that an unblemished case could still be made for Erasmus Darwin. And for fun we even imagined running therapeutic weekends for the afflicted of

North London: he to conduct the church service, Ronnie Laing to provide rolling thunder in the chapel, and me to sing songs in the farmyard. A shame we never tried it.

In the 1980s and 1990s it was usually supper at the Savile, where we were often joined by Vincent Brome for a pre-prandial. Boy Brome was and is a wonder (now well into his nineties), having manifestly found the secret of eternal youth: when pressed on the matter, he would become cagey but then confide that it had mostly to do with the love of woman—the which, we all agreed, was becoming increasingly difficult to find.

Ah, yes, the 1980s, when the unacceptable face of feminism came proud. We would sift the news like battle reports, and soon developed a kind of trench humour—

"Lost another regiment in the north salient last month."
"Silly buggers, shouldn't have been there anyway."

His feel for what was going on was remarkably astute: for example, I remember one evening he began, "I have just read Angela Carter's latest, and the news is not good." I had known and liked her a little, some time before, so off we went. What made him so good at this sort of thing was not just the erudition and the remarkable combination of conceptual power and extreme sensitivity, but also his unerring eye for class comedy in the metropolis and the slippery pole it rides on.

Sometimes the bad news came rather close to home—some of those regiments were *ours*. Charles had over the years dared not only to criticise Kleinian theory but even the woman's *person!* What's possibly worse, he was, as is often the case with sensitive men, not only keen on women and attractive to them, but in no great hurry to dismantle his gender—did he not, after all, point out in puckish mode that "Madonna" Winnicott, though extremely good on mother and child, had little to offer the beleaguered male?

Such a man was clearly for the high jump; and the hard fems of North London duly did him over, the old charges surfacing once again: "Upper-class, eclectic, popularizer, dilettante", to which could now be added "sexist bastard". I won't say he enjoyed all this, but I will say he took it remarkably well. Not only had he been through it before, but he was in his seventies by then, and though singularly young at heart, increasingly full of years. *D'abord il faut durer*, as they say over there; and this he had, rather prodigiously, done. The mask young Rycroft had started hammering in the Rhineland and at Cambridge had indeed stayed the course, seen him over some bumpy jumps without falling into phoniness, slipping only now and then—in the 1960s, for example, when everyone any good got into some kind of trouble.

Is it then, finally, a tale of melancholy stayed, accepted, and overcome? I think it is: his basic disposition was certainly melancholic (look at the face!) and his great strength the ability to look compassionately at sadness and suffering and evil without flinching—and at the same time without relinquishing his simple, old-fashioned morality. The combination is rarer than one might think. Two illustrations: first of all, his great talent as therapist and interlocutor. What I found in 1968 was a man in a chair, undefended by Freudian jargon or ritual, uncannily acute of hearing, with a voice prepared sympathetically to follow the argument, wherever it might lead—a voice that nonetheless remained capable of saying, having heard some enormity, "Ah, yes, but that was rather wicked, wasn't it?" Charles believed in what Cambridge still calls "the moral sciences", and this belief strengthened his therapeutic practice. Therapy is tendance, after all, and as the evolution of its Greek sponsor *therapeuo* indicates, it combines a kind of reverent attention with a knowing touch. Lying nearby in the Greek mind is the healing grace [*charis*] of charisma, whereby devils are exorcized and luck is restored or bestowed. It was ever thus, and Charles's gift was enhanced by his intuitive sense that the noise of Freudian theory must be minimized if the magic of grace is to make itself felt and heard. He wouldn't *quite* put it this way, but nor would it altogether displease him. [For an illuminating glimpse of how he would put it, see his essay on "Faith, Hope and Charity" in *Viewpoints* (1991)].

My second illustration of his "virtuous melancholy" involves briefly considering the life—a rich catalogue of loss and failure that nonetheless failed to subdue his spirits: first of all the rolling acres vanish, then the radical politics, the professional disarray, the written work not quite what it might have been, the marital failure (almost mandatory in the late twentieth), and, more generally, the decline of almost everything he cared about. And then, to round off the list, the feminist hammering as prologue to the dumbing-down.

This process, though well under way in his lifetime, has by no means run its course, and it is likely that what is left of Charles's reputation will be shredded within a few years. Those of you who think I exaggerate might like to consider the comparable cases of two other men who were famous long ago in the 1960s: R. D. Laing and Robert Lowell. Both died early and are now almost beyond recall. Laing, who did his analytic training with Charles, is the less compelling instance, not only because his existentialist radicalism seemed a bit foreign to many, but also because he took a hand in deconstructing himself before the end. Still, something of a giant among dwarves: I remember, for example, an evening out with Ronnie & co to the Roundhouse for Sam Shepherd and his latest. After the show we gathered in a circle, Ronnie stood on his head (India calling), Sam displayed the latest American graffiti, and the rapping went on for hours. This was not nothing: this was indeed something, though the seeds sown therein are now blowing in the wind.

The shredding of Lord Lowell is nothing short of astonishing: unquestionably a major poet, cherished as a national treasure even before the 1960s and his important role in the anti-war movement, he offered his wisdoms to the faithful in Harvard Yard for years and is now virtually unmentionable in any reputable university. [I may as well declare an interest here—Lowell was a friend, used to stay with me when teaching in our department in the 1970s, and so I am disposed to object personally to his liquidation].

All three of these rebels were intellectually distinguished, attractive to women, and unintimidated by their own masculinity; and yet their besetting sin may well have been, not the masculine thing, but the fact that they spoke for a while (quietly, in Charles's case) with the voice of *authority*. How one acquires this voice in a crazing culture is an interesting and difficult matter, not unrelated to the *charis* in charisma, which we cannot go into here: suffice it to say that these men were among the last to have it, and that the forces of the dumbing-down are implacably opposed to it. The major prophets in this regard are Orwell and Huxley (mix the two) but the 1960s voice that rolled it all into one deathless line was Andy Warhol's: "Henceforth everyone will be famous for 15 minutes"—great fun, until the penny drops.

And just in case you think that the present feminist silence augurs peace in our time, I would remind you that the knife-work continues: even as I write, the Home Office is promising legislation to enable a woman to claim that, though intercourse was consensual, she was mildly intoxicated; at which point the case for the defence will collapse, and the jury will be directed to return a verdict of Statutory Rape. Before such mind-blowing stupidity the analytic mind must, alas, lay down its arms and fall silent. Equally disturbing, perhaps, is the recently "resolved" Shieldfield Nursery scandal in Newcastle, which began in 1994 and clearly reveals that hysteria with regard to sexual abuse is still endemic among social workers and civil servants—not only in deepest Newcastle, but in the Home Office and Westminster, where The Protection of Children and The Youth Justice Acts were passed in 1999. The seeds of this collective psychosis, imported from America, were sown in the 1980s, and North London psychobabblers (not to say the Tavistock Institute) will be found more than a little culpable, should the history ever be written. Charles did what he could to keep the witch-craze contained (notably in his important piece *contra* Masson in the *New York Review* in 1984) but his licence to pronounce "with authority" was even then in the process of being revoked by the forces of feminism and the dumbing-down.

Cyril Connolly said in the 1930s that since it was closing time in the pleasure gardens of the West, a man will henceforth be gauged by the quality of his despair—which is to say, by the amount of bad news he can incorporate without faltering. It's a Nietzschean idea, and in its light Charles stands rather well. None of the items in my list of his "failures" did he seek to extenuate or deny: the eye remained open, the spirit undaunted, the cheerfulness undismayed. I call that remarkable.

Re-reading my manuscript, I notice one signal omission, and so, rather than following the old boy down into death where all the stories end, I shall finish with a brief meditation on one of his favourite jokes, which originated with Karl Kraus, that apocalyptic Viennese goofball who, together with the unsmiling Adorno, is my favourite Freudian critic: "Psycho-analysis is a symptom of that disease for which it purports to be the cure." Now this, you will readily grant, is not the sort of joke one expects a distinguished analyst to crack, in the Savile or anywhere else; and it nicely illuminates the difference (even the trendy *différence*) that was Charles: mischievous, commonsensical, erudite, rebellious, and deeply serious. It is inviting us to stand back a moment from whatever little *Sekurität-system* we happen to be riding and consider the occidental sclerosis that is taking us, as Nietzsche so presciently put it, into "the world as hospital, with everyone as everyone else's nurse". One could do worse than consult Herr Goethe on this matter, or even William Wordsworth. Serious fun, opening various doors on those primary and secondary processes, the major motif. I was very pleased that Boy Brome recalled this joke in his obituary of Charles.

Envoi

While dining with Charles at the Reform Club not so very long ago, we were approached by an old acquaintance of his, not seen for some years and perhaps not to be seen again. The exchanges were brief, courteous, affable, and then, momentarily, quite moving. Hail and Farewell: it was as if a great deal was being distilled into very little. As he left, the man said: "And may you continue to improve with age, dear boy, like the fine old vintage you are."

Appendix

I should like briefly to comment on Paul Roazen's remark that Charles once said to him that Melanie Klein and Anna Freud had "ruined his career" (see p. 39). This shocked me when I read it and will, I think, mislead those who didn't know the Rycroft. While not in the least disposed to question Paul's memory, I would venture to suggest that, perhaps because the wine was particularly good that evening, he missed the ironic inflections that accompanied so much of what Charles said. The deconstructive key lies in the word "career": Charles didn't have one of those, and so when he gives himself one, ironies are in play. The literal truth (in the bass line) is that these two foreign bruisers were central players in the back-biting that nearly drove him to distraction; and hence when in mildly misogynistic "monstrous-regiment-of-women" mode, he could certainly have made the remark. Its important meaning however, clusters on "career", which elegantly sends up (while preserving) the real sorrow and turns it to triumph both empty and full. Though saddened by his professional alienation, and doubtless somewhat reduced thereby (as Susan Budd speculates), he was also deeply grateful to have been released from a mad circus and would certainly have been further reduced had he stayed on. Moreover, though immensely polite and retiring, he was no pussycat, and not in the least intimidated by noisy women. You could look it up. The real ogre was Klein, and there he is, *new boy*, staring back at her: "If I cannot hold my own with you, then British psycho-analysis is not worth fighting for." And so he left it to her, more or less; and there is no doubt in my mind that British analysis has since then been much impoverished by being over-Kleinianized.

That's as may be; but on the question of whingeing Rycroft I am prepared to wax categorical. We discussed both it and, more gener-ally, the loneliness of the long-distance runner, at great length and over many years; and though he never denied the pain (and the shame) of those demeaning fights, his conscience was clear: he exited on the symbolism paper, serious stuff, and turned the rest to comedy. And thus he could remain adamantly pro-woman to the end, amply provisioned with lethal scorn for the harpies.

Notes

1. I quote from Wordsworth's 1805 Preface to the *Lyrical Ballads*, where he argues for parity with the "Man of Science" in the construction of a new identity (i.e. post-Christian, post-aristocratic) for modern man. *The Innocence* of *Dreams* is of the same party. Unfortunately, the gods of unpleasure prevailed against both.

2. Kant's line is so good (and pertinent) that it is worth quoting: "*Ich muss das Wissen aufheben, um dem Glauben Platz zu räumen*" [I must at once cancel, preserve and heighten knowledge in order to make room for faith]. The word *aufheben* is serious magic in Kant's hands, untranslatable *Ursprache*.

112   DUDLEY YOUNG

References

Freud, S. (1911). Formulations on two principles of mental functioning. *Standard Edition*, 12.

Jones, E. (1918). The theory of symbolism. In: *Papers on Psycho-Analysis*. London: Baillière, Tindall & Cox, 1948.

Rycroft, C. (1956). Symbolism and its relationship to the primary and secondary processes. In: *Imagination and Reality*. London: Hogarth Press, 1968.

Rycroft, C. (1962). Beyond the reality principle. In: *Imagination and Reality*. London: Hogarth Press, 1968.

Rycroft, C. (1984). A case of hysteria. *New York Review of Books*, 12 April.

Rycroft, C. (1985). Memoirs of an old Bolshevik. In: *Psychoanalysis and Beyond*. London: Hogarth Press.

CHAPTER NINE

A brief history of illusion: Milner, Winnicott, Rycroft

John Turner

> Panic seized her. Blood seemed to pour from her shoes. This is
> death, death, death, she noted in the margin of her mind;
> when illusion fails.
>
> Virginia Woolf, *Between the Acts*, 1941, p. 125

Illusion is a word that Raymond Williams might have included
among his list of keywords of British culture, since it is a word
that discloses "both continuity and discontinuity, and also
deep conflicts of value and belief" within its intellectual and political history (1983, p. 23). It is, as we shall see, a banner under which
the meaning of that culture has frequently been contested. My
purpose here is to indicate some of the more significant of those
contests, with occasional glances at the wider European context
and with special reference to the history of psychoanalysis, where
the conflicts that characterize the larger history of the word have
been interestingly re-enacted. In particular, I want to explore its
significance for the English psychoanalysts Marion Milner and
Charles Rycroft and, more centrally, for Donald Winnicott, not
least in Winnicott's case because it is a word that has been treated

only peripherally in the two books that are organized around the study of his language: Alexander Newman's *Non-Compliance in Winnicott's Words* (1995) and Jan Abram's *The Language of Winnicott* (1996).

I

In the sixth section of *The Future of an Illusion* (1927), the book in which Freud looks forward to the dispersing of the cloudy mists of religion before the strong light of reason, he offers a definition of illusion that may serve as our starting-point. *Illusion*, he says, is different from *error*: it may have been an error in Aristotle to believe that vermin developed out of dung, but it was not an illusion. To call a belief false is not necessarily to call it an illusion. Nor need an illusion necessarily be false. "A middle-class girl may have the illusion that a prince will come and marry her", and so, indeed, he may. But we think of her belief as an illusion, says Freud, because "we call a belief an illusion when a wish-fulfilment is a prominent factor in its motivation" (p. 31). He then goes on to distinguish *illusion* from *delusion*. Both words direct our attention towards erroneous beliefs that are shaped by wishes: the difference between them is that when we call a belief a *delusion* we are thinking of it in its relation to reality. Thus *error* belongs to the question of the objective truth of a belief, *illusion* belongs to its subjective quality, and *delusion* belongs to its subjective quality considered in relation to its objective truth.

There is one obvious question opened up by these distinctions, and Freud raises it at once at the start of Section VII: can we *ever* separate the question of the objective truth of our beliefs from our wish to believe them? If our religious doctrines are illusions, he asks, "must not the assumptions that determine our political regulations be called illusions as well? and is it not the case that in our civilization the relations between the sexes are disturbed by an erotic illusion or a number of such illusions? And once our suspicion has been aroused, we shall not shrink from asking too whether our conviction that we can learn something about external reality through the use of observation and reasoning in scientific work—

whether this conviction has any better foundation" (p. 34). Religion, politics, sex and science: how can we be sure that our beliefs in any of these areas are illusion-free, determined by reality rather than by pleasure?

It is clear that this question was an important one for Freud, perhaps even the most important question of all; and accordingly he reserves his answer for it until the final section of his book, when he asks it once again—not of politics or sex, which he places outside the field of his present inquiry, but of his own treasured belief in science. The question emerges out of a dramatized exchange (the only such exchange in all Freud's work) where Freud wrestles with an imagined interlocutor who is his own alter ego, his dialogic other. This imagined interlocutor is possessed by an anxiety both political and philosophical that leads him to argue on the one hand for universal scepticism and on the other hand for the need to retain the illusion of religion in order to preserve civilization from anarchy. His case is a familiar one among conservatives of the time who felt themselves threatened by the growing power of the working classes: people, he says, *the* people, need illusions. "Civilisation is hooped together, brought / Under a rule, under the semblance of peace / By manifold illusion": these lines from the start of Yeats's sonnet "Meru" (1958, pp. 333–334) might well have been written for Freud's alter ego in *The Future of an Illusion*—and of course the case had already been stated most famously of all in the "dialogue" between the Grand Inquisitor and Jesus in Dostoevsky's *The Brothers Karamazov*.

Freud concedes much to the argument of his imaginary opponent, implicated as he is in an elaborate *pas de deux* in defence of what he calls "our God, *oyos*" (Reason) against the Christian Word (Freud, 1927, p. 54). He is quite prepared to admit that his liberal faith in human rationality and its final triumph over the illusions of religion may prove itself to be illusory, and that he may have to modify his optimism in the future. His wry deification of Reason as the *Logos* of his choice concedes the element of wish-fulfilment in his own thinking. But what he will not admit is that science is an illusion; and science, for Freud, of course, included the "science" of psychoanalysis. "We believe that it is possible for scientific work to gain some knowledge about the reality of the world, by means of which we can increase our power and in accordance with which we can arrange our life" (p. 55). These gains, he argues, are real gains, not mere novelties reflecting the endless relativity of all human knowledges. Nor will he accept the neo-Kantian critique of science as invalidated by the limitations of our faculties, since it is the real world that those faculties have evolved to deal with, and all other worlds are mere abstractions, of no practical interest at all. "No", the book concludes defiantly, "our science is no illusion. But an illusion it would be to suppose that what science cannot give us we can get elsewhere" (p. 56).

Freud's conclusion is clearly intended to bring to an end the long debate with his alter ego; and yet, despite his attempt at closure, the assertiveness of his final statement still continues to bear within it the trace of a deep anxiety about the status of science and of human reason. Freud believed in science as the supreme work of human reason, and in psychoanalysis as his own special contribution to that science; its aim, he thought, was to bring patients through the illusions of the transference into what, in "Meru", Yeats called "the desolation of reality". Yet it seems that the very weight of Freud's concentration upon his "science" de-substantiated it: his bleak pursuit of an illusion-free existence threatened that same existence with illusion. His self-creation as a man of science simultaneously gave birth to the imaginary double of his sceptical opponent; and it is his long agon with this opponent, and not the easy demystification of religion that lies on its surface, that gives to *The Future of an Illusion* its discursive energy and its deepest structural organization. The palace of reason, we might say, is built upon the sands of doubt. Nor was Freud unique in discovering this: his agon repeated a pattern recurrent in European culture. Other men had been there before him, most notably perhaps Descartes.

II

In his *Meditations* (1641), Descartes confronted his scepticism about the possibility of ever finding certainty in human knowledge; and the way in which he did this may serve to remind us of the space occupied by the concept of illusion in the culture of early modern

Europe. The illusions of dreams, and the facts of human deception and self-deception, he wrote, had led him to doubt the knowledge of his senses; and so he decided to go back to the beginning and to doubt everything that may be known.

> I will suppose, then, not that Deity, who is sovereignly good and the fountain of truth, but that some malignant demon, who is at once exceedingly potent and deceitful, has employed all his artifice to deceive me; I will suppose that the sky, the air, the earth, colours, figures, sounds, and all external things, are nothing better than the illusions of dreams, by means of which this being has laid snares for my credulity. . . . [p. 84]

Where Freud wrestled with an alter ego, Descartes wrestled with a malignant demon; and the nature of his imagined opponent suggests that he, too, like Freud, was preoccupied not simply by epistemological problems that belonged to the conscious mind but also by ontological problems that belonged to the unconscious. The issue, in other words, was not simply of scepticism, which is a respectable philosophical position, but of the anxiety that often attends it, particularly among intellectuals who invest so much of their energy and self-worth in the activities of their own reason. Psychologically speaking, it was a question not only of doubt but of what Winnicott called "*doubt* about oneself" (1988, p. 94). In his book *The History of Scepticism from Erasmus to Descartes* (1960), R. H. Popkin has argued that Descartes's "malignant demon" may well have been suggested to him by the witch-trial at Loudun in 1634 (p. 184). Be that as it may, Descartes dramatized his philosophical *crise pyrrhonienne* in the iconography of those early modern demonologists and witch-hunters who devoted their energies to exposing the illusions of witches as counterfeits of the miracles that only God could perform. Such demonologists, by the logic of their own work, were often brought up against the alarming possibility that everything that they took for truth was in fact illusion, the work of the devil. The *scientia* of theology itself might prove to be illusion; and the only answer that the demonologists could find to their anxiety was to trust to the goodness of God, who would never let us be so comprehensively lost. Descartes's solution to the problem of doubt was little more than an idealized version of that of the demonologists; he trusted to the reality of his own thoughts (*cogito ergo sum*), one of which was an intuition of a perfect superior being who would never allow us to be the victim of a malignant demon. As we have seen, it would be by an assertion of his faith in the Logos not of Christianity but of science that, nearly 300 years later, Freud would similarly attempt to resolve the anxiety of his own scepticism.

Descartes's dramatization of his doubt reminds us of the dangerousness of illusion in early modern Europe. Whether a good Catholic or merely politic, he shared with the demonologists a sense that illusion threatened to destabilize not only the self but also the established religious and political order of the world. In Renaissance England, too, the word was a weighty one. It made its first appearance at the end of the fourteenth century, derived from the Latin *illudere*, meaning "to make sport of, to ridicule, to trick, to impose upon". To *illude* someone meant to play tricks upon them: *illusion* implied trickery and deception; and since in the world of early modern Europe the devil was the arch-deceiver, the trickster-in-chief, illusion was most commonly used to describe the kind of false seeing suggested by supernatural agents. The "illusion" of the "artificial sprites" that ensnare Macbeth (III: v.27–28) illustrates the typical literary use of the word and its customary theological weight. The deception practised by Hecate and the Weird Sisters, with their misleading prophecies of a moving wood and a man not born of woman, leads not only one man but a whole kingdom to ruin; the malicious tricks that they play unseam the body politic of Duncan's Scotland.

The sinister playfulness of the Weird Sisters reminds us that *illudere* derives from *ludere*, to play, and that if witchcraft was dangerous in Renaissance Britain, so too at times was play. Leontes in *The Winter's Tale* catches something of the complex ambivalences surrounding the term when he says to his son, in the mistaken belief that his wife has been unfaithful to him:

> Go, play, boy, play: thy mother plays, and I
> Play too; but so disgrac'd a part, whose issue
> Will hiss me to my grave. [I.ii.187–189]

The metadramatic implication of these lines underlines the fact that the business of theatre was illusion, and that illusion might be something to be celebrated as well as feared. The word, in fact, had considerable countercultural potential; and yet, because of its theological associations and because of the theological and political disapproval that relegated the dangerousness of theatres and plays to the margins of Puritan London, outside the city-walls, this potential rarely emerged. Puck may practise "illusion" upon Helena in the wood in *A Midsummer Night's Dream* (III.ii.98) but the subversiveness of the pleasure to be taken in his activities, as in the fairies and the play as a whole, is explored in the language of dream rather than of illusion.

Gradually, however, in Britain, with the passing of the late feudal civilization, whose various crises in religious and political authority had intensified witchcraft-beliefs and precipitated witch-hunting, the concept of illusion became secularized and entered upon its modern psychological meaning. After the bourgeois pacification in 1690, theological gave way to a psychological anxiety, in a range of meaning that fluctuated between that of delusion (irrational thinking and feeling) on the one hand and pleasurable fantasy ("pleasing illusions") on the other. This latter sense had always been part of the word's psychological meaning, especially in matters of sexual passion, although its demonological associations had prevented its being widely used in this way; but in the eighteenth century, as the episteme changed, this emphasis became much more prominent. Freud's definition of the word as signalling a belief shaped by wish-fulfilment belongs to this new bourgeois period. Freud was determined, of course, that illusions should be banished as far as was humanly possible. But the question raised by the instability of the word in the eighteenth century was precisely one of what was humanly possible and, indeed, of what was humanly desirable. Hard-headed people in hard-headed moods might still oppose illusion to reason, science, and common sense; but reason itself, in the shape of Lockean philosophy, now began to offer scientific reasons for valuing illusion.

Addison, in his book *The Spectator* (1712), popularized this new philosophy in his description of the *"secondary and imputed* qualities" that Locke had attributed to our subjective seeing rather than to the real objective world. These qualities, he wrote, were particularly those of light and colour, which gave to our existence the illusions of a magical romance, the spell of which bore now only the most distant trace of their demonological antecedents:

We are every where entertained with pleasing Shows and Apparitions, we discover imaginary Glories in the Heavens, and in the Earth, and see some of this Visionary Beauty poured out upon the whole Creation; but what a rough unsightly Sketch of Nature should we be entertained with, did all her colouring disappear, and the several Distinctions of Light and Shade vanish? In short, our Souls are at present delightfully lost and bewildered in a pleasing Delusion and we walk about like the Enchanted Hero in a Romance, who sees beautiful Castles, Woods and Meadows; and at the same time hears the warbling of Birds, and the purling of Streams; but upon the finishing of some secret Spell, the fantastick Scene breaks up, and the disconsolate Knight finds himself on a barren Heath, or in a solitary Desart. [Vol. 3, pp. 283–284)]

The witchery of Keats's "La Belle Dame sans Merci" partly originates in this passage. Addison's aesthetic, like the philosophy on which it was based, betrays an inexorable psychological split that lay deep in early bourgeois society and that had deepened still further by the time that Keats came to write a century later: a split between the objective reality of the world and the subjective illusions of romance, between fact and fancy, between science and poetry.

Countless works of fiction sprang up along this fault-line in eighteenth-century society, embodying or exploring the ambivalence surrounding the idea of illusion. The novels of Mrs Radcliffe afford a typical example. They seem at first sight to be exercises in the disciplining of illusion by reason. Emily St. Aubert in *The Mysteries of Udolpho* (Radcliffe, 1794) is haunted by visions that are the products of fear and desire—"the illusions of a distempered imagination", Mrs Radcliffe calls them (p. 95)—and she struggles hard to check them in the name of the patriarchal reason recommended by her father. Mrs Radcliffe's shimmering castles of romantic illusion, it seems, are securely founded upon the rock of reason. And yet this does not quite tell the whole story. There is a destabilizing ambiguity about the idea of illusion in her novels, suggested both by her choice of the Gothic genre and by her use of the word. Illusion is not only something to be checked: there is a strong countercultural movement within her texts that leads her to celebrate it as a source of value. It belongs to the joyous seeing of childhood and the precious seeing of love, to the enjoyment of art (such as her own) and the appreciation of landscape. It belongs to the workings of the fancy and the imagination, and these may be positive as well as negative. To appreciate "the magical illusions of twilight", for instance, was to exercise a sensibility that consciously flourished in opposition to the daylight world of rationality and common sense (p. 599). Yet at the same time the restriction of that sensibility to twilight, and to the worlds of pastoral and domestic life, reminds us too that such opposition was usually muted, an expression of political and psychological retreat. It belonged to a counterculture permitted by the dominant ideology that contained and emasculated it. Illusion offered no more than consolation for the rigours of reality, and it commonly did so in eighteenth-century Britain in a spirit of nostalgia, which, as Winnicott reminds us, "belongs to the precarious hold that a person may have on the inner representation of a lost object" (1971, p. 27).

There is, however, a moment in Edmund Burke's *Reflections on the Late Revolution in France*, written in 1790, that offers a more vigorous use of the word and foreshadows its future development. Burke was arguing against the egalitarianism of contemporary radicals who believed in the sufficiency of human reason to evaluate the political and religious institutions of their country; and he attacked their "new conquering empire of light and reason" by the consciously paradoxical celebration of all those "pleasing illusions, which made power gentle, and obedience liberal" in the *anciens régimes* of Europe (p. 74). Burke's position was fundamentally a conservative one, and he used the language of illusion to mystify a reality where power was not always gentle and obedience not always liberal. Yet implicit in his argument was a recognition of the important fact that any idea of a civilization was necessarily an imaginative construct, involving a set of objective relations mixed inextricably with subjective values in such a way that its worth could not be measured solely upon the scale of reason. The "science of government" (p. 58), as Burke called it, was paradoxically the work of "prejudice" (p. 84)—that is to say, of values, traditions, and habits of thought and feeling that necessarily preceded and informed all rational judgements. To use Winnicott's language, Burke saw nations as large-scale examples of groups held together (if at all) by the similarity of their common illusory experiences; and these illusory experiences were to be respected as the stuff of life.

Burke's emphasis on the subjective habits and traditions that inform perception was to be crucial in the development of English Romanticism, with its high valuation of those feelings that, in Wordsworth's phrase, constituted "the blood and vital juices of our minds" (1974, Vol. I: 103). Wordsworth, like Descartes before him, had tried to live by reason. He had belonged to that same radical movement attacked by Burke, but he had been brought close to breakdown by its failure in the early 1790s; and in that great crisis of his life he went through a period of painful philosophical scepticism, which he clearly identified in part as doubt about himself. Like Hume, who had suffered a similar scepticism some sixty years earlier, Wordsworth described that doubt not in pre-Enlightenment terms of demons and devil-possession but in more modern terms of mental and physical disease. He became "sick", he wrote in *The Prelude* (1805/1958): "demanding *proof*, / And seeking it in everything, I lost / All feeling of conviction, and, in fine, / Sick, wearied out with contrarieties, / Yielded up moral questions in despair" (X: 897–901). It was Wordsworth's survival of this crisis that made him a great poet, as he struggled to understand the process by which he had recovered his hold upon those primary feelings with which, he believed, his mother's "Presence" had first irradiated "all objects through all intercourse of sense" (1974, Vol. II: 258–260). Our assumption that life is worth while originates here, thought Wordsworth, in the maternal love that confirms the bounty both of the outside world and of our capacity to contribute creatively to it. One may quarrel at times both with the politics and the platonism of Wordsworth's bourgeois idealization of love and regret his neglect of rage and hatred; but his fundamental prioritization of feeling over reason marks a significant transformation of cultural paradigms. He was not arguing, as many Victorians would, that there were two worlds, one of reason and one of feeling, one of science and one of poetry. There was only one world, and what mattered was our capacity to find value in it. Similarly with the exercise of the human faculty of reason: what mattered was our capacity to find value in it. But as Winnicott might have observed, we can only find that value if we have first created it; and it was Wordsworth's appreciation of this that produced his resonant definition of Poetry as "the impassioned expression which is in the countenance of all Science" (Wordsworth, 1974, Vol. 1: 141).

Wordsworth's emphasis on the importance of subjectivity in perception ranged from the suffusion of external objects with feeling to the usurpation wrought upon those objects in moments of sublimity. The imperious power of imagination worked through illusion; and yet that power also brought with it a corresponding sense of the vulnerability of the percipient. If a sense of the worthwhile is the light that we bring to our seeing, it is a light that may go out. Moments of enhanced vision, symbolized by Wordsworth in the figure of the rainbow which "comes and goes", may decrease (1940–49, Vol. 4: 279); the habit of joy may be overthrown by suffering; and the faith and beliefs out of which we have built our lives may prove to be illusion. What saved Wordsworth from such catastrophic disillusion was the strength of his habitual disposition and his development of a stoical religious faith; but it was nevertheless characteristic of him that, even amidst his most stoical poems, he should retain a tender regard for the youthful illusions that had helped build up the present habits of his mind. Perhaps the most moving example of this is the poem that he wrote on the death of his brother in 1805, the "Elegiac Stanzas Suggested by a Picture of Peele Castle", where, wonderingly, revising the "delusion" that he had first written, he recreated the "fond illusion" of his youthful invulnerability out of which his newer serenity had now emerged (1940–49, Vol. 4: 259).

It is notable, however, that despite the value that he placed upon illusory experiences, Wordsworth reserved the word *illusion* itself to denote a category of superseded belief, once of value but now discredited by experience. It was not until the new conditions of modernism at the end of the century, with its new sense of cultural relativism, that the concept of illusion was to emerge among certain writers as a positive force, descriptive of the imaginative subjectivity that was the necessary condition of all human values and beliefs. Conrad was the most striking embodiment of this new spirit, and in *Nostromo* he epitomized his vision in the pencil-thin beams of a lighthouse attempting in vain to penetrate the all-consuming darkness that encompassed it. All the feelings and beliefs by which we live, religious, political and emotional, were seen by Conrad as illusions; and his fiction was the formal expression of a countercultural attack upon many of the certitudes of early twentieth-century imperialist and positivist culture. Many modernist texts explored a similar vision—Lawrence's *The Rainbow*, for example, or Virginia Woolf's *To The Lighthouse*—and Logan Pearsall Smith's popular compilation from Santayana's works, the *Little Essays* (1920), which Marion Milner liked so much, offered a comparable vision in philosophy. Even the most practical and scientific person, Santayana wrote, must from time to time fall back upon his soul in the recognition that "only his illusions have ever given him a sense of reality" and that all his practical strivings have only been "a dream and a symbol" of the truths that lay beyond (p. 139). Hence the panic experienced in the words of my epigraph by Miss La Trobe, the amateur theatrical producer in Virginia Woolf's *Between the Acts* (1941) and in some sense a stand-in for the author herself: "This is death, death, death, she noted in the margin of her mind; when illusion fails" (p. 125). It was in this world of English literary and philosophical modernism, with its widespread sense of the illusory nature of all human values and beliefs, that Marion Milner and Donald Winnicott were brought up, and its influence may be felt in their rethinking of the concept of illusion in psychoanalysis in the 1940s.

III

Where previously psychoanalysis had followed Freud in seeing illusion negatively as a failure to adapt to reality, Milner and Winnicott came to view it positively as a means of adaptation. Milner told her biographer designate, Margaret Walters, of the stimulus that she had found to her thinking about illusion in Christopher Caudwell's Marxist history of the social function of poetry, *Illusion and Reality* (1937). Classical Marxism had been as impotent as classical psychoanalysis in finding a way to value the artistic activities of human beings. Caudwell, however, typically of his time, had married the world-views of Freud and Marx and developed a view of art and science as parallel exercises in illusion through which individual men and women sought to resolve the contradictions between themselves and the world around them. "It is the characteristic of the artist", Caudwell argued, "that his products are adaptative, that the artistic illusion is begotten of the tension between instinct and consciousness, between productive forces and productive relations, the very tension which drives on all society to future reality" (p. 119). Artists in the subjective sphere of art, and scientists in the objective sphere of scientific theory, react to the constraints of reality by developing fictions; they pursue illusions that have been abstracted from the real phenomenological world, and that may prove useful in the unending struggle of men and women to accept or to resolve the tensions within their social experience.

Caudwell's belief that the illusions of art and science were fundamentally adaptive was influential on Milner and, through her, on Winnicott, although this influence took a depoliticized form that focused upon the individual struggle to maintain creative autonomy rather than upon the collective struggle to remove the contradictions of bourgeois society. Caudwell's Marxism was itself adapted by Milner to the liberal world of London psychoanalysis, with its professional interests in individual and family psychology. There were, moreover, particular tensions within that world which helped to shape the adaptation of Caudwell's ideas. Milner and Winnicott did not altogether agree about illusion, as we shall see; but it is significant that their ideas had a common origin during the 1940s, in the aftermath of the supposedly scientific quarrels within the British Psychoanalytical Society between the supporters of Melanie Klein and those of Anna Freud. Both Milner and Winnicott found in the concept of illusion a way of preserving their own individual creativity within that professional world; and in this way the concept was developed to perform the function that it describes. It recovered its long-standing countercultural value in their hands, as a weapon to be wielded against scientism and what Winnicott called "split-off intellectual functioning" (1971, p. xii). It was no accident perhaps, in the context of those "scientific" quarrels, that while Caudwell stressed the similarities between art and science, Milner and Winnicott so often stressed their differences.

Milner's explorations of the positive value of illusion came in her book *On Not Being Able To Paint*, first published in 1950 and revised in 1957, and in her long 1952 essay on aspects of symbolism in comprehension of the not-self, later revised under the title of "The Role of Illusion in Symbol Formation" (1955). The book is an account of her struggle as a painter to help her eye escape the tyranny of edge and outline. It was a struggle, she thought, between two kinds of seeing: a kind of denotative, or objective, seeing that is necessary to perceive the otherness of the created world in all its difference from the self, and a kind of poetic, or oceanic, seeing that is necessary to suffuse the otherness of the outside world with the sense of self. Both kinds of seeing, she thought, belonged to human beings, and both were necessary. Objective seeing helped to establish our sense of separateness as human beings, while poetic seeing reaffirmed powerful infantile experiences of fusion, before the boundary-line between inner and outer was drawn, when the breast that satisfied and the hunger that was satisfied were one. Such seeing might be recovered in later life in love, in art, in dream, in the analytic hour, in what she called "moments of illusion"; and such moments, she thought, were "the essential root of a high morale and vital enthusiasm for living" (1950/1957, p. 29). They were "a recurrently necessary phase in the continued growth of the sense of twoness" (1952/1955, pp. 100–101). Such moments were dangerous in that one cannot live only in illusion, but necessary in their place as the means to recover a refreshed sense of one's own separateness.

Milner's book and essay are interesting developments, closer to Jung than to Freud, of the distinction commonly drawn in classical psychoanalysis between two different ways of thinking: one strongly influenced by unconscious motives and the other, falling more under the influence of the rational conscious mind; and her argument is directed against what she calls the Puritanism of classical analysis for its excessive reliance upon denotative, or objective, thinking.

Her fundamental quarrel was with Ernest Jones's view of symbolism as regressive and unnecessary to the educated man; and while she pointed out that Jones himself was ambiguous in that he saw the necessity for symbolism in the development of new scientific paradigms, she added that she herself agreed with Melanie Klein that symbolism was the basis of all the talents, not merely those connected with science. All her writings and revisions of the 1950s show her struggling to work out the implications of this remark of Klein's in such a way as to accommodate states of mind that she valued profoundly, both as painter and as analyst. Symbolic thinking lay at the heart of the arts, of play, and of psychoanalysis too, she argued, and, invoking the example of Wordsworth, she celebrated those moments of ecstasy in which it originated: "Moments when the original 'poet' in each of us created the outside world for us, by finding the familiar in the unfamiliar, are perhaps forgotten by most people; or else they are guarded in some secret place of memory because they were too much like visitations of the gods to be mixed with everyday thinking" (1952/1955, p. 87). In her later book *The Hands of the Living God* (1969) she offered her definitive account of these moments of illusion and confirmed her view that they constituted the matrix of symbolism: "Moments of illusion: necessary for symbol formation, moments when the me and the not-me do not have to be distinguished. Moments when the inner and outer seem to coincide. Needed for restoring broken links, bridges, to the outer world, as well as forming the first bridges. As necessary for healthy living as night dreams seem to be—and as playing is" (p. 416).

To a lesser extent, however, the same ambiguity that Milner found in Jones's writing is also to be found in her work of the 1950s. Despite her valorization of symbolic thinking, her argument does not quite come clear. Like any creative thinker, she is thinking out of the powerful need to understand her own experience, primarily her experience as a painter. But in so doing, she submits to the influence of classical analysis in its insistence that there are two kinds of thinking and seeing that are categorically different—one characteristic of infancy and one of adulthood—and that they are as distinct and distinguishable one from another as a painting is from the world around it by its frame. It is curious, in an argument about the tyranny of edge and outline, to see the frame return in this way. I do not want to deny either the utility or the truth of Milner's typology but, rather, to ask whether difference is the only relationship that we can imagine between her two kinds of thinking and seeing. Need we think only in terms of either/or? A different relationship was suggested by Wordsworth, who strug-

gled as hard as did Milner to distinguish poetry from science and
came to the conclusion, as we have already seen, that poetry was
"the breath and finer spirit of all knowledge", "the impassioned
expression which is in the countenance of all Science". Here is a
suggestion that synthetic and analytic modes of thinking, identified by Wordsworth as opposites, may at their best be co-existent.
Winnicott comes closer to Wordsworth than Milner does here, and
I want now to turn to consider his understanding of illusion. It is an
understanding that escapes the dualism of Milner's thinking by its
rich emphasis upon a third way, an intermediate space, a play area
between subject and object where the self can mix itself with the
stuff of the world.

Winnicott starts at the beginning, where life starts, and says that
there is no such thing as a baby. This is a deliberately paradoxical
utterance, of a kind that I have described elsewhere (Turner, 1988),
and its aim is that of all epistemological paradox: to remind us that
the categories of language are not necessarily the categories of
experience. When we see a baby, we see a baby in relationship with
parents, or family, or those who care for it; so that the self from its
very beginnings is relational. And at the basis of all relationship, in
Winnicott's account, is illusion. The baby cries, and, if all goes well,
the breast appears, as it were out of the innermost of its need and
the infallibility of its power. Thanks to the bounty of the external
world, the infant experiences the bounty of its own capacity to
create. Here is an experience that Winnicott describes again and
again, often with different emphases but always with great care. In
the final version of his theory, as Masud Khan has shown, he
distinguished the infant's *"experience of omnipotence"* from defensive fantasies of omnipotence that belonged to "magical control";
the infant's experience was so rich because it included "the creative
aspect of experience" (Khan, 1971, pp. 263–264). Freud had described in *Totem and Taboo* (1912–13) the need incumbent upon men
and women, whether considered historically as a species or bio-
graphically as individuals, to renounce the aboriginal omnipotence
of their thinking; but in so doing he had seen that some of that
primitive omnipotence nevertheless survived "in men's faith in the
power of the human mind, which grapples with the laws of reality"
(p. 88). It was this area within psychoanalytic theory that Winnicott

opened up, tracing the origins of adult creativity to infantile omnipotence in a way that suggests an almost Wordsworthian concern for creative minds as "Powers" (1805/1958, XIII: 107). Often
Winnicott writes absolutely that "omnipotence is a fact" of the
baby's experience (1988, p. 106); elsewhere he writes, more interestingly, that "omnipotence is nearly a fact of experience" (1951b, p.
238). This delicate qualification suggests that, for the infant not in
the grip of defensive fantasy, there remains room within the experience of omnipotence to apprehend the otherness of the mother's
presence. The illusion of omnipotence nurtures in the undaunted
infant a faith in the value of what it may bring forth out of its inner
world, and its gradual apprehension of the mother's otherness
fosters a trust in the outer world as a safe and interesting place in
which to exercise that creative power.

What follows, in Winnicott's view, is well known. Gradually
the long process of disillusion begins, as the breast is withheld
more or less in line with the baby's capacity to wait; and so, little by
little, the child is ushered into the otherness of the outer world,
where the mother, after all, is only ordinarily good-enough in her
provision and not magically perfect. But this disillusion functions
only by means of further illusion: the same developmental process
that dispels the intensity of the baby's illusion also produces an
extension of its illusion as it passes into infancy. This is the second
of Winnicott's four stages of illusion, as a satisfactory entrance into
the outside world is mediated through a "transitional object".
Wordsworth thought that the process by which the infant mixed its
subjectivity with the objects of the world depended upon maternal
love and the infant's habitual responses to that love. This relationship created in the infant, he wrote, "a virtue which irradiates and
exalts / All objects through all intercourse of sense". In Wordsworth's view of infancy, that is, the objects were already present in
the world, ready to be suffused with value. Winnicott, however,
described the process differently, in such a way as to emphasize the
imperiousness of what was creative in the infant's perception. To
the adult it may seem obvious that the mother has presented the
transitional object to the infant—teddy-bear, silky tie, blanket,
whatever it may be. But to the infant the object has been created by
the infant itself: the blanket may exist for the infant where the

teddy-bear does not. Such omnipotence may be "nearly" a fact of experience for the infant, and hence Winnicott's paradoxical account of the status of the transitional object—while it must be found in order to be created, it must also be created in order to be found. Here, he thought, the parents must allow the infant to remain unchallenged, to inhabit an intermediate area where the blanket belongs neither solely to inner fantasy nor solely to outer reality but is variously at home in either and in-between.

This conceptualization of an intermediate area—a "potential space", between the inner and outer worlds—is Winnicott's most important contribution to psychoanalysis. Like the novelist D. H. Lawrence and the critic F. R. Leavis, Winnicott referred to this area as a "third area"—*das Dritte*, as the maverick Austrian psychoanalyst Otto Gross had called it before them all (1913, p. 1180)—and in so doing he offered a way of healing the split between inner and outer that had bedevilled Western thinking since Descartes. This third area is one served badly by language, which is so good at describing the outside and so good at describing the inside but so poor at describing what lies in-between. Winnicott's use of paradox was designed to restructure our understanding of these two categories of inner and outer, and his celebration of illusion was part of that programme. Illusion in his work does not constitute an alienation of the mind from reality; rather, it is the bridge between them, corroborating the individual sense of creative power within the holding environment of the world. The illusion that first creates the breast, then the transitional object, gradually, through further disillusion and diminution of intensity, extends its range into the playing of the small child; and with his interest in the playing child, Winnicott rescued the *ludere* at the heart of illusion, drawing attention to the intermediate activity of playing as an inseparable blend of fantasy and real work done in the real world in real time and space. The anxiety that had so often beset play in Elizabethan and Jacobean Britain had been alleviated within the limited but real play-areas opened up by bourgeois society, and Winnicott found himself able to celebrate play as a means of trustfully exploring the world. Play, he insists, belongs to health and creativity; hence his determination to separate it from the defensive fantasies of masturbation. The play that begins in the transitional object lies at the origins of our capacity to symbolize and facilitates the process by which we begin to mix ourselves with the world, to feel ourselves at home there, able to find value and pleasure in it and to bear solitude because to be alone is not to be lonely.

The role of illusion does not end with childhood, however, but is extended by further disillusion into the heart of adulthood. This is the fourth and final stage of illusion: the breast, the transitional object, and the playing of the child yield in due course the cultural activities of the adult. Winnicott has two distinct ways of conceptualizing this psychological history within the individual, and they are not fully integrated in his work. Both appear in his essay on "Transitional Objects and Transitional Phenomena" (1951b), and they reveal an important difference in his thinking between the primary creativity of the infant and what we might call the secondary, or defensive, creativity of the adult. Perhaps his richest statement of what belongs to primary creativity, both within the infant and the adult, comes in his review of Milner's *On Not Being Able to Paint*, where he writes:

> what is illusion when seen from outside is not best described as illusion when seen from inside; for that fusion which occurs when the object is felt to be one with the dream, as in falling in love with someone or something, is, when seen from inside, a psychic reality for which the word illusion is inappropriate. For this is the process by which the inner becomes actualised in external form and as such becomes the basis, not only of internal perception, but also of all true perception of environment. Thus perception itself is seen as a creative process. [1951a, pp. 391–392]

This is a large claim, comparable to Coleridge's claim in *Biographia Literaria* (1817) for the primary imagination as "the living power and prime agent of all human perception", "a repetition in the finite mind of the eternal act of creation in the infinite I AM" (p. 167). Illusion in Winnicott's scheme, like imagination in Coleridge's, empowers and authenticates perception; and in so doing it takes centre stage in his post-Romantic discourse of creativity. This claim seems to be repeated in a weaker form at the end of the slightly later paper on "Transitional Objects and Transitional Phenomena", where Winnicott concludes that the intermediate area of experience "is retained in the intense experiencing that belongs to the arts and to religion and to imaginative living, and to creative scientific work" (1951b, p. 242).

At other times, however, Winnicott's emphasis seems to fall rather upon the defensive role of illusion in adult experience, attributing to imaginative and cultural experience the same defensive function from which he had attempted to rescue play. One well-known formulation of illusion from the same paper is of this kind.

> It is assumed here that the task of reality-acceptance is never completed, that no human being is free from the strain of relating inner and outer reality, and that relief from this strain is provided by an intermediate area of experience which is not challenged (arts, religion, etc.). . . . This intermediate area is in direct continuity with the play area of the small child who is "lost" in play. [1951b, pp. 240–241]

For all its subtlety, and despite its important elaboration of a third area between self and other, this seems to me in two ways an imperfect formulation. It is not imperfect because Winnicott is necessarily wrong; he may be right to conceptualize adult creativity as a defence against strain, a reaction to what Caudwell calls "tension". In the first place, however, it is imperfect because he does not explain the development from primary infant creativity to secondary adult creativity, and does not explore the relationship between them. It may be that there is no inconsistency here. Perhaps primary creativity is reactive to the internal tensions of hunger and bodily pain, while secondary creativity is reactive to the wider range of tensions that accompany acknowledgement of the outside world; but we do not find this argued out. Instead, we find different emphases in different places, apparently conceptualizing creativity either as aboriginal in human beings or as a defence against strain. Second, Winnicott's formulation is imperfect because it offers no explanation as to why certain activities are included in the intermediate area and others excluded. In his review of *On Not Being Able to Paint*, Winnicott (1951a) stresses the importance of illusion to "true perception" in general, implying that creativity has to do with the capacity to find value and meaning across a range of activities. But in the passage from his 1951 paper he ties creativity more specifically to certain kinds of activity; and it is unclear why one has been preferred to another. What, other than a narrow class-based definition of "culture", distinguishes "arts, religion, etc." from politics, science, etc.? What unstated criteria sustain Winnicott's *etcetera* here? May not all lives, in all spheres of human activity, be lived creatively or uncreatively? This is a conclusion that Winnicott himself seems to have reached by 1970, when he wrote, in "Living Creatively", that "everything that we do can be done creatively or uncreatively" (1970, p. 48)—or to adapt Wordsworth's metaphor, poetry is the impassioned expression that may appear in the face of *all* human activity.

It may be that the same psychoanalytic pressures that hindered Marion Milner in her effort to reach a fully satisfactory statement of human creativity in the 1950s were also hampering Winnicott in 1951; nevertheless, even while confining creativity to particular kinds of activity, he successfully found a place for illusory experience within a scientific account of human development and embodied its value in a paradoxical formulation that encouraged precisely the kind of play that belonged to such illusory experience. Masud Khan thought that it was Winnicott's paediatric work with spatula and squiggle that had prompted his ideas about illusion. Doubtless he was influenced, too, by the rethinking of the question of the origins of symbolism then going on in the British Psychoanalytical Society and, in particular, by Milner's work in this field, to which he paid careful and generous tribute in *Playing and Reality*: "It was at an important point in the phase of development of these ideas in me in the early 1940s that Marion Milner (in conversation) was able to convey to me the tremendous significance that there can be in the interplay of the edges of two curtains, or of the surface of a jug that is placed in front of another jug" (1971, p. 115). Winnicott, like Milner, was concerned to respect the value that men and women ordinarily find in cultural experience; and such experience, as we have seen, had long been conceptualized in literary, artistic and philosophical circles in terms of illusion. Underlying these concerns with spatula and squiggle, with symbolism and art, however, was a fierce determination on Winnicott's part to protect his own creativity amidst a professional world that urged compliance upon him. As he put it in "Living Creatively": "I have this need to talk as though no one had ever examined the subject before" (1970, p. 41). The singularity of his style, like his cavalier treatment of other psychoanalytic authorities, belongs to his need to keep alive his own creativity and to ward off those who threatened it. The trick of his prose guards the playfulness of the illusion that it elaborates.

It seems probable, too, that, like so many people before him, Winnicott warded off the inner dangers of compliance by invoking the full countercultural force of the concept of illusion; probably his paradoxical use of the word was deliberately provocative. Adam Phillips (1988, p. 119) describes Winnicott's 1951 paper on "Transitional Objects and Transitional Phenomena" as "quietly scandalous" because of its coded message for the British Psychoanalytical Society to which it was delivered:

> I am here staking a claim for an intermediate state between a baby's inability and growing ability to recognise and accept reality. I am therefore studying the substance of *illusion*, that which is allowed to the infant, and which in adult life is inherent in art and religion. We can share a respect for *illusory experience*, and if we wish we may collect together and form a group on the basis of the similarity of our illusory experiences. This is a natural root of grouping among human beings. Yet it is a hall-mark of madness when an adult puts too powerful a claim on the credulity of others, forcing them to acknowledge a sharing of illusion that is not their own. [Winnicott, 1951b, pp. 230–231]

In the name of their scientific differences, the rival supporters of Melanie Klein and Anna Freud had brought the British Society during the Second World War close to collapse, necessitating measures that came to divide the Society into three groups for administrative and training purposes. From his own intermediate position in the Middle Group, Winnicott was inviting the supporters of Klein and Anna Freud to reflect upon the fantasies of omnipotence that inspired their "scientific" quarrels. He was also perhaps, in Phillips's words, questioning "the status of psychoanalytic theories and institutions as Transitional Phenomena" (p. 120).

The concept of illusion is clearly a powerful weapon here; and if we come to it in the essays of 1951 in a chronological reading of Winnicott's work, we might expect it to go on to play an equally powerful role in his later writings too, exerting a strong countercultural critique on all those whose beliefs, of whatever kind, deny their own subjective content and impinge too much upon the credulity of others. Still today the first-time reader of *Playing and Reality*, meeting the 1951 paper on transitional objects as its opening chapter, might well expect the concept of illusion to stand at the ideological heart of the rest of the book, inculcating the virtue of tolerance and the value of play in a world where both are undervalued. Illusion, it may be thought, will afford a political lesson to all kinds of authority in the relativity of all human knowledges. Yet this does not happen, and the concept of illusion actually diminishes in importance as Winnicott's work developed. This is not to say that he changed his mind. Infantile illusion retained its place in his developmental scheme, and he continued to value the kinds of thinking that illusion enabled. In 1965, for instance, we find him arguing the need to complement logical with intuitive thinking in science on the grounds that "we need to be able to reach out for symbols and to create imaginatively and in preverbal language; we need to be able to think hallucinatorily" (1965, p. 157). Psychoanalysis itself was included and redefined in this understanding of science; and yet after 1951 it was not in the name of illusion that such redefinition characteristically took place. The importance that the term had suddenly assumed in the 1950s waned; and, paradoxically, this was because its importance remained so great. Illusion, seen from the outside, lies at the heart of everything; but seen from the inside, from the standpoint of "psychic reality", the inappropriateness of the term seemed to Winnicott self-evident. The countercultural challenge of insisting upon the illusory content at the heart of belief would cause more trouble than it was worth; and so in Winnicott's writing the concept of illusion became subsumed into the more useful, less technical, more practical categories of playing and of creativity. Illusion became occluded behind the play that it enabled.

If Winnicott subsumed his understanding of illusion into the broader category of playing, Charles Rycroft subsumed it into the category of imagining; and in so doing he discovered one of the major concerns of his writing career: attempting to integrate the psychoanalytic concept of the unconscious with the Romantic literary concept of the imagination. Indeed, it was a Romantic poem— Leopardi's "The Terror by Night"—that prompted Rycroft to write his most significant contribution to the psychoanalytic debate about illusion, his 1955 essay entitled "On Idealization, Illusion, and Catastrophic Disillusion", reprinted in *Imagination and Reality* (1968). His purpose, he wrote later, was to "sort myself out" by discovering "how much value" he could find in Milner's and Winnicott's ideas of illusion and disillusion (Rycroft, 1984, p. 120). Leopardi's poem is a fragmentary and seemingly uncertain attempt to wrestle creative meaning out of an unbearable anxiety and, in its central image of the sudden dropping of the moon from the sky, it recalls Wordsworth's famous untitled "Lucy" poem that begins "strange fits of passion I have known". The name *Lucy* derives from the Latin *lux*, meaning "light", and the poems of both men express a fear that the light of their lives might suddenly go out. Their theme was the vulnerability of those values upon which they had built their lives. Both men, we might say, were haunted by uncertainty as to whether their inner hold upon good objects was sound or frail and unrealistic; and it was precisely this uncertainty that the word *illusion* had evolved in the eighteenth century to convey. It is one of the great strengths of Rycroft's essay that, with typical theoretical acuity, he distinguished between the negative and positive meanings that the word had come to bear in our culture, and thus in psychoanalysis too, before going on to describe the different dynamic factors operating in each.

Pathological illusion, Rycroft wrote, was the result of defensive idealization accompanying withdrawal of interest from the external world. The purpose of such withdrawal was to guard the self against its own ambivalence, while idealization protected the self against the ensuing feelings of emptiness and futility. This account enabled him to do justice to both meanings that *disillusion* has in our culture: "the disenchantment that is the emotional hazard of those whose stability is based on the over-use of idealization", and the "loss of the ability to find value and interest in things as they actually are" (1968, p. 36). It was this latter usage, he added, that provided "some" justification for the positive revaluation of illusion by Milner and Winnicott and their belief that "an element of illusion enters into the realistic cathexis of external reality" (p. 36). Here I have suggested some of the cultural influences that prompted Milner and Winnicott to celebrate illusion as the source of "value and interest in things as they actually are". Rycroft, with his usual scrupulous concern for the genealogies of psychoanalytic doctrine, traced the psychoanalytic influences more fully than either Milner or Winnicott themselves had done, and he identified their view as "an extension and elaboration" of Freud's idea of the tendency of wishes to seek for hallucinatory self-fulfilment (Rycroft, 1968, p. 37). Twelve years earlier, during the Controversial Discussions, this question of whether Freudian ideas of hallucination might be extended and elaborated into Kleinian ideas of unconscious phantasy had been one of the points of fiercest dispute. The balance of opinion had been with those who believed that it might; and in that spirit Ella Sharpe, writing of "the infant's breast hallucination", had said that "the first and deepest illusion is the belief in the actual incorporated object" (King & Steiner, 1991, pp. 338, 340). Yet, she had added, it was an illusion that must be dispelled. To Milner and Winnicott, however, this was mistaken. Illusion lay at the root of all creative living, not only for the infant but for the adult too; and their view encouraged Rycroft too to trace the health or sickness of the imagination to the quality of its most primitive imago.

There are two more papers on the topic of illusion in those collected in Rycroft's *Imagination and Reality* (1968). The first of these is his 1956 paper, "Symbolism and its Relationship to the Primary and Secondary Processes", in which he invoked Winnicott's idea of illusion with two complementary aims: first to argue, against classical analysis, that fantasy and reality are not always antithetical to one another (in illusion the real experience is simultaneously a hallucination), and second to argue, against Klein, that they do nevertheless remain importantly antithetical (illusion will help the relationship between them to develop creatively). With typical perseverance, Rycroft pushed Milner's ideas of symbolism and Winnicott's ideas of transitional objects to their logical conclusion. Symbolism, he said, is not simply a matter of primary processes, as classical psychoanalysis had maintained: it is a general capacity of the mind that may be used by either primary or secondary processes. The term "fantasy", he suggested, should be used for symbolism subserving primary processes and "imagination" for symbolism subserving secondary processes. Six years later, in 1962, in "Beyond the Reality Principle", he returned to Winnicott's idea of illusion in order to argue that the baby is born in an integrated state, that the primary processes that impel it have a powerful and lifelong adaptive function, that they function by means of what Susanne Langer called non-discursive symbolism, and that such non-discursive symbolism is accessible to the conscious mind in imaginative thinking of all kinds. The importance of illusion to Rycroft was, thus, that it provided conceptual space for him to argue that "the human infant begins life in a state of primary integration" and that imagination has a realistic function when sustained by the "primary relatedness" originating in a satisfactory relationship with the imago of the mother's breast (1962/1968, pp. 111–112). In Rycroft's later, more popular writings I have found only one further reference to illusion, in his 1972 essay on Winnicott; but since in this essay Rycroft declared that the idea of an intermediate area of experience was "perhaps the most important contribution made to psychoanalytical theory in the last thirty years" (1972, p. 145), we may assume that Winnicott's view of illusion continued to underpin his view of the way that imagination enriches and suffuses our perception of reality.

There is one aspect of Winnicott's treatment of illusion that Rycroft seems to regret, however, and that is its paradoxical presentation. "This seeming paradox of supposing illusion to play an essential part in the cathexis of reality", he wrote, can be resolved by recognizing "that the notion refers not to the individual's total relationship to reality but only to the erotic component of the total cathexis" (1968, p. 36). Winnicott himself knew full well that the paradox could be resolved but preferred instead to emphasize its value: "By flight to split-off intellectual functioning it is possible to resolve the paradox, but the price of this is the loss of the value of the paradox itself" (1971, p. xii). If it is indeed a function of epistemological paradox to subvert the categories of language, Winnicott's paradox here reminds us that the categories of subject and object, although distinct in theory, may not always be distinguished in practice—"the line invisible", in Wordsworth's phrase, "that parts the image from reality" (1977, ll. 576–577). Winnicott's paradox draws attention to that which is relational in experience, and he preserves in his theoretical writing something of the liveliness and intersubjectivity of his clinical work. At this point his prose enacts the creativity that it describes: it is a poetry of illusion, embodying the potency of the potential space. It generates *interest*; and *interest*, we might remember, derives from the Latin *interesse*, to be among. To be interested in the objectivity of the world is to be mixed in with it as a subject, and it is this relationship that gives our knowledge both its individual and its provisional character. Winnicott's paradox is also a reminder to the psychoanalyst that of theory, too, it may be asked: "Did you create that, or did you find it?"

Rycroft, however, was impatient of Winnicott's paradox and persisted in his "abstract formulation" of it (1972, p. 144). Perhaps he found the paradoxical structure of Winnicott's thinking quirky, a further regrettable instance of his "intuitive", "idiosyncratic" and "visionary" indifference towards the scientific theory-building at which Rycroft himself excelled (pp. 143–144). It is true that, considered from this point of view, the individuality of Winnicott's mind has the weakness of its strength. If Winnicott wrote a Romantic poetry of illusion, Rycroft wrote its prose; but he wrote it with the same sense of its provisionality, its subjective components, and its cultural determinants as Winnicott had done. In "Beyond the Reality Principle" (1962) he acknowledged the limits of theory by preferring an epistemological paradox of his own: the paradox that the "science" of psychoanalysis used secondary-process thinking to observe and analyse the primary-process thinking that science itself had evolved to exclude. In this way it was a symptom of the same disintegration that it sought to cure. During its observations and analyses, moreover, it had destabilized the ego upon whose powers of objective observation its scientific status rested. Thus, Rycroft concluded, psychoanalytical theorizing "poses problems relating (1) to the pathology of the Western intellectual tradition, and (2) to the status of the observer in scientific work" (p. 109). Like Winnicott, Rycroft was aware of the constraints placed on thinking by language, and like him he struggled to integrate into his theoretical frame the problematization of the subject–object antithesis caused by Klein's view of the omnipresence of unconscious phantasy in mental life. Here too, Rycroft believed, was a paradox that might be resolved, not by the paradoxical and poetic language of Winnicott, but by the wholesale reconceptualization of psychoanalysis as a hermeneutical activity closer to the humanities than the sciences. Its business, he came to believe, was as much with meaning as with cause and effect. The essentially symbolic, culturally specific language that it used, both in its clinical and theoretical work, relied not simply upon secondary-process thinking but upon an imaginative and realistic integration of primary and secondary processes. Properly understood and practised, psychoanalysis should embody the reintegrated mental life to which it sought to help its patients.

In his 1800 Preface to *Lyrical Ballads*, Wordsworth had argued that the opposite of Poetry was Science (1974, Vol. 1: 134); the synthetic power of imagination was antithetical to the analytic power of reason. To T. S. Eliot, looking back in 1921, this distinction was an expression of a long-standing "dissociation of sensibility" that dated back to the middle of the seventeenth century, to the scientific revolution and the establishment of bourgeois society. In Rycroft's own gloss on Eliot's remarks, that was the time when men and women had first come to view reality from "two unconnected and incompatible standpoints, one scientific and objective, the other imaginative and subjective" (1962, p. 108). It was at around that time, too, as we have seen, that illusion became increasingly valorised as part of the countercultural resistance carried out by the imaginative subject. Rycroft's aim was to heal this dissociation within psychoanalysis as a step towards healing it more generally within our culture. Armed with a newly integrative idea of the imagination which united the two kinds of thinking proposed by psychoanalysis, he sought to bridge the gap between the arts and sciences and, as he wrote in *The Innocence of Dreams* (1979), to "marry" the thinking of Freud and Coleridge (p. 167). For Rycroft, as for Winnicott, it would be a "marriage" of imagination and reality, originating in the illusion of infants that they had created the breast that was already there.

IV

We have come a long way since *The Future of an Illusion*. In his rethinking of the role of illusion in human life, Winnicott rescued religion from the obloquy of Freud; he found space for the arts, which Freud's essay deliberately set aside; he celebrated the value of illusion in human sexuality; he argued that the concentration at the heart of scientific thinking is a species of illusion; and, more important, he argued that such thinking is itself a falsification, a defence, a false-self activity, when divorced from its roots in the illusions of the inner self. It is not quite what Milner says, that there are two kinds of thinking; it is rather that, at the heart of whatever kind of thinking we do—and surely there are many kinds—we find illusion. What is at stake is a whole new way of thinking about what it means to be alive in the world. For Freud, life was justified primarily in terms of science and reason, the anxiety of knowledge; but for Winnicott it was justified not in terms of knowing but of being, in terms of our capacity to find *value*—*value* rather than *pleasure*—in the things that we do. For Winnicott, illusion is not the *ignis fatuus* that it was to Freud. It does not baffle and bewilder our relationships; it is the necessary precondition and condition of them all, including the therapeutic relationship between analyst and patient. The purpose of analysis is no longer primarily to bring the patient into a knowledge of reality but, rather, to bring someone unable to play into a state where he or she can play and thus find value in reality. The aim of the psychoanalytic transference, we might say, is to enable the patient to pass through illusion into illusion; and in understanding this, Winnicott found himself able to discard the word *illusion* as no longer the word that he wished to use.

There are three sentences in *Playing and Reality* in which Winnicott confronts the same question that had haunted Freud as to whether or not his own psychoanalytic theory was illusion-free. For Freud, this had been the question of questions, threatening to desubstantiate the whole of his life-work. But for Winnicott the question posed no threat: he felt free to trust himself playfully to the same world that for Freud had been demonized by doubt. This is what he wrote: "In some way or other our theory includes a belief that living creatively is a healthy state, and that compliance is a sick basis for life. There is little doubt that the general attitude of our society and the philosophic atmosphere of the age in which we happen to live contribute to this view, the view that we hold here and that we hold at the present time. We might not have held this view elsewhere and in another age" (1971, p. 76). The work done by these three sentences is very clear: they define the nature of the group, and of the whole post-Romantic British cultural tradition to which Winnicott thought that he himself belonged, on the basis of a shared similarity of illusory experiences. It was a group with which Rycroft, too, aligned himself; but, with greater theoretical rigour, he thought through the implications of Winnicott's hypothesis about illusion in such a way as to draw out its revolutionary implications for psychoanalytic theory. In particular, he insisted upon the realistic and adaptive function of primary-process thinking and proposed that the integration of primary- and secondary-process thinking was a feature within all healthy living and communicating. "Imagination", he wrote, "is necessary for a full appreciation of reality" (1956, p. 59); and in choosing this Romantic concept and marrying it to the scientific psychology of Freud, he espoused a cultural theory that enabled him both to diagnose a widespread dissociation in modern culture and to propose a remedy that would reintegrate the language of illusion with the language of reality from which it had so long been separated.

References

Abram, J. (1996). *The Language of Winnicott*. London: Karnac.

Addison, J. (1712). *The Spectator* (4 vols.). London: Dent/Everyman, 1945.

Burke, E. (1790). *Reflections on the Late Revolution in France*. London: Dent/Everyman, 1910.

Caudwell, C. (1937). *Illusion and Reality: A Study of the Sources of Poetry*. London: Lawrence & Wishart, 1946.

Coleridge, S. T. (1817). *Biographia Literaria*. London: Dent/Everyman, 1965.

Descartes, R. (1641). *Meditations on the First Philosophy*. In: *A Discourse on Method*, trans. John Veitch. London: Dent/Everyman, 1912.

Freud, S. (1912–13). *Totem and Taboo*. S.E., 13.

Freud, S. (1927). *The Future of an Illusion*. S.E., 21.

Gross, O. (1913). Notiz über Beziehungen. In: *Die Aktion, Vol. 3* (pp. 1180–1181).

Khan, M. M. R. (1971). The role of illusion in the analytic space and process. In: *The Privacy of the Self* (pp. 251–269). London: Hogarth Press, 1974.

King, P., & Steiner R. (Eds.) (1991). *The Freud–Klein Controversies 1941–45*. London: Routledge.

Milner, M. (1950/1957). *On Not Being Able to Paint*. London: Heinemann; revised edition, London, Heinemann.

Milner, M. (1952/1955). The role of illusion in symbol formation, revised edition. In: Melanie Klein et al. (Eds.), *New Directions in Psycho-Analysis*. London: Tavistock Publications.

Milner, M. (1969). *The Hands of the Living God*. London: Hogarth Press.

Newman, A. (1995). *Non-Compliance in Winnicott's Words*. London: Free Association Books.

Phillips, A. (1988). *Winnicott*. London: Fontana.

Popkin, R. H. (1960). *The History of Scepticism from Erasmus to Descartes*. Assen: Van Gorcum.

Radcliffe, A. (1794). *The Mysteries of Udolpho*. Oxford: Oxford University Press, 1966.

Rycroft, C. (1955). On idealization, illusion, and catastrophic disillusion. In: *Imagination and Reality*. London: Hogarth Press, 1968.

Rycroft, C. (1956). Symbolism and its relationship to the primary and secondary processes. In: *Imagination and Reality*. London: Hogarth Press, 1968.

Rycroft, C. (1962). Beyond the reality principle. In: *Imagination and Reality*. London: Hogarth Press, 1968.

Rycroft, C. (1968). *Imagination and Reality*. London: Hogarth Press.

Rycroft, C. (1972). D. W. Winnicott. In: Peter Fuller (Ed.), *Psychoanalysis and Beyond*. London: Chatto & Windus, 1985.

Rycroft, C. (1979). *The Innocence of Dreams* (2nd edition). London: Hogarth Press, 1991.

Rycroft, C. (1984). Psychoanalysis and beyond. In: Peter Fuller (Ed.), *Psychoanalysis and Beyond*. London: Chatto & Windus, 1985.

Santayana, G. (1920). *Little Essays*, ed. Logan Pearsall Smith. London: Constable.

Turner, J. (1988). Wordsworth and Winnicott in the area of play. *International Review of Psychoanalysis, 15*: 481–497.

Williams, R. (1983). *Keywords: A Vocabulary of Culture and Society* (revised edition). London: Fontana.

Winnicott, D. W. (1951a). Critical notice of *On Not Being Able to Paint*. In: *Psycho-Analytic Explorations*, ed. Clare Winnicott et al. London: Karnac Books, 1989.

Winnicott, D. W. (1951b). Transitional objects and transitional phenomena. In: D. W. Winnicott, *Through Paediatrics to Psycho-Analysis*. London: Hogarth Press, 1975.

144   JOHN TURNER

Winnicott, D. W. (1965). New light on children's thinking. In: *Psycho-Analytic Explorations*, ed. Clare Winnicott et al. London: Karnac Books, 1989.

Winnicott, D. W. (1970). Living creatively. In: *Home Is Where We Start From*. Harmondsworth: Pelican Books, 1986.

Winnicott, D. W. (1971). *Playing and Reality*. London: Pelican Books, 1974.

Winnicott, D. W. (1988). *Human Nature*. London: Free Association Books.

Woolf, V. (1941). *Between the Acts*. Harmondsworth: Penguin, 1953.

Wordsworth, W. (1805/1958). *The Prelude* (2nd edition), ed. E. de Selincourt, revised by H. Darbishire. London: Oxford University Press.

Wordsworth, W. (1940–49). *The Poetical Works of William Wordsworth* (5 vols.), ed. E. de Selincourt & H. Darbishire. London: Oxford University Press,.

Wordsworth, W. (1974). *The Prose Works of William Wordsworth* (3 vols.), ed. W. J. B. Owen & Jane Worthington Smyser. London: Oxford University Press,.

Wordsworth, W. (1977). *Home at Grasmere*, ed B. Darlington. Ithaca, NY: Cornell University Press.

Yeats, W. B. (1958). *The Collected Poems of W. B. Yeats*. London: Macmillan.

CHAPTER TEN

On bridging continuity and precision: the hidden music of psychoanalysis

Robin Higgins

> Love means to step away from the ego
> To open the eyes of inner vision and
> Not to take this world so seriously.
>
> Rumi, "Hidden Music", 2001, p. 18.

When someone asked him when he meditated, Rycroft with a half-smile replied: "All the time." The reply was no joke, as anyone who has studied his writings or was lucky enough to converse with him must know. His imagination sparked on connecting the precision implicit in his *Critical Dictionary* (1968) with that sense of continuity he singled out as the one idea he might choose to deify (Rycroft, 1985, p. 293). It is this connection between precision and continuity that imbues his essays and a book like *The Innocence of Dreams* (1979) with a lively humorous surface clarity and a depth that, as I experienced in his sparse comments during our sessions together, might last a lifetime.

In what follows I would like to illustrate this depth of connection from one aside he threw out in an essay on Carl Jung and analytical psychology:

One cannot incidentally help regretting that none of the pioneers of the unconscious thought naturally in auditory terms. If
they had, we would perhaps have a psychology in which
thoughts are conceived of as themes, which can occur in different modes and keys, which can vary in their audibility, which
can be harmonious or discordant, and which can undergo
development and variation. [Rycroft, 1985, p. 115]

In this short paragraph, Rycroft selects as examples of thinking in
auditory terms, themes, and their audibility, central structures
(mode/key), tensions (concords/discords) and change over time
(growth and variation). I will expand on each of these examples.

Audibility

In any passage of music or conversation, we are immediately
struck by the degrees of audibility. Certain notes or words, poly-
phonic lines or sentences, phrases or sections stand out. These
points may stand out because they are louder (and the dynamic
range our ears can cope with is enormous) or because we select
them. Our auditory perception acts as a filter for what we find
audible: we are more ready to hear this than that; it fits in more
appropriately with our personal interpretation of the universal
way. Conversely, for the same reason, we may block it out.

Such perceptual filtering goes for all our sensory channels but is
particularly relevant to our hearing, partly because of the flow of
sounds and partly because the audible is always balanced by the
inaudible. In Indian music the *ahata*, the played note, is balanced by
the *anahata*, the unplayed. The played note is seen as the symbol of
the unplayed, which provides its foundation and is unceasing. So
the inaudible provides the shadow of the audible, the opposite and
the extension of it. It also provides an ever-expanding background
of possibilities, like the unfolding of Bohm's implicate order
(Bohm, 1980).

The inaudible, *anahata*, silence is that nothingness out of which,
as Meister Eckhart and other mystics have said, all things are
created. And as these sounds or insights emerge, silence persists as
an unhurried support. As the basis for meditation, silence, as
Rycroft implied, is there all the time, and the distinction between

the audible and inaudible may have been at the back of his mind when he was teasing out a new way of looking at primary and secondary processes and the paradox that faced Freud "when he tried to formulate in words the nature of a type of thinking (primary-process thinking) which is essentially non-verbal and which is, therefore, of necessity falsified by being put into words" (Rycroft, 1985, p. 263).

Improvisers, like Mbira players (or patients and therapists), may take hours listening to sound/silence before finding the next "right" step on the journey. In the right frame of mind, we become aware that the opposite of silence is not sound but noise: auditory pollution.

In the aural tradition of improvisers, the oral tradition of the voice plays a key role and often carries something of the paradox Rycroft detected in Freud's treatment of primary-process experience. Craig points out that in a dialogue, psychotherapeutic or everyday, what we seek to hear is the "characteristic utterance" of my own and the other's voice. Often it is our own authentic voice that we find hardest to hear. When we read a poem aloud and, less starkly, whenever we open our mouths to speak, we, "like the poet, must reveal the nature of our venturing in a performing which we can never wholly order". We can easily slip into "premature crystallisation" when we attempt to "cast into discursive-analytic words" what we've intuitively heard in the moment of speaking (Craig, 2000). The declarative cuts short and withers the procedural (Squire & Cohen, 1983).

Linked to this disturbing element is the way any of us, patients or therapists alike, may use degrees of vocal audibility to bamboozle, tease, or otherwise control each other.

The idea of "audible conversations" (verbal and non-verbal) opens up two further dimensions. The first has to do with Time. In the womb, the human foetus is responsive to sound from the sixth month and reaches sophisticated recognition levels with regard to human speech by the time of birth (Eimas, 1975). The early auditory competency may well serve a variety of developmental functions such as mother–infant bonding (Bell, 1974). The new-born's earliest voice preferences (maternal > female > male) are among the growing evidence for links between pre- and post-birth auditory experiences.

These earliest "conversations" are among the "neural organisa-tions" that Edelman singles out as what gets encoded in memory (Edelman, 1985). They are the original imprints the contents of which can only later be drawn out in words, like a fossil imprint the meaning of which can only later be revealed, after a latex mould has been poured over it (Rossi & Cheek, 1988).

The second dimension opened up by the idea of "conversa-tions" concerns the axis which Rossi (Rossi & Cheek, 1988), Pert (1997), and others have mapped between:

- culture/society;
- brain;
- body;
- molecule/gene.

The part plated by auditory channels in culture, mind, cortex, and neuro-transmission has long been recognized. The further part played by neuro-modulators (such as neuro-peptides) acting through, for example, the nervous, endocrine, and immune sys-tems on cell-molecules and genes has only been recognized much more recently. "Conversations" are now accepted as occurring at and between all four levels of the above axis. (A recent article speaks of the "science of cellular conversation" going on between cells and micro-organisms in our mouth—Henderson, 2002.) The flow of information running up and down this axis through such conversations provides a central platform for mind–body therapy and stems directly from Rycroft's intuitive hunch. The force in the flow has been styled an "affect bridge" (Watkins, 1971), a scientifi-cally more respectable metaphor, perhaps, than Rumi's "love".

Central structures in themes

The ear, like the nose and unlike the eye, has no cover. Smelling and hearing, we experience the world directly, and, perhaps partly because of this exposed position, we are given, in the case of hearing, instruments of immense precision. If we think in terms of octaves alone, the range of frequencies we can hear is ten octaves: for the eye it is one octave (Berendt, 1988, p. 17). Small wonder that the old Indian and Indo-European root AR signified both harmony and number (*armonia* and *arithmos*) and that for thousands of years sounds provided us with the basis for measuring the proportions of temples, seasons, planetary movements (McLain, 1984; also Berendt, 1988 p. 160).

The frequencies of possible sounds can, of course, extend in either direction beyond our human range, and between any two frequencies there is an infinite number of microtones. So we can begin to appreciate that in theory for any theme there is an infinite choice of possible shapes. In practice, as Rycroft reminds us, themes tend to follow a particular core pattern: a mode, scale, raga, etc. This imposition of pattern on infinite choice has been observed widely in nature. In the world of the ear, what strongly influences the pattern is the presence of the harmonic series in any sound: overtones and undertones of the fundamental. The presence of this series—the relation between fundamental and these over- or under-tones—shapes the musical intervals, the scale, and the timbre, the quality, of our voices and instruments. In turn, intervals, scale, and timbre, shape harmonies and discords.

Through the precision of our two cochleas (those miraculous and minute analysers in our two ears) we can appreciate the constant feedback between the shifting fundamentals and overtones. This is one key example of precision scanning infinite choice in auditory terms. Another access to infinite continuity is through the multi-dimensions of sound. In any passage of music or conversation, a voice not only has different qualia (rhythms, dynamics, textures, words, etc), but it may hive off along a vector that may be quite different from, though related to, the direction of any other voice. Everything flows—a vision that prompted Bohm to update Heraclitus with the term "holomovement": that flux of which a hologram is like a photograph, a fixed image of one process in this movement. According to Bohm, this holomovement can best be comprehended through Total Listening (Bohm, 1980; also Berendt, 1988, p. 108).

In this holomovement, the part is inseparable from the whole. Any holographic photograph gives us an abstraction of the whole. With any sound in a piece of music or a word, we hear condensed into the present NOW the memory of what has gone before, as well as the possible expectations of what is to come (on hope and prospective emotions, cf. Rycroft, 1991, pp. 9–31). Connections here are to dreams, where the super-position of images renders them co-present and separate (Comfort, 1984; Hayward, 1984), and to the evolving memories of neural organizations, the "neural Darwinism" of Edelman, already mentioned.

In outlining how the theories of psychoanalysis might be re-phrased in auditory terms, Rycroft chose a medium that reflects his gift for combining precision with infinite continuity. He points to a map that takes us deep into the territory of experience because the structures of observer and observed overlap.

It so happened (perhaps not completely fortuitously) that the time he wrote this aside coincided with a re-dressing of the balance between eye and ear in the writings of physicists, mathematicians, and biologists (Bohm, Matte Blanco, Shelldrake—see Arden, 1998). On the musical scene, a similar move was taking place in the reinstating of improvisation and the escape from the tyranny of the written score in the Western tradition (see Prevost, 1995). Note also the rich testament to auditory sensation (hearing through inner sight) of blind or partially sighted musicians like Frankie Armstrong (Armstrong & Pearson, 1992) or Sleepy John Estes.

Tensions

For us humans, hearing and balance go together and make up our earliest sensory channel. This channel, the stato-acoustic, has gone a long way to maturation by the 28th week of foetal life (Feess-Higgins, personal communication—cf. Feess-Higgins & Larroche, 1987). Take the well-established cycle:

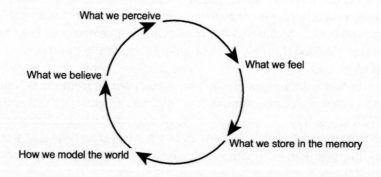

It is not difficult to see why this primacy of the stato-acoustic channel of perception carries such significance.

The discords that Rycroft mentioned are one way we can be thrown out of equilibrium, put under tension, and find our emotions aroused (Meier, 1956). Discords may be used to delay fulfilment, analogous to the dialogue that Winnicott spelt out in his concept of the "good-enough mother". Rhythmic delays or precipitations, unexpected accents and articulations (syncopations, premature beats) provide further analogies.

Or we may displace our natural body symmetries: our left and right hands may, for example, pursue opposite directions, as in the "dual brain" of a good Boogie pianist.

These shifts in and out of tension, between balance and imbalance, play a significant role in the *holomovement* noted earlier. They fire it with energy and are themselves ever changing. Yesterday's discord becomes today's concord and tomorrow's cliché. There is a constant flow of parts becoming wholes and, in turn, becoming parts again of bigger wholes.

Another aspect of tension/balance in the auditory world is that between the players: composer, performer, and listener; between patient and therapist. Is the balance one between two equals, the tension ebbing and flowing like a game of tennis, the interactive rhythms of two dancers or four string players or singer and accompanist? Or is it one between superior and inferior, one who gives and one who carries or responds to the message? Or is it between one who has made a discovery and waits for the other to find his own version of it?

Improvising, like psychotherapy, contains instances of these and many other types of tension/balance.

Change over time

In his essay on "Model and Metaphor in Psychology", Rycroft noted that we use metaphor and the language of observation when talking about subjective experience.

> And yet subjective experiences lack many of the attributes of the physical world which the language of the natural sciences has been constructed to describe and explain. In particular they

lack location in space, they lack size, shape, and weight. Perhaps indeed the only property they share with material phenomena is duration in time. They last for a certain length of time, they can be arranged serially, and perhaps synchronously. They display continuity, discontinuity, and recurrence. [Rycroft, 1991, pp. 52–53]

These last properties, duration in time, discursiveness, repetition, the unfolding of the themes, lie at the core of our ear world. They link with the filter of auditory perception I touched on when considering audibility. They link with empathic participatory voicing and listening. Am I—are you—ready to take in or reveal this particular bit of information? Is this really the truth we are both seeking at this moment? They link with that crucial neurological network, our episodic memory, without which all ordering of memories falls apart.

Repetition and recursion, with its highly significant offshoots of ultradian and circadian rhythms (see Lloyd & Rossi, 1992); selection and variation (the key forces identified in evolution); amplification and simplification: these are among the many phases that occur in the continuous flow, the holomovement, of our auditory imagination.

Such, then, are just a few ideas that spring to mind in a brief expansion of some examples Rycroft selected to illustrate an aside. There have, of course, been many much weightier studies on the part our auditory imagination may play in psychotherapy—for example, Theodore Reik's *Listening with the Third Ear* (Reik, 1948), together with its musical hands-on companion by Berendt (Berendt, 1988); the background of much of Winnicott's thinking (see my extended review of his *The Family and Individual Development* entitled "Theme for two with variations"—Higgins, 1965); Anthony Storr's many reflections on music and the mind (e.g. Storr, 1992); the expanding literature on music therapy, with valuable contributions from David Aldridge, among others (Aldridge, 1996).

My aim has been more circumscribed: to celebrate Charles Rycroft for the live historian, the integrationist, that he was, one who in his writings lights up so deftly the present from the depths of past and future, the precise moment from the infinite. My aim will have been achieved if this paper prompts you to return to these writings with their ever-present pedal-suggestion that we reveal and be revealed in the music.

References

Aldridge, D. (1996). Music therapy research and practice. In: *Medicine: From Out of Silence*. London: Jessica Kingsley.

Arden, M. (1998). *Midwifery of the Soul: A Holistic Perspective on Psychoanalysis*. London: Free Association Books.

Armstrong, F., & Pearson, J. (1992). *As Far as the Eye Can Sing*. London: The Women's Press.

Bell, R. (1974). Contributions of human infants to caregiving and social interaction. In: M. Lewis & L. Rosenblum (Eds.), *The Effect of the Infant on the Caregiver*. New York: John Wiley.

Berendt, J.-E. (1988). *The Third Ear: On Listening to the World*. Shaftesbury/London: Element.

Bohm, D. (1980). *Wholeness and the Implicate Order*. London: Routledge/Ark Paperback, 1983.

Comfort, C. (1984). *Reality and Empathy*. Albany, NY: State University of New York.

Craig, G. (2000). Talking to himself being together. *British Journal of Psychotherapy, 17*: 203–214.

Edelman, G. M. (1985). Neural Darwinism: Popular thinking and higher brain function. In: M. Shaffto (Ed.), *How We Know*. New York: Harper & Row.

Eimas, P. (1975). Speech perception in early infancy. In: L. Cohen & P. Salapatek (Eds.), *Infant Perception: From Sensation to Cognition, Vol. 2*. New York: Academic Press.

Feess-Higgins, A., & Larroche, J.-C. (1987). *The Development of the Human Foetal Brain*. Paris: Inserm.

Hayward, J. W. (1984). *Perceiving Ordinary Magic: Science and Intuitive Wisdom*. Boulder, CO/London: Shambala.

Henderson, B. (2002). Oral bacterial disease and the science of cellular conversation. *Journal of the Royal Society of Medicine, 95*: 77–80.

Higgins, R. (1965). Theme for two with variations: A review of D. W. Winnicott: *The Family and Individual Development*. *New Society*, 1 April 1965.

Lloyd, D., & Rossi, E. L. (Eds.) (1992). *Ultradian Rhythms in Life Processes: An Enquiry into Fundamental Principles of Chronobiology and Psychobiology*. Berlin/London: Springer-Verlag.

McLain, E. G. (1976). *The Myth of Invariance: The Origin of the Gods, Mathematics, and Music from the Rg Veda to Plato.* York Beach, ME: Nicholas-Hays.

Meier, L. B. (1956). *Emotion and Meaning in Music.* Chicago, IL: University of Chicago Press.

Pert, C. B. (1997). *Molecules of Emotion: Why You Feel the Way You Feel.* London: Simon & Schuster.

Prevost, E. (1995). *No Sound Is Innocent.* Matching Tye, Harlow: Copula.

Reik, T. (1948). *Listening with the Third Ear: The Inner Experience of a Psychoanalyst.* New York: Noonday Press.

Rossi, E. L., & Cheek, D. B. (1988). *Mind–Body Therapy: Ideo-dynamic Healing in Hypnosis.* New York/London: W. W. Norton.

Rumi (2001). *Hidden Music,* trans. M. Mafi & A. M. Kolin. London: Thorsons.

Rycroft, C. (1968). *A Critical Dictionary of Psychoanalysis.* London: Penguin. Second edition: London: Penguin, 1995.

Rycroft, C. (1979). *The Innocence of Dreams.* London: Hogarth Press.

Rycroft, C. (1985). *Psychoanalysis and Beyond.* London: Chatto & Windus.

Rycroft, C. (1991). *Viewpoints.* London: Hogarth Press/Chatto & Windus.

Squire, L., & Cohen, N. (1983). Human memory and amnesia. In: R. Thompson & J. McGaugh (Eds.), *Handbook of Behavioural Neurobiology.* New York: Plenum Press.

Storr, A. (1992). *Music and the Mind.* New York: Free Press/Macmillan.

Watkins, J. (1971). The affect bridge: A hypnotic technique. *International Journal of Clinical and Experimental Hypnosis, 19*: 21–27.

CHAPTER ELEVEN

Charles Rycroft
and the historical perspective

Edgar Jones

Although Charles Rycroft is principally known for his work on imagination and symbolism and for re-thinking Freud's concept of primary and secondary processes, a consistent sub-text in his writings is the need for a historical perspective. History has three possible roles in analytical psychotherapy. First, studies of the psychoanalytical movement itself can help us to understand how it has evolved and highlight its truly influential ideas and the forces that shaped its leaders. Key principles and their impact on treatment can be evaluated only if their context is known. Indeed, to assess Rycroft's own contribution to the debate, it is essential to take account of his social background, Cambridge education, medical training, and other formative experiences, such as the death of his father. Second, as therapists, we need insightful histories of individual patients to create an environment in which they feel recognized. The significance of the therapeutic alliance has been emphasized in determining positive outcomes (Roth & Fonagy, 1996), and a sense of understanding can follow from an appreciation of where our clients come from. Third, it has been argued that analysts, or historians who have had a personal analysis, will, when they turn their hand to history, gain insights into personality, groups, and even culture.

But before exploring these themes further, I have to declare a personal interest. When I interviewed Charles Rycroft on 7 May 1998, shortly before his death, he had been my analyst for almost thirteen years. As a result, I cannot claim the objective stance of a biographer, and some of my memories may be distorted by the tendency of analysands to idealize their training therapist.

History within therapy

Rycroft had originally studied economics at Trinity College, Cambridge, before turning to history. It became an abiding interest, despite the fact that he had abandoned academic research in favour of psychoanalysis and medicine. He argued that it was important not only to gather an accurate factual account of a patient's life, but also to grasp the social, political, and economic context in which individuals grew up. Nuances—subtleties of speech, dress, or behaviour—could often tell more than a lengthy discourse. Rycroft once commented, for example, that my impatience was revealed by the way that I rang his doorbell before sessions.

The essay that particularly reveals Rycroft's belief in the importance of history is "On Ablation of the Parental Images" (Rycroft, 1985a). In this paper, he argued that individuals who dealt with parental conflicts by disowning them then have to find ideal ancestors to replace those that they have dismissed. Although this rewriting of history is an imaginative and creative act, it involves deception and the destruction of a genuine and potentially valuable inheritance. Rather than attempt to erase the past, Rycroft believed, individuals should seek to discover its realities to serve as a foundation. It is difficult to feel at home, or grounded, in a self that has been manufactured internally, like a castle built on sand. Ablators find it almost impossible to be truly creative, as they rarely acknowledge a sincere debt to the work of others. Furthermore, by not having been forced to re-evaluate the ideals and values of their parents, they have never learned to be original. Without history, there can be no novelty.

A meta-analysis of the effectiveness of psychotherapy by Roth and Fonagy (1996) identified the therapeutic alliance as a key factor in generating positive outcomes (pp. 350–352). Defined as a conscious collaborative, rational agreement, it relies on both the acquired skills and the personal qualities of the therapist. On the client side, beliefs about the value of therapy are obviously important, and these may be sustained throughout what is often a distressing exploration of past traumas by feeling recognized and taken seriously. A therapist is more likely to tune into his client's wavelength if he is able imaginatively to reconstruct the patient's life and view of the world, a process that has much in common with a historian attempting to understand a past figure or culture.

Rycroft's personal history

Others have written more fully on Rycroft's own history, and I make only a few personal observations. His trademark independence, the ability of think things out privately, was perhaps underpinned by his social background. As the son of a squire, he was known by everyone in the locality but divided from them by the class system. Coming from an established family, surrounded by portraits and memorabilia, it probably gave him a strong sense of his own history. Most of us have to hunt quite hard to find out anything very much about our antecedents (hence the burgeoning passion for genealogy), but I sense that Rycroft grew up with a strong feeling of belonging to a dynasty that was both integral to the social hierarchy and yet divorced from the majority. He preferred to work solo rather than join a group analytical practice. An inveterate walker, Rycroft needed space and time to explore his ideas before committing them to public inspection.

Rycroft also acknowledged a debt to his Cambridge education and, in particular, to British empiricism. Much of classical psychoanalysis fell into the European tradition of rationalism, by which formal deductive systems serve as paradigms for knowledge. Hypotheses were often formulated by introspection, and Freud's structural model of the mind is an intra-psychic one. Analysts educated in the rationalist school believe that references to external events would reflect the structure imposed upon them by the psyche, and so its organization and processes should be the focus of any therapeutic theories. By contrast, empiricists place greater emphasis on the senses (and instruments that extend their range) and experiment to frame ideas (Grayling, 1995, pp. 486–487).

Rycroft and other members of the "Independent Group" explored the way that the external world interacted with the psyche and highlighted factors such as the quality of mothering. Although not a perfect distinction between subgroups of analysts, this difference of approach may in part explain why the British Psychoanalytical Society was not particularly receptive to some of Rycroft's essays.

"Known among his friends as a survivor", Vincent Brome (1998) wrote that Rycroft "always regretted that he had not put himself to the ultimate test, but would not specify what that was. He claimed that one of his work's main themes was people under pressure in extreme situations." It is interesting to speculate what Rycroft believed was "the ultimate test". My feeling is that this may have been combat. He came from a military family. His father had served in the Boer War, an elder brother had been decorated when serving in the Royal Navy during the Second World War, and Rycroft himself went to Wellington College, where it was expected that he would enter the Army. Many there assumed that his father had been killed during the First World War (Rycroft, 1985b). He once told me that he remembered the Armistice as a time when people stopped counting the dead in towns and villages. The intense emotions stirred on the battlefield, risking one's own life for the sake of comrades, coping with the ever-present threat of death, led some veterans of the First World War to conceive of battle as the ultimate initiation test, a *rite de passage* into adult reality (Leed, 1979, pp. 12–13). Men who had survived this trauma, it was argued, shared a new, common identity—an experience that separated them from those who had not fought and one that could not be communicated to them. I have no compelling evidence to establish that Rycroft conceived of combat as the ultimate challenge, though he believed that individuals had the capacity to adapt to almost any form of adversity.

Having qualified in medicine in August 1945, Rycroft worked at the Maudsley as a "house physician". The hospital had recently re-opened at Denmark Hill under the leadership of Aubrey Lewis, its staff having been evacuated during the war years either to a converted public school at Mill Hill or to Sutton EMS Hospital. Little information survives about Rycroft's clinical work at the Maudsley. He had told me that he was unusual among the junior medical staff in not feeling intimidated by Lewis, a formidable intellect and once described as a man with a question for every answer. Subsequently, I recounted this comment to Dr J. J. Fleminger, a friend and colleague of Rycroft. Dr Fleminger observed that he thought it difficult to imagine him being intimidated by anyone (interview, 13 December 2001). There was a tough, combative side to Rycroft, revealed by his nose, broken in a school boxing match, and his sparing and careful use of English.

History of psychoanalysis

Rycroft once remarked that a thorough comprehension of the laws of physics did not entail knowledge of Newton's character, but to understand psychoanalysis it was necessary to know something of the personality and history of Freud and his followers as their hypotheses reflected innate characteristics, prejudices, blind spots, and so forth. Rycroft went some way to illustrate this principle in an autobiographical essay in which he placed senior figures in an historical context. The theoretical differences between Winnicott and Klein cannot be fully explained, he wrote, without research into their professional relationships within the British Society. "Winnicott", Rycroft observed, "always seemed to be pleading to be understood and appreciated by Klein. When I discovered that throughout this period Mrs Winnicott was in analysis with Mrs Klein, and that some years previously Mrs Klein's son had been in analysis with Winnicott, I began to wonder what I was doing sitting in on a family quarrel" (see chapter 15 herein).

The particular nature of the British Society (the way that students are selected and trained), Rycroft argued, increased the need for an historical perspective. Ablators who train as analysts "prefer to believe that psychoanalysis arose as an autochthonous idea in the mind of the genius they have discovered" (Rycroft, 1985a, p. 228). This ahistorical approach was, he suggested, assisted by two features: first, the fact that some key ideas derived from Freud's self-analysis and therefore appear to have arisen from an unconscious source quite distinct from the history of ideas, and, second, the fact that the first generation of analysts deliberately hived off psychoanalysis from the various medical and scientific groups to which it arguably ought to have remained attached.

Furthermore, Roazen (2001) argues, the theme of ablation in psychoanalysis has heightened the need for scholarly histories to question received wisdom and to find out who owed what to whom. "A typical lack of respect for historical sequences has", he wrote, "bedevilled writing about psychoanalysis". To serve as models of the problems that creative people face in unsympathetic environments, Roazen urges studies of the pioneering analysts "whose ideas and lives will continue to be of historical interest" (p. 274).

During the First World War, the epidemic of shell shock that swept through the British Army, and the associated problems of treatment led a number of talented doctors to explore psychoanalytical ideas. William Brown, Frederick Dillon, T. H. Pear, Grafton Elliot Smith, T. A. Ross, H. Crichton-Miller, J. A. Hadfield, William McDougall, C. S. Myers, and others trawled through Freud's writings, modifying and adopting them as they saw fit (see Jones, in press; Jones & Wessely, 2003). However, once the war was over, Ernest Jones made no attempt to recruit them, and he wound up the pre-war London Psycho-Analytic Society to exclude those who were sympathetic to Jung's ideas (Roazen, 1976). When he established the British Psycho-Analytical Society in February 1919, Jones was able to admit only those who, he believed, were truly loyal to Freud and his principles (Rayner, 1990, p. 11). Of the enlightened shell-shock doctors, only W. H. R. Rivers, Millais Culpin, David Eder, Maurice Wright, Bernard Hart, and Sylvia Payne became psychoanalysts during the interwar period, and of these only Payne took executive office; Rivers, who died in 1922, Hart, who resigned in the 1930s, and Culpin remained associate members.[1] In part, this closing of ranks was a defensive reaction against post-war criticism of psychoanalysis by broad sections of the medical profession. Yet, it could be argued that, but for Jones's caution and misplaced loyalty, an opportunity had been lost to build on the achievements of the war years and to establish psychoanalysis as a radical, multi-disciplinary profession. Indeed, the hostility shown to the Tavistock Clinic by the British Society during the interwar period is difficult to comprehend unless one considers the personalities of its leaders and their desire to create a pure Freudian strain of psychoanalysis (King & Steiner, 1991, p. 27; Roazen, 1976, p. 351).

Analysts doing history

The third theme is that the psychoanalyst, by virtue of his own analysis and reading will gain insights into personality, group dynamics, and culture. Should he turn his hand to history, and particularly to the biography of past figures, it is argued, the analyst will be able to discover things not available to historians unschooled in unconscious processes. Such research has earned the generic term "psychohistory". Peter Gay, author of *Freud: A Life for our Time* (1988), though not a fully trained analyst, argued that psychoanalytical ideas can be used to illuminate the past, and he wrote a primer: *Freud for Historians* (1985). In reviewing this work, Rycroft agreed that Freudian theory could be of legitimate interest to any historian attempting to illuminate the motivation of individuals and groups. "There is the literature", he wrote, "which elucidates the origins and interrelationships of the various emotions of self-regard and the sense of identity.... The psychodynamics of pride and shame should ... be of particular interest to historians studying nationalism, militarism, chivalry and gentility" (Rycroft, 1991, p. 85).

But this is not to claim primacy for psychoanalysis. It is simply one of many disciplines that the historian can draw upon, depending on the area of his inquiry. One UK analyst who is also an academic historian, Daniel Pick, has, for instance, written with profit on nineteenth-century ideas of degeneration and on the ways that war, or mass slaughter, have been rationalized by modern society (Pick, 1989, 1993).

Concluding thoughts

In his later years, Rycroft achieved international recognition. He was, for example, asked to present degrees at Regent's College graduation day (chapter 15 herein), his books were widely available in the United Kingdom and the United States, and he continued to review for the *TLS*, *New Statesman*, and *New York Review of Books*. Yet during my training, I cannot recall a tutor who referred to his writings, nor did they appear on reading lists, though the work of his contemporaries was discussed. I suspect, however, that his *Critical Dictionary of Psychoanalysis*, which in 1995 ran to a second edition, was more widely consulted than many would care to admit. Nevertheless, there is a troubling discontinuity between the recognition of his ideas in the wider fields of psychology, psychiatry, and the social sciences and their muted acceptance by the major analytical societies. Although a literature survey by Susan Budd shows that Rycroft continued to be referenced in the main psychoanalytical journals after his withdrawal and resignation from the British Society, these were limited to his papers on symbolism and dreams (Budd, 2001). John Turner's paper published in the *International Journal of Psycho-Analysis* and reprinted here as chapter 10, which contrasted his contribution to our understanding of illusion with that of Milner and Winnicott (chapter 9 herein), may imply a change. I wonder whether his death, and the fact that Rycroft has himself become a historical figure, may allow a growing acknowledgement of his ideas within analytical circles. Although he disliked the idea of creating followers, Rycroft's writings will have served as an inspiration to those who set store by independence of thought, integrity of behaviour, and the synthesis of knowledge from diverse sources.

Note

1. List of members, *International Journal of Psycho-Analysis*, 12 (1931): 529–530; 20 (1939): 504–506.

References

Brome, V. (1998). Obituary. *Guardian*, 1 June.
Budd, S. (2001). Insiders and outsiders. *British Journal of Psychotherapy*, 18: 281.

Gay, P. (1985). *Freud for Historians*. Oxford: Oxford University Press.

Gay, P. (1988) *Freud: A Life for Our Time*. New York: W. W. Norton.

Grayling, A. C. (1995). The empiricists. In: A .C. Grayling (Ed.), *Philosophy: A Guide through the Subject*. Oxford: Oxford University Press.

Jones, E. (in press). Doctors and trauma in World War One: The response of British military psychiatrists. In: P. Gray & K. Oliver (Eds.), *The Memory of Catastrophe*. Manchester: Manchester University Press.

Jones, E., & Wessely, S. (2003). The impact of total war on the practice of British psychiatry. In: R. Chickering & S. Förster (Eds.), *The Shadows of Total War, Europe, East Asia and the United States, 1919–39* (pp. 129–148). Cambridge: Cambridge University Press.

King, P., & Steiner, R. (Eds.) (1991). *The Freud-Klein Controversies 1941–45*. London: Tavistock/Routledge.

Leed, E. J. (1979). *No Man's Land, Combat and Identity in World War I*. Cambridge: Cambridge University Press.

Pick, D. (1989). *Faces of Degeneration: A European Disorder c.1848–c.1918*. Cambridge: Cambridge University Press.

Pick, D. (1993). *War Machine: The Rationalisation of Slaughter in the Modern Age*. New Haven, CT: Yale University Press.

Rayner, E. (1990). *The Independent Tradition in British Psychoanalysis*. London: Free Association Books.

Roazen, P. (1976). *Freud and His Followers*. London: Allen Lane.

Roazen, P. (2001). Charles Rycroft and the theme of ablation. *British Journal of Psychotherapy, 18*: 269–277.

Roth, A., & Fonagy, P. (1996). *What Works for Whom? A Critical Review of Psychotherapy Research*. New York: Guildford Press.

Rycroft, C. (1985a). On ablation of the parental images, *or* The illusion of having created oneself. In: P. Fuller (Ed.), *Psychoanalysis and Beyond* (pp. 214–232). London: Hogarth Press.

Rycroft C. (1985b). Where I came from. In: P. Fuller (Ed.), *Psychoanalysis and Beyond* (pp. 198–206). London: Hogarth Press.

Rycroft, C. (1991). Freud for historians. In: *Viewpoints* London: Hogarth Press.

CHAPTER TWELVE

The innocence of Charles Rycroft

Harold Bourne

The innocence, or rather, pseudo-innocence of Charles Rycroft covertly brought about a grievous waste of himself. "Lamentably, there is no Rycroftian school of psychoanalysis", I wrote in 1993, reviewing his book *Viewpoints*. And I went on: "if Rycroft is not recognized as one of the major revisionists not only of psychoanalysis but of our perception and understanding of the human organism, it is his own doing." It was indeed a momentous self-defeat, and a huge loss not only for psychoanalysis which, a century after Freud, is a network of studies, theories, applications, and clinical methods, but also for psychiatry, psychology, and much else.

It was, moreover, a muffled self-defeat, obscured by success in the day-to-day meaning of the word. He was highly respected in the psychoanalytic community in London; he was well connected both in society at large and with persons outstanding in various cultural fields; and as a psychoanalytic book reviewer, his name was among those familiar to the educated public in Britain. Nevertheless, he did not fulfil the mission that went far beyond this, and nobody prevented him but himself. At the end, I believe he knew this when it was too late.

Unlike other psychoanalytical revisionists since Freud, such as Jung, Klein, Kohut, who have commanded widespread professional attention, dispute, acclaim, and followers, Rycroft offers not a revision but a radical reconstruction of psychoanalysis—convincing, elegant, primarily concerned not with amending or adding to its component formulations but with re-writing its entire script. However, he gives this forth in a mode almost designed to elicit no such attention at all. Marx claimed to have found Hegel standing on his head and to have turned him the right way up. Were he less averse to proclaiming his message, Rycroft could have said the same of himself and Freud.

In an epic process of labour, Freud gave birth to psychoanalysis, but he was forever a physician, and it therefore grew swaddled in medical clothing. Consequently, notwithstanding its unprecedented illumination of the human mind in its everyday workings, psychoanalysis became foremost an account of the sick mind. In a sense, Rycroft turned Freud the right way up by reformulating his discoveries so as to be an account of the healthy mind. In this way, the Freudian unconscious came into its own as a reservoir nurturing creativity, and only secondarily as a cauldron of the repressed throbbing to return and of primitive instincts and drives to be kept safely in check.

Freud's dictum was that where id was, there ego should be, and he likened psychoanalytic therapy to draining the Zuyder Zee both to extend the Netherlands and safeguarding them from flooding. The id is characterized by what Freud called the "primary process" of mind—timeless, non-rational, iconic, self-centred, unconscious, and governed by the "pleasure principle". His discovering it altered our knowledge of ourselves as radically as Columbus altered the map of the earth. But for Freud, it was primitive, as if to be outgrown, and the "secondary process"—rational, verbal, cognitive, self-inhibitory, conscious and "pre-conscious", and governed by the "reality principle"—characterizes the ego and accounts for humanity's achievements. Rycroft shifted the focus contrariwise—that for the human species' unique evolutionary attainments, imagination, unconscious phantasy, and symbolism were faculties no less essential than the prehensile forelimb and the bipedal erect posture.

In the clinical world, Rycroft conferred on the imagination, on the symbol-forming function, and on the unconscious workings of mind that Freud first brought to light in dreams, as central a role in healthy well-being and living as a properly functioning kidney or heart. Freud, the one-time neuro-anatomist, struggled to delineate the mind's structure in quasi-anatomical terms of discrete, inter-relating organs—the id, the superego, and the ego—and he seemed to track them entering into conflicts, alliances, and compromises with each other. For Rycroft, it was sufficient to be empirical—to make sense of clinical phenomena without some Continental com-pulsions, Hegelian, Marxist, or Freudian, to have them generate and subserve grand, global theories.

Rycroft also put his finger on Freud's having invented an en-tirely novel and richly productive relationship and dialogue be-tween two people—the psychoanalytic procedure—and then mistaking it for a version of the detached and objective physician's clinical procedure for detecting the sick patient's underlying physi-cal pathology, with all kinds of obfuscating and long-lasting results.

All of this is merely to provide some flavour of the liberating and refreshing impact on psychoanalysis that Rycroft almost per-versely debarred himself from transmitting far and wide. However distinguished he was in the English cultural scene at large, the misfortune for the international world of psychoanalysis and re-lated disciplines is that Rycroft, far from making himself a leading figure and an influence, made himself virtually invisible and inau-dible in it. He alienated himself from its organizations and its learned literature so that professional awareness of his work is restricted mostly to personal acquaintances in Britain and scattered admirers in the United States. The loss to psychoanalysis is exas-perating and heart-breaking, even if, somehow or another, it be retrieved in the long run.

My twin purposes here are to examine what lay hidden in Charles to generate so preposterous a sabotage of himself and to pinpoint the devices by which he secured that. It will emerge that his revolutionary creativity, on the one hand, and his undeclared scheme for minimizing its impact, on the other, share common sources and are inseparable.

This came into view in the course of our relationship, but far too late—barely a decade before his death aged 83 in 1998. The discovery induced an upheaval in him and a whirl of painful self-discovery in me. To explain it all, I must outline the story of our long friendship, which became the context of that discovery.

The story begins in the 1920s with two outwardly different clusters of events, one in his life, one in mine. Unbeknown to us until some 48 years after we first met in 1940, we already had in common, touched off by events long before, certain powerful but contradictory forces harboured deep within: rage against the English social order, opposed to and not quite quelled by an intense and reparative identification with it. Neither of us recognized this in the other, nor did either of us know at that time that the other had a strong interest in psychoanalysis or that the other was a medical student, not by spontaneous choice but by arm-twisting. Charles took up medicine as a condition for acceptance for psychoanalytic training. I did so because my father insisted that I enter a profession that would give me a living anywhere in the world, if the Fascists gained power and the Jews were kicked out of England, as was happening in Germany: "They can take what you own away, but they can't take away your knowledge." In those pre-Holocaust days of the 1930s, he little thought that "they" might take your life away along with everyone else's.

In Charles's case, the aforesaid events began in 1925, when he was 11 years old and his boarding-school headmaster summoned him in to be told that his father had died. He was told to go back to his class and get on with his schoolwork. To make it even more agonizing, he and his siblings, the four children of Sir Richard Rycroft's second marriage, at the same time as losing their father, lost the beautiful eighteenth-century country house at Dummer in Hampshire where they were growing up. The rule of primogeniture was, as Charles put it, "ruthlessly applied", and his older half-brother inherited the house and land along with the title, while the children and their mother were evicted to live in "aristocratic poverty" in the Dower House of their cousin's castle in Essex. I was to visit Charles in that house later, around 1943, for tea served by his mother with Charles commenting *sotto voce* "she's proud of herself because before the war she wouldn't have known how to boil a kettle of water!" For Charles, Dummer House was a kind of lost paradise of which they had all been robbed by the unjust laws of English society.

This was the beginning of a deep anger and revolt against the proprieties and order of the English social world. In adolescence, while at public school, Charles rejected Christianity, hurting his depressed mother, as well as deciding against the military career that had been designated for him by his riding-to-hounds family. Simultaneously conjured into being, surely for reparative purposes, was an intense and lifelong identification with the English order of things, so that arriving at Cambridge in 1933, aged 19, he actually joined the Conservative Association and the Communist-run Anti-War Movement at the same time! It was not long before he switched to the Socialist Club and then, at 20, to the Communist Party, after which he wore a hammer-and-sickle badge, made a pilgrimage to the Soviet Union, and looked forward to violent revolution. In later life, referring to his views when young, he said that he had come to think that it would take generations for a country to recover from violent change. Jenny, his widow, recently described Charles as "somewhat enigmatic . . . at the same time a traditionalist and a rebel". I will later discuss the dire restriction that these two early developments engendered. First, I want to relate how a curiously similar combination of developments came about in myself and how my friendship with Charles proceeded.

In my case the signal events go back to 1928, when I was sent to school, aged 5. The teacher said, "Harold, choose an empty place!" I surveyed the class, spotted a delectable blonde girl next to an empty seat, and happily put myself alongside her. I can still see her blue eyes fixing me and hear her throaty whisper: "I don't want to sit next to a Jew boy!" *En passant*, whether connected or not, my love life ever since has been devoted to winning gentile women, and so far I haven't even held the hand of a Jewish girl. While never having heard of Jesus and only vaguely, if at all, of Palestine, in a few days I realized that the bigger boys who sidled up to inquire why I didn't go back to Palestine could be violent, and that "You killed Jesus" meant "Now I'm going to bash you!" Like other Jew boys, I learnt to avoid ruffianly side-streets and to be cautious about playing in the park and wary about passing gentile boys in the street if there were two or more of them, or one if he was bigger than myself.

My mother, a teacher herself, could become a prototypical English school-ma'am on occasion, and in response to my pleas for help, she would tell me: "You must learn to fight your own bat-tles"—utterly impractical advice, given their size, number, and ubiquity, leaving me with the notion that it must be I who was craven. Looking back on it, given that she could not patrol the streets for me, what else could my mother have said?

My childhood plight with anti-Semitism stirred a lividly venge-ful phantasy, which settled into a limitless drive to up-end the terrifying gentiles and their England that spurned me, and led me at 17 to my two years in the Communist Party. It was the trajectory that has made Jews disproportionately conspicuous in revolution-ary and reformist movements. However, in my case, as in Charles's, this rage with the social order was counterbalanced by another development, classical over-identification with the aggressor, rein-forced by reparative identification with my "English school-teacher" mother and her brother, a local doctor and a central figure for me. Among her idols were Jane Austen, Dickens, George Eliot, while he venerated John Stuart Mill, Gladstone, and Palmerston. It was in his library that, at 14 or so, I encountered Frazer, Malinowski . . . and Freud.

By this process of over-identification I came to illustrate, well and truly, Arthur Koestler's remark that Jews are like everyone else but more so. Surpassing in Englishness my Jew-baiting peers, I throbbed with patriotic pride at the mention of Boadicea, Agin-court, Magna Carta, Drake, and the Charge of the Light Brigade, while at Crowland School, Tottenham, they had hardly heard of them. I even nagged my mother into buying me an Eton collar, absurd in working-class London in the hard-up 1930s and too unsafe to wear at school.

In sum, like Charles, I came to be emphatically English in values, caste of mind, and culture and at one and at the same time a dissenter and a rebel. And so, after I left the Communist Party in 1942, discarding Marxism and any penchant for Continental grand theories, it became easy to feel at one with Charles, and a friend-ship began and prospered naturally with, of course, no awareness of these parallels in our personal development. At about that time, now involved in clinical studies, I had the wondrous revelation as I was browsing in a bookshop that in opting reluctantly for medi-cine I had inadvertently set myself on the very pathway to a career, via psychiatry, that could enable me to regain one of my schoolboy fascinations that I thought I had forfeited by entering medical school: psychiatry would take me back into the realm of Freud! My gleeful announcement of this did nothing for my image at medical school, still overshadowed by my recent past as a communist activist!

Our first meeting two years earlier had been remarkably predictive, had I known it then. It was December 1940, the first term of pre-clinical sciences, and Charles, Ruth Jackson, and I were sitting in the sunlight on a long oak table in the hallway of a stately house in Surrey where staff and students resided. The faculty had been evacuated there from University College London. The setting was academic, rural, serene, occasional air raids being distant. We had no thought at that moment that Jews were being slaughtered in droves, for sport, by German soldiers in Poland, soon to be murdered in millions in the concentration camps. Poland was far away, Jews were no news, and nobody knew much. Instead, there we sat, debating student politics.

Ruth (now Ruth Fleminger), a friend to this day, had decided that Charles and I ought to meet. I was 17 and a busy bee in the limelight, or so I imagined: Secretary of the Student Union, organizer of Soc. Soc. (the Socialist Society), mastermind of the Communist "fraction"—supposedly secret, but hardly so with many students by then recruited into the Party. I had just caused a flutter by screening, in the ballroom, *The Battleship Potemkin*, accompanied by Brahms' Second Piano Concerto, to an audience disgruntled by my advertising it as a masterpiece.

I was one of a handful of students from local authority and grammar schools, surrounded by self-assured young people who actually came from the legendary public schools that everyone attended in story books: young people who had holidays abroad and winter sports in Switzerland, who played rugby not soccer and called the ditch bounding the great lawn a ha-ha.

Charles was 26, nine years older than I, and I quickly sensed that while he, too, came from that different world, he was of some rare quality as well. Ruth explained that she had brought us together because Charles supported our political aims and wanted to help, but he hadn't come to join the Party. We chatted about how our leftist activities were going in the student body and then, plucking up courage, I asked why he would not enlist with us. He said it wouldn't be helpful to support us openly and that he could do more as a sympathizer, promoting our ideas and advising me on strategy. Some people were best in activities out in the open, but that was not his forte: he was best out of sight as a guerrilla. I remember being at a loss when I heard this: obviously he was no faint-heart, but something wasn't right. Inarticulately I tried to plead that his stance was ineffective, that our cause needed exponents on the scene, not behind it without an audience. I felt baffled without being able to put my finger on what he was about. At the same time, what he conveyed to me then impressed me so deeply that ever since, whenever I come across the word "guerrilla", an image of Charles, seated on the table back then in 1940, flashes across my mind.

With hindsight, I realize that this first meeting of ours was also my first encounter with the pseudo-innocence of Charles Rycroft— an obdurate, would-be innocence sabotaging his immensely subversive creativity. These were, I think, residual expressions of an ancient childhood rage with the parental world and social order, combined with an intense identification with that world, mobilized in reparation.

The second such encounter came after my liberating discovery that a career I really wanted, psychoanalysis, was there ahead of me after all. My friendship with Charles had taken off, and we often lunched together. Sometimes he spent a day or a weekend with my family, as I still lived with my parents. Being nine years older than I, he was becoming something of a guru for me. In an interview over fifty years later, Jeremy Holmes (1996) asked Charles if there had been a conflict between his being in analysis and being a medical student at the same time. He replied as follows:

"I do remember the occasional arguments with consultants on ward rounds. There was an exact contemporary of mine who was much more militantly pro-analysis—Harold Bourne. He and I were a bit of a team and we used to put the psychological point of view forward. You might call it tact or moral cowardice but he aroused much more opposition than I did. And he was very aware of the fact. In fact, he wrote me a letter not so very long ago saying that I had spent my life provoking other people into being much more militant than I admitted to being."

That letter of mine was combined with a poignant encounter, which I will be describing, in which Charles came up against the finding that he had devoted his creativity to subverting psychoanalysis by a revolutionary reconstruction of it, while always blindly ensuring that any commensurate influence and recognition should never come.

Also with hindsight, I can discern now that my being Jewish was of more than ordinary, if obscure, importance for Charles. Having left Wellington, his public school, at 18 in 1933, he spent six months in Germany before the academic year at Cambridge began. He witnessed the street violence and mass rallies that Nazism ushered in, and he arrived with introductions to upper-class people like himself. At one dinner party they were voicing indulgent views of Hitler's rabble, and the urbane chatter was taking an anti-Semitic turn when Charles brought it to a ghastly halt. "I'm awfully sorry", he interjected, "I'm afraid I should have told you before, but actually I'm a Jew!"

Probably Charles had not yet got to know or even met any Jews. By the time we were becoming good friends, ten years after this, he was on the way to being driven to distraction by Jews, whereas at Cambridge he had once had a juvenile phase of exaggerated respect for the supposedly superior Jewish mind. Writing about himself at Cambridge and his first application for psychoanalytical training in 1936 at the age of 22, four years before we met, he recalled, "I tacitly assumed it was a profession reserved for Central Europeans who, at the time, I believed to be intrinsically more intelligent and cultured than the English." Central Europeans, in practice for him, usually meant Jews. From its start with Freud, who was still active in 1936, the International Psychoanalytical Society was largely Jewish, except in England and Switzerland. Soon the British Psychoanalytical Society would be overrun by "Central Europeans" in flight from Nazism, becoming a hotbed of doctrinal factions and Talmudic disputation.

In fact, psychoanalytic training bears a suspicious resemblance to classical rabbinical training. The aspirant sits beside his Rabbi for years, imbibing his words and analysing the multiple meanings of each line of the sacred texts. It is only when the Rabbi thinks the pupil has learnt and matured enough that he grants him Semicha and a new Rabbi is born. The so-called training analysis, the cardinal feature in the training of psychoanalysts, doesn't seem to be so very different, somehow.

As our friendship developed in the 1940s, Charles came to my home, stayed the odd weekend, engaged with my parents who very much appreciated him, met other relatives in my extended Jewish family, and, in short, gained experience of the world I came from, so different from his. Mine, too, was cultivated, but in a tradition more intense, intellectual, and outspoken, where relationships were warm more immediately. I remember once Charles nervously reached inside his jacket for a cigarette during an argument with a quick-witted uncle of mine whom he had just met, who instantly remarked, "Oh! So you're looking for your notebook, Boswell, to take down what I'm saying!" Thereafter he would now and then greet Charles as "Boswell". Later on he asked Charles to find an analyst for him, and Charles chose Michael Balint on the principle that they deserved each other. My uncle was aware that one's analyst never laughs but claimed that he could sometimes make Dr Balint laugh.

Nowadays I like to think of Charles's relationship with me and my family in the 1940s and 1950s providing a corrective emotional experience to his concurrent involvement in another Jewish milieu, the British Psychoanalytical Society, with the conflicts, the certainties, the immoderate theorizing of "Central European" doctrinal issues, where he was to find that it could be maddening to be a gentile among Jews. Decades later, he wrote in a letter to me: "All the elder statesmen and stateswomen have died, apart from Anna Freud, and it has become possible for a gentile to criticize classical psychoanalysis without being accused of anti-Semitism." Years later it was a phantasy of mine that but for the corrective experience my family provided, Charles would have dropped out of the Society much sooner than he did.

In October 1945 I became a father, as did Charles in 1947. Thereafter it became a steady friendship between two couples with professions and interests in common and their children, coming together of an evening or a weekend, for birthdays and so on. Once I retreated from a marital crisis to the Rycrofts for three or four days until Chloe negotiated my return home. Charles steered my wife into analysis with Wilfred Bion, and I followed, in the Society's clinic, with young Joseph Sandler. Twenty years later, in my second analysis with Henri Rey, I would ruffle his Kleinian poise by declaring that he was no different from the non-Kleinian Sandler.

There came another instance of open subversion by me, aided by Charles out of sight. In 1953, *The Lancet* published my paper "The Insulin Myth", which contended that the insulin coma treatment of schizophrenia, the jewel in the crown of psychiatry worldwide, was worthless. This brought the editor irate letters from the establishment and me some notoriety, along with brusque rejections at job interviews. However, it was not very long before the insulin treatment went on the scrapheap. Unpublished was the fact that Charles, labelling my text "Germanic", helped me to rewrite it presentably. Since then, writing is always an agony, straining in vain, as if Charles is looking over my shoulder, to reproduce his economical and felicitous prose. "The Insulin Myth" was, not altogether unintentionally, really subversive of official psychiatry. Charles's part in this was, again, a hidden part.[1]

In 1955, fifteen years after we first met, this pleasing, enriching, and gratifying relationship with the Rycrofts came to an end when I took my family to New Zealand. We exchanged letters for a while. I wrote to Charles that I was abandoning the superego; he wrote back that he had abandoned the ego and the id as well; I replied asking, what about the ego's autoplastic and alloplastic functions? He sent his iconoclastic paper on Symbolism (1956), which I now regard as a classic. Then came the shock: Charles wrote to say, knowing how deeply it would upset us, that he and Chloe were separating. We were stunned and felt that, whoever left whom, it was a terrible mistake.

We met again 13 years later, when I had a fellowship enabling us to have three months in England in 1968. Chloe had become my friend before Charles, being my first Communist ally when we began medical school in October 1940, and she was as affectionate and hospitable as ever. When we got together with Charles, it was, perhaps, not quite the same. A few times he an I met together on our own, reported on our personal lives, and talked a great deal. It worried me to hear that he no longer took much part in the British Psychoanalytical Society for what, to me, seemed specious reasons. I argued that you don't abandon the field because you disagree with your opponents. Charles was tolerantly amused, and as a result I felt rather juvenile. However, with the passage of time I changed my mind and realized that I had not been juvenile and that it was in Charles that something had gone wrong. This became clear to me after I returned to live permanently in London in 1973, five years later, and could exchange ideas with well-informed friends.

Having returned, I quickly made contact with Charles, and he took me to dinner at the Reform Club. Explaining his distancing himself from the British Psychoanalytical Society, he said disdainfully, "I can't possibly be associated with people like that." I wondered, uneasily, what he meant by "people like that". I had long grown out of the ethnic minority tendency to suspect racism in any contretemps, but for a mad moment it crossed my mind that Charles had gone anti-Semitic, and I came back at him with "People like what?" He then told me much of what he has put on record about why he had dropped out, along with some wickedly comic gossip and anecdotes.

In writing about himself, Charles offered the following reasons for dropping out of the Society. He could not abide the feuding between the Kleinian and Anna Freud orthodoxies, the accusations of heresy, the appeals to authority when opinions conflicted, and "ways of conducting business and engaging in controversy that were entirely alien to me". He contrasted it disparagingly with the standards of Cambridge and his education at University College Hospital: the Society "by medical standards, lacked common sense . . . nor, I came to realize, did Englishmen cut any ice in it". The last straw was the quasi-theological response at a society meeting to a paper presented by James Home in 1964 (Home, 1966). Thereupon he and Peter Lomas, an analysand of his, left in disgust and never attended a meeting of the Society again.

Long ago, I decided that all this was half-truth, at most, and a tissue of rationalizations for what propelled Charles from within into walking away, and, moreover, doing so at a time when, as will emerge here, he knew that the prospect for him was leadership in the Society and becoming an international force in psychoanalysis. Explaining himself to me during our Reform Club meeting in 1973, Charles made no mention of how Cambridge and University College Hospital standards put the British Psychoanalytical Society standards to shame, and I would not have gone along with him if he had. In universities, as in any large institution, there are always place-seekers, power-mongers, old-boy networks, intrigues, and nepotism, and Cambridge is known to be no exception. Its mode of selecting students so that local authority sixth-formers have a fraction of the chance enjoyed by those from so-called public schools remains shameful, a national disgrace, one repeatedly denounced. As for University College Hospital, Charles and I were pleased to be there but we also shared considerable scepticism and serious criticisms of the place. As for the British Psychoanalytical Society lacking common sense by medical standards, Charles must have forgotten what he once knew! In our day, if not now, medical education could transform any bright teenager into a psychological imbecile: after decades in hospitals and medical schools, I still have not lost my capacity for surprise at how lacking in common sense medical practice can sometimes be.

Soon after the Reform Club evening of 1973, my brother, Sandy Bourne, who knew and admired Charles, dismissed the reasons he had given me for leaving the Society as hogwash. "Sure, there still were these old-style *Juden* whose motto is '*Steht geschrieben*' (thus it is written) and who came in from Vienna and beyond twenty or twenty-five years before Charles departed. But the whole picture wasn't like that even ten years ago, when he went off, let alone now. God knows why he left. Maybe he just wanted to!" He mentioned other psychoanalysts he knew well who, like himself, shared Charles's values and intellectual outlook, who were every bit as English, to whom it had not occurred to walk out, who were dismayed and sorrowful about Charles doing so. I heard much the same from other friends in the Society, and it became impossible for me to believe that the version Charles gave of the Society was realistic and correct and that all these reputable people didn't know what they were talking about.

Later in the 1970s I met Charles a few times, but always at my initiative, until I gave up. After that, I met him once at a small party of my brother's. Depending on my mood, I ascribed the decline of our friendship either to life separating our paths or to my not being of fine enough stuff, now, for Charles, or even to our friendship not having been as solid or deep as in my memory of it. At some point my Italian wife suggested writing to Charles: if he was an old friend, it would be wrong not to do so. But I couldn't think of anything to write.

All of this was suddenly dispelled by an unforeseen *Eureka* experience in 1985. Pottering about my desk to no purpose one midnight, I picked up Charles's *Psychoanalysis and Beyond* (1985), a book that had come out recently but that I had not yet read. I was tempted, dipped in here and there, felt some consternation, and began to think, "What is Charles up to?" The same question, I recalled, had bothered me when I had read his 1979 book *The Innocence of Dreams*—a virtuoso piece that had entranced yet vaguely troubled me. On an impulse, since it was past any sensible bed-time with my early morning start, I turned to the autobiographical essay, "Where I Came From". It begins with a paragraph about the two publishers who had previously required him to write an account of himself, here rewritten. One publisher had a background "very similar" to his own and was amazed and amused that a scion of fox-hunting gentry should have become a psychoanalyst; the other was a "foreigner" with a "preposterously romanticized" vision of the English upper classes. Reading this, I was suddenly electrified, flooded with *aperçus* and insights, not only about Charles but about myself, and I knew exactly what I was going to put to him in my letter.

Thereupon, I feverishly wrote ten pages and over the following weeks, mostly at midnight, I kept writing more. The result was left as an unfinished treatise that I did not give to Charles until three years later after we met, by chance, in the middle of 1988 and talked as we had not talked for two decades. At this meeting I told him what I had written in my unfinished and unposted letter. Here I quote the overwhelming moment touched off by the opening paragraph of his autobiographical essay, "Where I Came From":

> instantly I knew both what you thought you were doing and much else that you have been, so to speak, up to, as well; I became certain now about our friendship—not only had it been real as I remembered it but also I now knew what lay at its foundation . . . something much more psychologically substantial than I had ever appreciated before.

This was a reference, of course, to what I have narrated earlier about having in common an unconscious rift harboured within ourselves, with childhood rage against the social order of our world pitted against over-identification with it. My midnight letter being unfinished and undelivered, I had to convey all that by word of mouth to Charles when we met three years afterwards. The letter continues:

> This letter is a kind of gift but I wonder how you will receive it, as it comes too late to bring about a productive change, or tries to do too much. About the two publishers, one true blue and acknowledged to be like yourself, but with the other, the foreigner with his preposterous vision of the English aristocracy, you apparently are not at all at one. Actually, so I suspect, they both are highly significant figures for you and also for me—whoever they happen literally to be. They impersonate in the external world two forces in conflict on either side of a schism within ourselves.
>
> It was a moment when all sorts of things about you and me—my unease about *The Innocence of Dreams* and much, much else which had been there but not in clear focus, became sharp and inter-linked in a flash. And I was startled and awe-struck by the audacity and clear sweep of your life's enterprise—the subverting and take-over of psychoanalysis by anglicising it, which would rectify it beyond measure and yet, and all unaware, covertly sabotaging your own invaluable contributions so that psychoanalysis can go safely bumbling along unchanged.

I will eventually indicate later how this sabotage was accomplished, but here meanwhile is more of the letter.

> For a few wild minutes, intrigued by the discovery that you had wondrously forged a beguiling pseudo-solution to a fiendish conflict in yourself that also survives unresolved in me, I imagined that I had spotted something that you weren't in touch with at all. Then modesty returned because obviously you must be clear about your programme of anglicizing psychoanalysis, even though unaware both of its subversive motivation and of how you ensure reparatively that it has neither impact nor recognition.

The next evening, too late to resume writing, I read Peter Fuller's introduction to *Psychoanalysis and Beyond* and was struck by how, far more vividly and completely than I could have done, he spells out *in extenso* your anglicizing of psychoanalysis. It is a badly needed unified exposition of the work of Charles Rycroft and his reconstruction of psychoanalysis. However, as an introduction to Charles Rycroft himself, he gets it wrong in three large, if not fatal, respects: he seems to see you as a man without conflicts, let alone any formative, unresolved, and pervasive ones; he overlooks the paradox of how, with a nature and mind so purely and resoundingly English and empirical, you could ever have been so seduced by the Weltanschauung and continental grand theorizing of Marxism as to enlist in the Communist Party and world revolution and then, at the age of 22, devoted your life to so Continental a growth as psychoanalysis; and, above all, Fuller doesn't perceive that you are a profoundly subversive person with a masquerade of innocence.

> Yet he does have an inkling. About your self-styled "peculiarly English point of view", he remarks "Rycroft's Englishness is of a peculiar, indeed an *exceptional* kind; it is perhaps only *half* Englishness." However, Fuller's reasons for arriving at this are neither here nor there.

I must leave my letter at this point to say that, living in Italy, I am conscious of peculiar Italian virtues, but even more am I conscious of English ones because of their absence around me; though given immodestly to valuing them in myself . . . and immodesty is un-English. Charles made much of his Englishness, but the reality in his case was not straightforward, as Fuller obviously sensed but could not quite make out when he described it as peculiar and half English. Returning to my letter:

> As for your being profoundly subversive, no! That is not sentimentality, nor is it a projection of mine. On the contrary, the first thing you ever told me about yourself meant just that, no more and no less, had I the wit to realize it at the time.

The letter goes on to remind Charles of our first encounter nearly fifty years previously, in 1940, as I have already described it, with him sitting on the long oak table in the sunlit entrance hall and explaining to me that he saw himself best as a guerrilla, out of sight, while other people were best at activities in the open. The letter continues:

You don't need me to tell you there has been streak of subversion within, nor would you have it otherwise, nor would it be conceding anything much to say so. But I am not talking about any streak, much less one overcome and properly tamed long, long ago, but about subversiveness as a motor force, hard at work lifelong . . . and energetically denied! My focus is on that denial with its attendant self-deception, self-disempowerment and masquerade of innocence.

Your autobiographical essays "Where I Came From" and "Memoirs of an Old Bolshevik" offer flagrant examples of denial. "My left-wing interests and activities required no moral courage. Marxism was fashionable, my family took the view that it was proper to engage in political activity and that it was best for them to start on the left."

This sounds good but it happens to be implausible. Marxism greatly appeals to the Continental mind and has been a force to be reckoned with across Europe, but you, better than anyone, know that for the English mind it is most unsuited. Therefore its political influence in England has been negligible, with none or one Communist in Parliament at the best of times, and it has never been "fashionable"—even at Cambridge. When you were there in the 1930s, students from the moneyed class and fee-paying schools were very much in the majority, and poor candidates for Marxism. Those for whom it was "fashionable" were only a minority, albeit a noisy one that made waves.

As for your family's easy-going attitude to your politics at the age of 19 and 20, I find it hard to believe and in those days particularly, unless perhaps they had quietly given up on you for the time being. Nobody would have been pleased at your record; rejecting the military career long anticipated; openly giving up Christianity and turning into a Communist. It was no surprise that in 1944, by which time the Communist Party was nine years in the past for you, your naval commander brother was still in the mood to say "Jolly glad not to have a traitor on my ship" when you were in Portsmouth and didn't visit him. We laughed about it then, while you said nothing to suggest he was the odd man out in your family and all the rest were comfortable with your left-wing convictions.

Likewise, how you took up psychoanalysis—"at Cambridge we all read Freud"—so Karen Stephen persuaded you to apply for training when you were 22; your family were not opposed except to you becoming a non-medical analyst; and you took up medicine to meet the requirements of Ernest Jones—never a mention that doing medicine might also placate the family and killed two birds with one stone. Oh well! This story also leaves me wondering—could it really have been like that?

Here, I interrupt my letter for a moment to point out that in 1993, five years after we had come together again and I had sent him this letter, Charles gave a very different and more credible account of how he got into psychoanalysis. I now quote from an address he gave then to an audience of psychotherapists and counsellors (reprinted here in chapter 15; the emphases are mine):

> I should explain that in the 1930s Freudian psychoanalysis was regarded as *deeply subversive*. In progressive, advanced circles, Marx and Freud were regarded as the arch-enemies of capitalist society and middle-class morality, and to announce that one wanted to become an analyst was, indeed, a gesture *pour épater les bourgeois*. In fact, of course, British psychoanalysis in the 1930s was more an offshoot of Bloomsbury than a wing of any revolutionary movement, *but I did not realize that at the time*, despite the fact that it was Karin Stephen, a sister-in-law of Virginia Woolf, who pushed, prodded, and *dared me to apply for training*.

Coming back to my letter, it continues as follows until it ends, unfinished,

> If "Where I Came From" is suffused with denial to the point of blandness, "Memoirs of an Old Bolshevik", while likewise suffused, is witty, seductive, and, in a way, fiction, the more accurate title being "The Innocence of an Old Bolshevik". Self-deception having no limits, it is faintly possible, I suppose, that you even believe now it was like that in Cambridge in the 1930s—that people there joined the Communist Party and worked for revolution without any of the urges that drive people into revolutionary movements anywhere else. They had

no anger, neither righteous indignation nor destructiveness, no envy, and, apart from the very few, no seriousness of purpose. Some bumbled along to Spain; some got mixed up in well-intentioned treason, and some like you only took a trip to the Promised Soviet Land . . . quintessentially English amateurs all, let's say. . . . And for that matter, I've met an ex-Fascist with the very same innocence and denial these days, who manages to obliterate how, once upon a time, he would have relished doing in a Jew like me. The device you employ in your ex-Bolshevik memoir is to confuse being an ingenue, which you and I and most other Bolsheviks were then, with being innocent and innocuous, which we were not. In so far as your memoir is a symptom (which, as well as being a *jeu d'esprit*, I think it is) it amounts to a parade of innocence for bolstering up denial of subversiveness. By completely omitting your pilgrimage to the Soviet Union and any reference to the atmosphere of the 1930s—mass unemployment, hunger marches, strikes, the rise of Nazism, the rape of Nanking, and the wilful impotence of the League of Nations, the surge of Indian nationalism and the British Empire's response—you can these days depict your Communist Party activities as comically ritualistic but harmless play. "Looking back on it", you say "I don't think we did either ourselves or anyone else much harm." Maybe so, but only by the grace of God and the English Channel. And couldn't Mosley and the British Union of Fascists say the same thing? Sadly, your equally harmless and communist opposite numbers in universities in Berlin, Vienna, Prague, Paris and so on were never to be able to say the same.

It was sensational news recently in Italy when a dozen middle-aged doctors were imprisoned for murdering a fascist years ago. My wife knew them well, as they belonged to a left-wing party's medical student group which she led, and she was sure it must be a frame-up. While entirely ignorant of murder, she risks arrest for "moral responsibility"—seemingly, Italian law acknowledges the unconscious! At the moment therefore it is safer for her not to go to Italy on holiday. Haven't you had the same surprise as my wife about the treason of Anthony Blunt who was in your group that visited Moscow, about Michael Straight who edited *New Republic*, and others you knew well?

When Burgess and McLean went missing and the newspapers guessed they were in Moscow, you told me confidently that it was absurd and Guy Burgess certainly would be dug up drunk in Paris or somewhere.

Blunt and Co. directly caused the death of opponents to Soviet tyranny, but how did they do so? Innocently? Idealistically? With no anger, malice or destructiveness? Come off it, Charles!

Do we too have some residual "moral responsibility"? And whom am I rebuking? Perhaps myself more than you, since I probably have more reservations and dislike for some of the things that made me a Communist 45 years ago.

My letter petered out unfinished at this point. I will now try to give some of the intended sequel. It was to illustrate how Charles relentlessly pursued the path of a guerrilla and thereby ensure self-defeatingly, if unconsciously, that his subversive but acute re-reading of Freud and his masterful reformulating and rewriting of psychoanalysis should go as little noticed as possible wherever they might exert an influence, be appreciated in depth, and acquire permanence and successors to take them further.

Among other demonstrations of this, the story of his relationship with the British Psychoanalytical Society is an extreme example. I have quoted reasons he gave for dropping out of the Society, for all practical purposes, in 1962, and I dismissed them as a tissue of rationalizations for whatever, buried within himself, really impelled him to do so. Reliable witnesses, with the same values and intellectual outlook as Charles, convinced me that his account of the Society was overheated, unbalanced, and distorted in 1962, when he walked off, and even more unrecognizable in 1973, when he explained his departure to me over dinner at the Reform Club.

Furthermore, his own career in the Society simply nullifies his assertion, "nor did Englishmen cut any ice in it". He himself, in an interview in 1996, refers to his career in the Society as "meteoric", as indeed it was, obviously because his remarkable promise was recognized very early. He qualified as a psychoanalyst in 1947 at the age of 33 and, as soon as he presented his paper that gave full membership in 1950, he was made Training Secretary, then Training Analyst, Scientific Secretary, and invited speaker at an international gathering of psychoanalysts for the Freud Centenary in London, in 1956. He sat on committees of the Institute and Society for altogether 14 years.

When he walked away from the Society in 1962, it could not have been for the reasons he dreamed up and told me ten years later and put on record in the 1980s, nor was it because "only God knows", as my brother said. It was very much in the pattern of other actions of his, which I shall enumerate, in which he seemed to walk out with poise and decision, but really he fled. Perhaps not entirely unbeknownst to himself, he fled in phobic avoidance of the risk of becoming a public figure instead of a guerrilla and, manifestly, a powerful revisionist of psychoanalysis across the world. This would have followed, had he stayed on to become President of the British Psychoanalytical Society and, thence, a force in the committees and policies, world-wide, of the International Psychoanalytical Association. We have his own words for this prospect in the 1996 interview: "I remember thinking, I shan't be able to prevent people making me President. At some point, it was bound to happen, particularly as at one time . . ." And here Charles almost wipes out his previously stated reasons for dropping out: "the refugee community, on the whole, took the view that they were guests of the British Society and therefore shouldn't throw their weight about too much".

After his departure, or, rather, his flight from the affairs of the British Psychoanalytical Society in 1962, Charles operated on his own and in no organizations, at times talking of this as a splendid and sensible liberation, not once dwelling on his ambivalence about it, plainly expressed by paying his subscription for no less than a further 16 years until 1978. Even if he preferred to boycott meetings of the Society, that would still have allowed him to go back and attend meetings, present papers, and be heard at the annual scientific conferences of the International Psychoanalytical Association and at the regular international conferences of its European societies, but with singular tenacity, as a guerrilla, he avoided any risk of professional visibility and weight. Thus he never offered papers to the annual conferences of the Royal College of Psychiatrists or the conferences of its important Psychotherapy Section, nor did he take part in these conferences. He could probably have found a podium for his message in academe, where psychoanalytic units in universities were coming into being, but he made no attempt to reach for one.

He might nevertheless have up-ended or reformed psychoanalysis by publishing appropriately—his nascent ideas in the journals of the clinical and psychological disciplines, and the body of his work compendiously structured and in book form, so as to be properly and easily available to the professions, to academicians in their fields, as well as, though less important, to the general public. He did nothing openly like this, lest subversion might succeed. Instead, he kept sniping from the sidelines as a guerrilla, squandering his formulations in a scatter of bits and pieces addressed to the educated readership at large—a readership that could admire and be informed by these writings but could not possibly descry their larger significance. Moreover, this transmission of elements of his opus was in barely perceptible form. Charles expended himself to excess in explicating the work of others in a cascade of book reviews with Rycroftian flavouring, for the most part on books of ephemeral quality.

His superb monograph in 1971 on Wilhelm Reich, a model of its kind, is one exception among his explication of others, because it is published in book format that places it fittingly in the professional literature. The other such exception is *The Critical Dictionary of Psychoanalysis* (1968b), a gem that places on view a mind of formidable clarity, originality, and energy. Again it explicates and defines the concepts of others, but in the process some of his own seep through. It has been deservedly acclaimed as a classic and steadily reissued in paperback, but it has not properly achieved the status it merits as a basic text world-wide in psychoanalysis. Perhaps this is because Charles committed himself to writing so as to be intelligible to the general reader and does not come across as catering for the learned one. However, I believe it is more likely that by dropping out of the British and International Psychoanalytical Associations and the professional arena in general, and by ceasing to publish in the learned journals and steadily addressing his writings to the general reader, Charles made his dictionary too easily overlooked by compilers of reading lists for students and trainees.

I have heard it said that for the psychoanalytic establishment Charles became a non-person, cast out like a priest or a rabbi turned atheist. I am not alone in thinking that this is fanciful and that, on the contrary, he would have been welcomed, had he chosen to take part at any time. Eric Rayner, a senior figure in the Society, gives considerable and positive attention to Rycroft in *The Independent Mind in Psychoanalysis* (1991), a book that was not greeted with even a murmur of heresy.

In summary, Charles, the *soi-disant* guerrilla, could seldom come forth and say it out loud but, instead, sprinkled his message in obscure fragments, as the record of his publications over forty years makes distressingly clear. His work is a scatter of some 200 book reviews, essays, and papers, amid a spread of periodicals from the *Sunday Observer* to *Nature* and the *New Left Review*. The year 1962, when he dropped out of the British Psychoanalytical Society and its Institute, marks the end of his writing for learned journals. By then he had contributed, beginning in 1951, seven papers and five book reviews to the *International Journal of Psycho-Analysis*, but, ominously, these twelve items were soon to be out-numbered by book reviews in the ordinary press. These began to appear in 1959, in *the Observer*, and by 1962 twelve had been published. By 1991 Charles had published a total of 145 book reviews in twelve periodicals and reviews for the general public, and it is a truism that today's newspaper is forgotten tomorrow. In that time he also published three introductions to books authored by others, a chapter each in two books for the general reader: "The God I Want" (1967) and "Steps Towards an Ecology of Hope" (1979b); a chapter on the effect of psycho-neurotics on their environment in *The Role of Psychosomatic Disorders in Adult Life* (1965), edited by a philosopher and a physician; and an editorial contribution to *Psychoanalysis Observed* (1966).

In book form, he published three compilations of previously published items, with the addition of some essays newly written. The first, *Imagination and Reality* (1968c) contains, foremost, his seven papers that appeared in the *International Journal of Psycho-Analysis* between 1951 and 1962. The second, *Psychoanalysis and Beyond* (1985) contains 25 sections, of which 17 are book reviews reprinted from periodicals and newspapers and three are reprinted essays with a similar provenance. The third such book, *Viewpoints* (1991), contains 13 such reviews out of 19 items.

Peter Fuller, whom I quoted before, touched on something more serious and deep-seated in Charles than he realized when he says, "The position he elaborated is nothing if not clear. Nonetheless, its impact has been dispersed in a plethora of publications." To point the contrast, Freud would have got nowhere if he had published mostly in Viennese newspapers and Austrian periodicals and if, as Charles did, he had delivered his addresses to cultural societies and hardly ever to learned or professional meetings. Like any other discipline, psychoanalysis would be as nothing if its advanced concepts and the language to enunciate them were *totally* intelligible to the common reader, let alone instantly so, as Charles adamantly sought to make them.

Only twice did Charles put together certain of his novel and far-reaching theoretical concepts so as to be properly available in book form: in *Anxiety and Neurosis* (1968a) and *The Innocence of Dreams* (1979a). The former is much less radical than the latter, a disarming masterpiece, with a title that I think unconsciously reflects his pseudo-innocence—the compulsion to stifle and render innocuous his age-old subversiveness and to diminish the potential impact and influence of the creativity and iconoclasm by which that subversiveness could express itself.

Again, in my view perversely and self-defeatingly written for Everyman, *The Innocence of Dreams* received notice on the radio, where Charles Rycroft himself answered callers' questions about their dreams, and in reviews, some of them by novelists, poets, and literary critics, far and wide in the press, from coast to coast in North America, in Britain, and elsewhere. The book was therefore as triumphant a success as any fine book offered to the reading public can be. However, for original work to have a pervasive and lasting influence and be woven into the hard knowledge of psychoanalysis, psychiatry, and the social sciences and into professional practice in their fields, it has to be conspicuous in their own specialist literature. Otherwise it inspires nobody to carry it on and evolve it further. The ordinary press cannot serve that purpose.

Charles inflicted other damaging and dismal self-deprivation by not publishing his creative work, with its highly innovative ideas, in the professional literature, where it belonged. It could only be there that his work would receive learned evaluation, criticism, and modification—in other words, be digested and healthily absorbed, becoming part of the body of psychoanalysis. Certainly, some of Charles's seductive theorizing is not above correction and improvement. An example of this is his over-evaluation of common sense, which, he complains, is so lacking in the psychoanalytic fraternity. Actually, common sense ceased to be a reliable guide to the nature of things long ago when the earth turned out to be not flat but spherical and, worse still, in ceaseless motion.

The Innocence of Dreams was in fact thoroughly and favourably reviewed in *The International Journal of Psycho-Analysis* and a lesser journal or two, but twenty years on Charles's influence and presence can be felt no more than before. He had an inner restriction on allowing himself full-force, on saying it out loud, saying it to a learned audience where it really matters, where he would win followers and where his work could take root, live on, and be extended by others.

Jenny Rycroft has pointed out to me that Charles would never repeat himself and that once he had spelt out a concept, a theory, an observation, a formulation, that was that, over and done, never to be spelt out again. Charles himself put this down to having a low boredom threshold. Was this also a phobia of being really heard, having a real effect and being properly influential? It is irrational to eschew repeating oneself if one is to be effective.

My letter undertaken in 1985, and left unposted at the time, had an extraordinary sequel in 1988. Leaving a conference with my wife at the lunchtime break, unexpectedly we found ourselves walking alongside Charles. We greeted each other, I introduced Flavia, and I suggested that we had lunch together. Flavia, who has an Italian taste-blindness for the *spirito degli inglesi*, the English genius, might have been tempted to savour what she had been missing by having lunch with Charles, so notable (according to me) for his English-ness. However, she had heard the story I have presented here and so, to our surprise, she dismissed us briskly, saying, "You two guys have a lot of talking to do to each other. I will look after myself for lunch!" Rather sheepishly, Charles and I went off together, found a restaurant, sat down, and began to talk. It turned out that he had distanced himself from me because of something he thought I had done years ago: he had the impression that at the time of their divorce I had been disparaging about Chloe. I insisted that this was impossible because Chloe had been a friend that I had loved. He was obviously both shaken and relieved. Then we really began to

talk and talk and talk, going on too long to get back to the conference.

I was able to pour forth much that I have written here and in my
unfinished letter, written three years previously. He asked me to
send it to him. It was a relief to be friends again, though the paths
of our lives had long diverged, and to know that we could meet
once more. I sensed that Charles was moved by what came up in
this conversation about us and our friendship, but his composure
was unruffled, and I was left wondering what effect our lunch
together might have had. Not long afterwards I received a letter,
which I will now quote.

> *Dear Harold,*
>
> Thank you for sending me the two papers on the Connoly unit
> and for the unfinished letter of 1985, which I am putting to one
> side to read when I am feeling stronger. The lunch we had at the
> conference had the most extraordinary effect on me: it acted as
> what Paula Heimann used to call a global interpretation.

Here he mentioned dramatic repercussions in his life; then he went
on:

> One day perhaps I will explain in detail to you how and why it
> had such effects, but at the moment I will just say how grateful
> I am to have had my rather boring equilibrium disturbed. It was
> good to see you so well and happy . . . when I have quietened
> down we must meet again.
>
> *Charles*

The stance that Charles came to have in psychoanalysis was rather
like George Orwell's in regard to socialism. Orwell was averse to
"smelly Continental ideologies" and so was Charles; Orwell felt
alien to much that passed as left-wing, as was Charles to much that
passed as psychoanalytic; both were subversive, yet both were
quintessentially English.

Vincent Brome relates that "Charles always regretted that he
had not put himself to the ultimate test, but would not specify what
that test was". What could that test have been other than to abandon his age-old role of mischievous guerrilla and come out into the

open, to declare himself clearly and extensively, and systematically to set about the fulfilment of his mission?

The grand mission that inspired Charles was to de-doctrinize and de-dogmatize psychoanalysis, to cure it of ideology, and to make it English, empirical, commonsensical, and innocent—a far from innocent enterprise.

Notes

1. *Editor's note*: I remember Charles talking to me about this paper and his own contribution to the writing of it. He commented that "That is the most important piece of writing I have ever done!" [*J.P.*]

References

Bourne, H. (1953). The insulin myth. *The Lancet*, 2: 964.

Bourne, H. (1993). Review of *Viewpoints* by Charles Rycroft. *Changes*, 11 (March).

Home, H. J. (1966). The concept of mind. *International Journal of Psycho-Analysis*, 47: 42–49.

Holmes, J. (1996). Interview with Charles Rycroft. *Psychiatric Bulletin*, 20: 726.

Rayner, E. (1991). *The Independent Mind in British Psychoanalysis*. London: Free Association Books.

Rycroft, C. (1956). Symbolism and its relationship to the primary and secondary processes. *International Journal of Psycho-Analysis*, 37: 137–146. Also in: *Imagination and Reality*. New York: International Universities Press, 1968.

Rycroft, C. (1965). The effect of the psychosomatic patient on his environment. In: J. Wisdom & H. Wolff (Eds.), *The Role of Psychosomatic Disorders in Adult Life*. Oxford: Pergamon Press.

Rycroft, C. (Ed.) (1966). *Psychoanalysis Observed*. London: Constable.

Rycroft, C. (1967). The God I want. In: James Mitchell (Ed.), *The God I Want*. London: Constable. Reprinted as "On Continuity" in: *Psychoanalysis and Beyond*. London: Hogarth Press.

Rycroft, C. (1968a). *Anxiety and Neurosis*. London: Allen Lane/Penguin, 1971: London: Karnac, 1988.

Rycroft, C. (1968b). *A Critical Dictionary of Psychoanalysis*. London: Penguin. Second edition: London: Penguin, 1995.

Rycroft, C. (1968c). *Imagination and Reality*. London: Hogarth Press.

Rycroft, C. (1971). *Reich*. London: Fontana.

Rycroft, C. (1979a). *The Innocence of Dreams*. London: Hogarth Press.

Rycroft, C. (1979b). Steps towards an ecology of hope. In: R. Fitzgerald (Ed.), *Sources of Hope*. Oxford: Pergamon Press.

Rycroft, C. (1985). *Psychoanalysis and Beyond*. London: Chatto Tiger-stripe.

Rycroft, C. (1991). *Viewpoints*. London: Hogarth Press/Chatto & Windus.

Rycroft, C. (1995). *A Critical Dictionary of Psychoanalysis* (2nd revised edition). London: Penguin Books.

CHAPTER THIRTEEN

Glimpses of a life

Jenny Pearson

T o begin at the beginning: Charles was the second of four children, of the second marriage of Sir Richard Rycroft Bt, who owned, as Charles would say, the village of Dummer in Hampshire. He described his family background as "more country gentry than aristocracy", the first baronet having been a country rector who was offered a choice between a baronetcy and a bishopric in 1794. Charles's mother, Emily Mary, had slightly grander origins than her husband. She was the daughter of Col. The Hon. Henry Lowry Corry, youngest son of the Third Earl of Belmore, and Lady Edith Blanche, daughter of Charles Wood, First Viscount Halifax, who was at one time Chancellor of the Exchequer. Charles looked very like Lord Halifax: visitors sometimes asked if the pencil portrait of Halifax by Richmond, hanging in our house, was a portrait of him.

Dummer is quite a small village near Basingstoke, still surprisingly rural when I was last there in the 1980s. At that time we were living at Kew Gardens and occasionally drove to Dummer at weekends, to walk among woods and fields, which were full of primroses and violets in spring and bordered with cowslips in the early summer. The elegant white house where Charles was born and spent his first years is an eighteenth-century building of beautiful proportions, set back from the road behind tall cedar trees, in one of those large gardens with areas of "wilderness" that children remember as Paradise. It stands next to the village church of All Saints, a small twelfth-century church full of Rycroft graves, where his mother sometimes played the organ for Sunday service. We would stand in the churchyard and look over the wall at the house where Charles lived until he was eleven years old, when his father died and the bereft family had to move out of their home to make way for the new baronet, his older half-brother Nelson.

Life at Dummer was fairly typical of children of the gentry in those days, looked after by servants and not seeing a lot of their parents, particularly when they were small. There were four children: Richard, Charles, Alice, and Eleanor. Nanna, their nursery nurse, was a rather sinister figure, inclined to sadistic behaviour. Alice recalls that "she was very fierce: she used to wallop us a lot". Charles told me how Nanna would talk to them about the next life, when she would be able to sit in Abraham's bosom and look down on the gentry frying in hell. She used to take them for long walks by the side of the road so that she could flirt with the local AA man.

There was a butler who polished the silver: Charles always felt that polishing silver was a man's job, and it was one of the household chores he assumed quite naturally in our home. A groom called Fisk looked after the horses, drove the family coach, and, with the march of progress, went on to being the chauffeur who looked after cars. There is an endearing picture of Fisk, dressed in a formal coat and bowler, leading a donkey with the two-year old Charles seated on its back, looking important. Charles remembered Fisk and the donkey with affection. He also retained an eccentric behaviour that he learnt from Fisk. One evening as he was driving us home, the engine of the car began to fail, and I noticed that he was rocking backwards and forwards in the driving seat. When I asked what he was doing, he thought for a few moments and said, "It's what Fisk used to do to help the horses up a steep hill!"

One day when he was quite small, Charles wandered off into the village and came across a number of people he didn't know at all. He was surprised to discover that they clearly knew who he was, addressed him as "Master Charlie", and offered to take him home. When he told his mother about this and asked her, "How do they know who I am?" she replied rather sternly, "More people know Tom Fool than Tom Fool knows!" He got the message that she didn't want him to get big-headed. I often heard Charles, his brother Richard, and his sisters, Alice and Eleanor, reminiscing about their childhood at Dummer. Charles told me how his sister Eleanor had reported indignantly after a visit to Dummer: "They've cut down one of the Cedars of Lebanon!" Her sense of continuing ownership and outrage struck him as both sad and funny, many years after the family had moved out and lost their rights over this place that they still thought of as home.

Alice Harvey.   Charles's sister Alice was particularly close to her father. She was his first daughter, and he had the church bells rung when she was born. She remembers:

> "Father used to come into the nursery in his dressing-gown before breakfast and fool around, have a few laughs with us. He did things with us that Mother never did. He took us for walks. Sometimes he would come to the nursery and say he just wanted to take me for a walk. After Richard went to school, there was a time when Mother and Father thought they would teach Charles. Father stammered a bit, and Charles used to get furious with him and say that he was spitting, and then Father would get cross. But Charles was fond of father—we all were. Mother never came to the nursery to play with us. We only saw her when we went downstairs. Sometimes she would come to the nursery after lunch and have a cup of tea with Nanna and take no notice of us at all."

* * *

I have been told many stories of that time. There is the story of their old Cousin Izzie, aged 90, who saw a young bull at the local market looking sad and bought it: the *News of the World* carried a headline "Lady of 90 Keeps Bull for a Pet". Occasionally, ghosts made an appearance: one day when Alice was ill she woke up to see a strange woman in a very big skirt with a tight waist standing in the room. Charles, aged 7, was visited by a man who stood by his bed and blessed him. His interpretation of this episode appears in a long, as yet unpublished paper entitled "On Visitations". There was a local ghost known as Parker Terry. One day a Mr Parker Terry from Australia came to visit their parents. The children were excited and puzzled, wondering if their visitor was a ghost. They decided that the way to find out was for one of them to creep round the furniture and pinch him. There is some argument as to who actually performed the experiment: Charles claimed he was the one who pinched their visitor, while Alice is emphatic that she did. Whoever the culprit was, the outcome was satisfactory: Mr Parker Terry was pinched and jumped, proving he was not a ghost, and he was so amused at their story that he sent the children a box of chocolates "from the ghost who came to tea!" A prank that didn't go down so well was definitely committed by Charles. He was angry with one of the governesses for favouring him over his older brother, Richard: one day, before his parents were giving a garden party, he wrote in red paint across the lawn, "Miss Muskett is a bugger". All efforts to remove the message failed, and it had to be concealed under trestle tables for the occasion.

Another project that got Charles into trouble while living at Dummer left a deeper impression. He discovered a facility for writing humorous sketches featuring some characters modelled on real people who visited or worked in the house—an early attempt at fiction. He was pleased with his new accomplishment, but Nanna found the stories and showed them to his mother, and he was told off for "telling lies". He was very upset by this reaction to his creative efforts, especially as the stories were then destroyed. He told me about this episode when we were living at Kew and he was contemplating a fresh venture into fiction, perhaps a detective story, wondering if the notion that stories were "lies" was getting in the way. His presenting reason for going into analysis with Marion Milner some years before was that he enjoyed writing, wrote with great facility, and wanted to get away from writing about professional matters, but he couldn't get started on anything fictional. I remember him describing a series of dreams in which he found himself living in the country and each dream brought him nearer to the house at Dummer, until he was living in a cottage on the edge of his father's estate. However, his dreams never got back into the house itself, and he never did get started on writing fiction.

Life at Dummer came to an abrupt end when his father died in 1925, after a long illness. The children were not prepared for his death in any way, and nobody comforted them. Alice and Eleanor were sent to a cousin on the day that he died and had a good time in the park "looking at the beautiful deer". The next morning, as Alice describes it, the governess told them they could go along to their parents' bedroom to say morning prayers:

"We hadn't been allowed in the bedroom for two or three weeks. So we asked, 'Is father better?' We were told 'Yes, he is', and we raced along to the bedroom and burst into the room, and there was Mother sitting on the bed, and there was just one single bed instead of two. I remember feeling dreadful: I thought the top of my head was going to blow off. Then we went back to the Nursery and said that he was dead, and the governess shouted at us and was horrible to us.

"Richard and Charles were both away at school. Mother asked the headmaster at Durnford to tell Charles, which he did. He didn't come home. For several nights he went to bed feeling absolutely terrible, but he didn't want to cry because he was in a dormitory and felt the other boys would laugh at him. It did him a lot of harm, I am sure, tied him in knots mentally. He was only just eleven, and he wasn't even a very grown-up eleven: he was still a little boy. Richard was at Dartmouth, and she didn't get anyone to tell him, she just wrote to him direct. That gave him a terrible shock. I suppose he was just running from one class to another, and he got this letter."

The children didn't attend their father's funeral, and no one ever talked to them about his death. In losing him, they also lost their home and all that was familiar. The title and estate were inherited by their half-brother Nelson. They left Dummer almost immediately and went to stay with their maternal grandfather, who didn't have much understanding of children. Alice remembers,

"Charles and I made a snowman on the lawn outside his study window. He came out and stormed at us. He was furious with us for doing such a thing. Another time Richard and Charles dammed up a little bit of a stream that ran through the park and made this little lake so that they could sail their yachts that they had for Christmas. When Grandfather discovered this, he roared at Mother and made her cry. And he was awful to Richard and Charles. They had to go down and un-dam, which was only a matter of moving a few sods of earth.

"We stayed there for six months. Mother wanted to find a house near a big town: somewhere like Cambridge, where Eleanor and I could go to school, because she didn't want to be bothered with any more governesses. But Grandfather wouldn't allow her to. He insisted on her having a house in a village, with a governess. That's why we went to Castle Hedingham, to Damyons, which belonged to our cousin Musette Madgingly. She lived in Hedingham Castle, and Damyons was the dower house nearby. We got it cheap, on condition that Mother took over some duties: the Mothers' Union, and the Women's Institute, and so on. When it came to the school holidays she didn't want to do these things, but Musette insisted that she must.

"Mother was very, very sad when we moved there. Not only had she lost her husband, but she was almost impoverished. She had only £1,000 a year with four children, and there were Nelson and his wife Ethel living at Dummer and really well off. She must have felt very humiliated, having been the great lady, as it were, in the Parish and the Village. She was in a bad state for quite a few years. She used to do a lot of talking to herself and make sobbing noises. I think she took ten or twelve years to get over it."

No wonder the children looked back on their life at Dummer as a kind of lost paradise and held on to a feeling that they still belonged there. It still felt that way on our walks around the village and through the woods when Charles was in his early sixties. The last time we were there, a man with a gun came up to us in the woods and informed us that we were trespassing. Charles said politely "Oh, are we? I'm so sorry!" Then he turned and walked quietly back to the road where we had parked the car. These had been his father's woods, but it would have been out of character for him mention this to a stranger.

At Castle Hedingham, Alice and Eleanor were taught by a very strict governess until Alice was 14 and Eleanor 11 when they were sent off to finish their education at boarding-school. Charles always felt bad that he and Richard had a better education than his sisters. In the holidays the boys came home, and all the children ran wild:

> "Mother didn't do anything about entertaining us in the holidays, and we just used to do what we wanted. I had a bicycle, and I used to go tearing about the countryside. Charles did too, and we went together sometimes. One of the things we used to do was to go up Sudbury Hill and come down the hill with our feet on the handlebars. How we never came off I don't know, because we used to go at a tremendous pace.... I once heard we were described as 'the forgotten children'."

Charles spoke of the condition under which they lived at Castle Hedingham as "aristocratic poverty". It was here that he formed his lifelong habit of going for long, solitary walks—something he did for the rest of his life. At Wellington College he distinguished himself as a long-distance runner but was otherwise uninterested in sport. The idea behind sending him to Wellington was that he should become an officer in the Army, but as time passed it became obvious to both Charles and the school that this was not the right path for him. He referred to himself, along with his friend Gavin Ewart, the poet, and a few others, as "Wellington type B", relishing English lessons with an outstandingly imaginative teacher called Rollo St. Clare Tallboys, who introduced them to the poetry of T. S. Eliot, and singing madrigals, on at least one occasion to prisoners at nearby Broadmoor. He became interested in art while still at school and told a story about a dance in a nearby country house during the holidays and how he stopped mid-dance in front of a picture to take a closer look, remarking to his partner that it looked like a Claude, and she drew away from him in horror, saying, "Christ, you're not cultured, are you?"

I was not the only person to feel disappointed that Charles never wrote an autobiography. I remember Carmen Callil putting the idea to him when Tigerstripe publishers got going in the mid-1980s. He replied, "I'll think about it." It was obvious that such a book would be a good read, describing with his sharp eye and wicked humour the life of the English country gentry of his childhood as well as the extraordinary convolutions of the psychoanalytic scene.

However, he held back from writing it: the more he was pressed for it, the more he resisted, saying: "I'm counter-suggestible!"

Emily Rycroft.   Charles once said that he could not write an autobiography while his mother was alive. He was protective of her and clearly loved her, while being aware that a lot of his troubles arose from their early relationship. When he was born, she was grieving for a favourite brother, recently killed in the First World War: it could be said that he drank in sorrow with his mother's milk. Alice has described how distant she was from her children when they were young and how dismally she failed to help them over the loss of their father. As the children grew older, she related to them better: Charles was a lively child—as witness Alice's stories—and he was aware that his mother enjoyed his liveliness. She used to say that he was the most spiritual of her children. After she died in 1982, there was no obvious barrier in the way of his autobiography, but he was sad to lose her and possibly still protective towards her. It is also possible that, being essentially a private person, he simply didn't want to enter the public arena with his own story. The expression of early sorrows and anger against mothers, which can feel liberating in an analyst's consulting-room, becomes quite exposing in print, and Charles's awareness of complexities, including his mother's own emotional scars, points to a story that would have been painful to write.

Emily, Lady Rycroft, lived for 99 years and was a widow for over half her life. I remember her as an old woman of quiet dignity and style who inspired real affection in those around her.

She lived in a rather grand country house near Taunton that had been turned into an old people's home. When my eight-year old daughter first met her and gave her a small present, a handkerchief she had embroidered with flowers, my mother-in-law thanked her warmly, saying, "My dear, how wonderful! I'm so glad you like embroidery. You must always keep your interest in sewing: it will give you pleasure for the whole of your life!" Her comment had the energy of genuine enthusiasm: embroidery was a pleasure that had helped her to keep going through a difficult life. She had an energy about her that reminded me of Charles: a local Hedingham paper described her as an "intrepid traveller" in the days before her marriage. It was her great misfortune as well as her children's that through their later childhood and adolescence she was grieving for a husband she had loved dearly and a marriage that had been all too short. At 99 she was still interested in politics and current affairs, taking a dim view of Mrs Thatcher. She was appalled when a local paper reported that a centenarian in the area had received a telegram of congratulations from Mrs Thatcher as well as from the Queen. When she died peacefully in her sleep after a slight stroke, Charles commented that she had found her own way of making sure that she didn't get a telegram from Mrs Thatcher.

* * *

This history of childhood deprivation and loss within a privileged setting may well have some bearing on Charles's rather paradoxical character. He talked to me of a childhood "spent in beautiful houses full of beautiful paintings, in which a series of father figures died, one by one". After his father there were uncles and much older half-brothers, and he seems to have lost every older man to whom he became attached. Idealization of the lost places and privileges of his childhood masked a deeply buried anger in the face of this loss. He grew up a traditionalist and at the same time a rebel. As a young man he retained a strong feeling for his aristocratic connections, while at the same time joining the Communist Party at Cambridge. It is said in the family that his Aunt Alice, his mother's sister, never forgave him for coming to tea wearing a tie that bore the insignia of the hammer and sickle.

Where religion was concerned, he would describe himself as "a cut flower", by which he meant that he had a religious attitude to life severed from the roots of belief. He was fascinated with mystical experience and always kept *The Oxford Book of English Mystical Verse* (Nicholson & Lee, 1917) and *The Cloud of Unknowing*[1] (anon., 2001) in the small bookcase beside his bed. He enjoyed church services at Christmas and Easter, especially the hymns, which he sang lustily. However, he did not subscribe to any conventional religion, and he knew how to hold his boundaries. When the Eucharist was announced at a family funeral, he said quietly, "I think it's a case of sit down and be counted!" At a Christmas service in Norwich Cathedral, I can remember him lustily singing the words of the alternative carol, "While Shepherds washed their socks by night"—right through to the "bar of Sunlight soap"!

The family's plan in sending him to Wellington College had been that he should become an officer in the Army like his father, but as he progressed through the school this prospect attracted him less and less. Eventually he went to his house master and announced that he didn't want to go to the Army, but to Cambridge. The house master expressed relief: he had already come to the conclusion that the Army was not for Charles, but he had not liked to say so. Charles's mother made no problems about his decision, and he was accepted by Trinity College to read economics, starting in the autumn of 1933.

With six months to spare before going to Cambridge, he decided to spend the time in Germany. Staying in a family and observing the social scene, he soon came to recognize the seriousness of the Nazi threat and was shocked to discover on his return that no one in Britain seemed to be aware of this except for the Communists. It was this that took him into the Cambridge Communist Party, a much more serious move at the time than his amusing "Memoirs of an Old Bolshevik" suggests (1985a). He attended meetings regularly and took part in demonstrations, including a big march through London, which did have its funny side: he used to recall how he dropped out of the march with Anthony Blunt for tea at the Reform Club, rejoining the tail-end of the march afterwards. Blunt was a research fellow at this time. Charles enjoyed his parties and liked him personally. He met Burgess and Maclean at Cambridge and many years later, after they had been unmasked as spies for the Soviet Union, Charles was invited out to dinner by a man from MI5 and asked if he thought Anthony Blunt could also be a spy. The meeting gains depth and mystery from the fact that some time after this, when Blunt was exposed as a spy and stripped of his knighthood, it turned out that MI5 had already known about him at the time of Charles's dinner. He was saddened by the dishonouring of Anthony Blunt and also puzzled, wondering whether Blunt would one day turn out to have been a double agent and on the side of Britain after all.

Judith Hubback. Judith Hubback, the Jungian analytic psychologist, was at Cambridge with Charles. She was drawn to the

Communists for the same political reason as Charles and recalls:

> "We were all very anti-Nazi, but we were also illogical and denied what we knew about the Soviets, although we had all read Koestler's *Darkness at Noon*. It was a version of denial, which I came to understand later when I became an analyst. In retrospect I'm really rather ashamed at how much we denied."

Judith was at one time approached by a woman at Newnham College who wanted her to become a 'contact'—the word they used for 'spy'—but she declined the invitation. She went to only one Party meeting and declined to become a member, being "appalled" at the Party line. When her husband David Hubback was subsequently in a senior position in Whitehall, a young man from MI5 came in to interview her and she was surprised to discover that MI5 had dossiers on everyone who had been involved with the Communists at Cambridge.

At Cambridge Charles seems to have been quite extreme in the conflicting values that Harold Bourne has written about: an emotional identification with his origins, combined with political affiliation to the arch opponents of the class system. Judith often met him socially as he was friendly with her husband, David Hubback, who was at King's. She recalls: "He was always very elegant, and he always appeared to be very keen to let everyone know he was a baronet's son, which was vaguely irritating when we were all undergraduates together. My father was knighted, and I was always rather careful not to mention that, being rather left-wing." Judith gives a clear description of the distant social manner behind which Charles invariably protected himself, outside the company of the few people he knew well. "His manner was partly distant, partly protected. That's my impression when I think about him now. There was a protection around him. There was an extreme importance about privacy to him."

* * *

Charles did very well academically, obtaining first-class degrees in Economics Part 1 and History Part 2, and he did a year's postgraduate research in modern history. He always retained an affection for Cambridge and was particularly fond of the fellows' garden at Trinity, which he showed me on a visit, pointing out the yellow flowers of the winter aconites. But he found academic life too cloistered and decided to apply for training in psychoanalysis. The idea came to him after reading Freud's *Psychopathology of Everyday Life* (1901), which he bought with some prize money at the end of his first year, and he talked to Karin Stephen about it when he met her socially. She was married to Adrian Stephen, Virginia Woolf's brother, who was a an analyst. He described the conversation to Samuel Stein in an interview for *Psychotherapy in Practice* (Stein & Stein, 2000).

> To be rather frivolous about it, I must have said something like "when I read Freud I thought it was rather interesting and I would quite like to become an analyst." She said "why don't you?" and I replied "surely only foreigners become analysts." But a group of us all applied to train as analysts during our last year at Cambridge. Two of us were accepted but I was the only one who went through with it.

As ever, this is Charles giving an impression of extreme lightness over a decision that was in fact deeply serious, or he would surely not have accepted Ernest Jones's condition that he also study medicine, spending his whole inheritance on training. His choice of profession was well in line with the spirit of rebellion against his social background. He wrote, in "Reminiscences of a Survivor" (see chapter 15 herein), "in the 1930s Freudian psychoanalysis was regarded as deeply subversive. In progressive, advanced circles, Marx and Freud were regarded as the arch-enemies of capitalist society and middle-class morality, and to announce that one wanted to become an analyst was, indeed, a gesture *pour épater les bourgeois.*"

On another level, well concealed by all this subversive panache, a more personal motivation was at work. Behind the brilliant scholar and the classy revolutionary was a young man in need of rescuing from the deeply buried grief and rage of early loss. Training, of course, involves having analysis for oneself, coming to grips with disturbing inner forces as well as mastering the theory. In his interview with Ernest Jones and Edward Glover, when asked if he had any questions, Charles inquired whether they considered, in selecting people for training, whether a candidate might be too neurotic for the work. He was amused and relieved at Glover's reply. "If you are not neurotic, you are going to find the training extremely boring!"

The requirement for candidates to undertake a medical training at that time was part of the campaign to get psychoanalysis accepted as "scientific". In fact several candidates did not complete their medical training, and some refused it altogether: Pearl King recalls that James and Alix Strachey walked out of medical training after six weeks, but "they went and got analysed by Freud, and no one could say anything about it after that!" Charles, however, was determined to become a doctor and demonstrate that he was not "an upper-class dilettante", as Jones had hinted in that first interview. In spite a difficult start and failing some early exams, he persevered and qualified with MB and BS in 1945, took a further qualification in psychiatry, and spent a year as a house physician at the Maudsley Hospital before going into private practice as a psychoanalyst in 1947. His training analysis, beginning with Ella Sharpe in 1937 and continuing after her death with Sylvia Payne, took place concurrently with his medical training. His two training supervisors were Marion Milner and Helen Sheehan-Dare. In an interview with Peter Rudnytsky, he described his supervisions with Milner as "very helpful—quite an education", while those with Sheehan-Dare were "a total waste of time" because even though the patient was schizophrenic, she nevertheless insisted on analysing his amazingly obsessional material "exhaustively". Characteristically, Charles added: "A nice woman otherwise. Nonmedical" (p. 67).

Pearl King. Pearl King, a distinguished psychoanalyst who has served at different times as Secretary and President of the British Psychoanalytical Society, was a close contemporary of Charles's from his early years as an associate member. I recently talked with Pearl in her home, where she has been writing prolifically about the history of the society: her books include a comprehensive account of the famous Controversial Discussions, edited with Riccardo Steiner (King & Steiner, 1991), and her recently published biography of John Rickman (Rickman, 2003). Pearl was an exact contemporary of Masud Khan. They were both in training analysis with Rickman in the early 1950s, and Masud was at that time a close friend of Charles's. All three were then active in the running of the Society, and it was they who set up the 1952 Club, in that year, inviting senior analysts to come and present new papers for discussion. Pearl was also friendly with Sylvia Payne, Charles's second analyst, as she attended a regular painting class that Payne organized in her consulting-room; Pearl kept in touch with her after her retirement and up to the time she died.

From talking with Pearl, I came to realize that there were people around at that time, including herself, who saw through Charles's bright, ironic stance to the well-defended young man who needed the protection of his outward persona. Looking back, she said:

"Sylvia was a great support to Charles, and he respected her. He had a good mind and really respected people who could organize things. He didn't like things in a muddle, and she certainly pulled the whole Society together after the controversies. She was the first President to be elected in 1944, after Ernest Jones retired, and it was she who mended the rift between Anna Freud and Melanie Klein. It was Sylvia Payne who approached them and said, 'Look, can't we find some way of working together? We've got a Society, we've got so many things in common, it's absurd that we can't find a way.' In the end it was decided to have two parallel trainings: the A Group, comprising the British Group, which arranged training as it had been before the Viennese came, and the B Group, which went along with what Anna Freud wanted.

"When Sylvia was thinking about retiring, I remember her saying that it would be impossible for her to retire and stay in London, because there was one patient who would never stop seeing her, and that was Charles Rycroft.

"Most people saw the grand defence that he put up, and they didn't see past it. But I have always been skilled at picking up young men who were vulnerable underneath. Masud Khan was certainly one of those, but Masud was very different from Charles. He was very open, very affectionate: he always gave me a big hug when we met. Charles never did that. I kept my distance from him because that was what he needed."

Pearl saw a lot of Charles in those early days, but he always kept his personal life very much to himself. She knew nothing of his early history: his father's death, the family title going to his older half-brother and his own family being shunted off into a social backwater. Not knowing the facts, she nevertheless sensed the feelings arising from them. She recalled that Winnicott had been protective of Charles, because he would also have recognized that he was troubled. "While Winnicott was around, Charles would have felt a bit comforted, because Winnicott would understand the inner rage, the little boy who lost his father and his home and wasn't even allowed to cry." I said, "I don't expect he ever told Winnicott!" Pearl smiled. "I'm sure he didn't, but you can pick these things up, can't you? It would just make sense to Winnicott that something like that must have happened. Winnicott always kept clinical issues to the forefront of his mind. He would pick up when something was a bit wrong, when somebody was having trouble, while other people would just see them in their roles. And you didn't have to have many bits of information without it coming to your mind that it could have been this, or this, or this. You could pick it up from the way he was behaving, from him being so anxious." I said, "So there were people who realized that he was troubled?" "Yes, but they probably would have done what I did: sort of withdraw from having much contact with him, because that was what he seemed to need."

I find myself recalling Charles's story about Winnicott seeing him across a room at a party of psychoanalysts and walking over to him, saying, "Doctor Livingstone, I presume!" When he told it to me, I had an impression of real pleasure at a shared joke in a room full of analysts who at that time would have been predominantly mid-European. Now I see it as perhaps something of deeper significance: a father figure, such as he had always needed, making him welcome in his chosen profession. Pearl said, "While Winnicott was around, I think he felt a bit comforted. When Winnicott died in 1971 he would have lost his last chance of being protected."

* * *

Those early days as a practising analyst were an extremely creative time for Charles, when he was thinking his way through the labyrinths of Freudian and post-Freudian theory while at the same time feeling his way into the dynamics and mysteries of practice. It has been my impression that he experienced his analytic practice as a protected place in which he felt able to relate to people in a more direct way than ordinary social life allows. He enjoyed the fact that people tend to be more "real" in sessions than in social life with its pretensions and small talk. Paradoxically again, he seemed to feel freer within the boundaries of professional practice than in other, less structured situations. Having talked with a few of his patients, I have the impression that they felt fully met by him within the parameters of the professional relationship. After his rather sudden death I spoke with a number of patients who were then seeing him at our house in Kentish Town, and I was struck by the depth of the affection some of them expressed for him. I remember one elderly lady saying very warmly, "He was such a *dear* man!"

When he first went into practice, Charles made two resolutions: that he would always treat patients with the courtesy to which he was brought up and that he would allow himself to make jokes in sessions. He was very shocked by stories of analysts who adopt a bullying manner with patients, and he designated them "the new brutalist school of psychoanalysis". It is my impression that people who knew only his rather awesome "public face" had little idea of the warm side of him that his patients encountered. He was shocked and hurt when a patient reported another analyst's suggestion that perhaps she had had enough of "all that intellectual stuff with Rycroft" and should go to another analyst who worked from the heart.

His practice was, of course, the experiential base for those papers in which he grappled with Freudian and post-Freudian theory, including the early papers, which were greeted with excitement and, from some quarters, disapproval. He gradually came to realize that his original thinking was not being met by open minds but was being judged in relation to the factions that divided the analytic establishment. Coming from a rigorous academic background, he found this, by turns, surprising, exasperating, and occasionally comic. Writing about his early experience of the British Psychoanalytical Society at that time in the title paper of his book *Psychoanalysis and Beyond* (1985b), he recalled that

it was only some years after I had qualified as an analyst that I
realised what intense loyalties and enmities were imperfectly
concealed behind a façade of tolerance and broad-mindedness.
And only then did I appreciate that the divergences of opinion
about theory between the three groups were really differences
of substance; that Anna Freud, Melanie Klein and D. W. Winnicott really did have different conceptions of human nature, of
health, of how analysis should be conducted and what constituted a successful one. Anna Freud and her circle seemed to
believe that the aim of analysis was understanding and mastery
of man's inheritance of uncivilised and unruly impulses; Melanie Klein and her circle that it was reconciliation of man's original and innate propensity to destructiveness, greed and envy;
while Winnicott was a meliorist, believing in the efficacy of
maternal love in leading man towards faith, hope and charity.

It was, indeed, most confusing, and several of my own early
writings, those collected in *Imagination and Reality*, were attempts to sort myself out, to discover how much value I attach
to the libido theory and the mechanism of defence as taught by
Anna Freud, to Melanie Klein's view of symbol formation, to
Winnicott's and Milner's views on illusion and disillusion.
Most of them were in fact read to scientific meetings of the
British Psycho-Analytical Society, at which Anna Freud,
Melanie Klein and Winnicott were present—or were conspicuous by their absence—and their contribution to the discussions
afterwards had to be scanned as much for their often conde-
scending tones of approval or disapproval as for any substan-
tial contribution they might be making to the topic of the
paper. [pp. 120–121]

* * *

While all this was occupying his energies professionally, Charles
also had a burgeoning family life with his first wife, Chloe Majolier,
whom he married in 1947, and their three small children, Julia,
Catherine, and Francis—now called Frank—all born between 1947
and 1950. Charles was a man some women found very attractive,
while to others he was "invisible", as he once observed lightly.
Chloe was very beautiful, also a doctor and a psychiatrist in training at the Maudsley when they met. They were a glamorous
couple, and the photograph albums portray an idyllic family on
seaside holidays and in Hampstead, walking over the heath with
Masud Kahn occasionally pushing a pram.

How or why it came about that Charles left home while the children were quite young, first going to live during the week in a flat near his West End consulting-room and eventually moving out altogether, has never been clear to me or, as far as I know, to anyone. He seems to have felt neglected by Chloe after she returned to her interrupted psychiatric training, once Frank was old enough to be left with an *au pair*. Charles suffered from sudden rages, which were frightening to children: though he was never violent, these rages did feel almost out of control. It is possible that they also frightened Charles himself and made him anxious, and that this had something to do with his withdrawal from the marriage. He was working extremely hard on many fronts and seemed unable to manage the change of gear that is needed in order to be at ease in the presence of small children. When Chloe was absent doing hospital work, he found other women to keep him company. So their family life gradually disintegrated, and in 1963 Charles and Chloe were divorced. When I met him years later, he was still grieving over the separation from his children, though he always kept in touch with them and was in many ways a very supportive and understanding father. Long after they were grown up, he told me that never a day went by without him thinking about all three of them. The three brief memoirs they have written bear sad testimony to the impact of his withdrawal on his children, creating a distance between him and them that tragically repeats some aspects of his own childhood loss.

Julia Jama [b. 1947]:

"My first memory is from when I was very young: in the house at Heathurst Road, watching at my window after I had gone to bed for a wave from Daddy as he parked his car on his return from work. I don't remember the infamous occasion when I painted Catherine with emulsion from head to foot while he was supposedly looking after us and he told Mum on her return that we'd been awfully quiet! My mother described his stance with us, maybe a bit unfairly, as 'benign neglect'. I also remember, from this time, how attached he was to Clementine the cat, who was somehow his cat rather than just the family cat.

"Slightly later memories, probably from Lawn Road, include walks on the Heath and 'good night' visits upstairs, which we tried to prolong by getting him to teach us to count to ten in German, and his 'good night' in German: *'Schlafe gut, traume Süß'*. There were visits to the consulting-room in Park Crescent, always of a separate nature to everyday life: it was a special sanctum, incredibly tidy, silent, and with a special smell, probably just stale air and furniture polish! This was demystified some years later when I did a summer vacation stint as a receptionist for him in Wimpole Street. I remember a holiday in Italy up a mountain with fireflies, lots of boiled eggs, and a trip to the seaside where Mum and Dad blamed each other for forgetting the picnic and we had delicious calamari and chips on the beach instead.

"These later memories begin to get an overlay of anxiety. I can remember quite clearly the day of his departure from the family home: us running down the street waving goodbye at the car as if he were going away on holiday, though a bit of me knew he wasn't. I was somehow aware of the irony and falseness of the scene, even at the time. Then began the weekend-Dad syndrome, a confusing mixture of presence and absence, when for a long time he was there on family occasions and sometimes holidays as well as weekends. I probably caught my anxiety from Mum, who wanted him to return. There was a feeling that he should be accommodated as much as possible: not too much noise, letting him be undisturbed in the sitting-room after lunch, and generally going along with whatever he wanted. It was at this time that his silent rages, jingling coins in pockets, and irritable wringing of hands were most in evidence.

"On the positive side, he was always reliable, consistent, there when he said he would be, and, by his own lights, child-centred. When the break with Mum had actually been made, I saw him a lot more, without Mum, and enjoyed a much better relationship with him. He visited us regularly at boarding-school, indulged us with meals in restaurants, and was always ready to comply with requests for items to be purchased. When he died, we found a pile of letters that he had kept from all of us from our earliest days. Mine for many years are full of commands—*please bring me a new hairbrush; send me a ten bob note; book me an optician's appointment; meet me off the train*—with a coda ordering him to let me know immediately if the required task couldn't be done. I find it hard to recognize myself in these letters, but perhaps my nearest and dearest don't.

"After Mum moved to the country, I stayed with him regularly, and our relationship grew. Then I lived in London for two years, staying with a girl friend while I did my A levels, and quite often went out with him to the theatre or art exhibitions and sometimes socialising with his friends. During the summer holidays I worked in London and stayed in his flat. Meals out figure largely in my memory of this time. He was at his best playing host to us children and our friends or his, and sometimes with visiting relatives. When our cousins Charles and Bruce were 21, he arranged a big meal out and a visit to the theatre. It was in term-time, but somehow I got flu and didn't go back to school, miraculously recovering in time to join the party. He bought us tickets for a Beatles' concert and partly spoilt the occasion by coming along himself and inhibiting our screaming. Weekends away in the country with him, staying with Peggy, our mother's sister, or at Alice's (his sister), or occasionally with other relatives, were a feature of this period.

"Friends of mine have told me they envied my informal relationship with Dad. However there was a depth lacking, which I only fully grasped later on as, growing into adulthood myself, I started to realize his inability to truly empathize, to see someone else as completely separate. He had a very bad memory for things I had done unless they impacted in some way on him, like a visit to a place where he himself had been.

"Even at that time I appreciated his non-judgemental attitude to us as young adults and to our friends. Unlike many parents, he was willing to accept our friends as part of accepting us, and he had a genuine respect for young people, their opinions, and their experiences. He also had a forgiving nature: when two friends of mine cleaned out his whisky in a night and I apologized, he said that it was there to be drunk; when I splashed coffee on a new art book, he said that showed it had been read. And he was trusting: I used his flat for a party with a *carte blanche* from him. He was never petty, always seeing the bigger picture.

"As I grew up myself, I became more aware of his problems with relationships, with his social life, with small talk involving anyone outside his cultural circle, and in relating to interests in the lives of others. However, he always treated anyone who worked for him in whatever capacity with utmost respect: the cleaner, waiters, his receptionist, even the flats' porter after it had been shown he had forged two of Dad's cheques! Cherry, Frank's girl-friend and later his wife, suffered particularly from his lack of everyday conversation in long evenings with him. I was only 'involved' in one of his relationships with women, before Jenny: she found him too difficult on a day-to-day level and their 'living together' only lasted for a few weeks. In the aftermath, Dad had the first of his serious depressions, which I had no idea how to deal with, and he eventually sought medical help. My mother always said he wanted a woman 'who could discuss Goethe while darning his socks', and I think in Jenny for a time he found this combination.

"As an adult I enjoyed discussing books, news, and people with him, and visits to places like stately homes and art exhibitions. We both enjoyed town walks. He was always game for something new—he came to both *Grease* and *Return to the Forbidden Planet* with the children and me, taking out his hearing aids as a precaution. He always kept in touch with phone calls, postcards, and occasional letters, often semi-legible. I miss his encyclopaedic knowledge of almost any subject (other than those of a practical nature) and his willingness to discuss almost anything. However, we rarely talked about psychoanalytical matters. It was many years before I knew Laing had been a patient, though the story of the patient with a hammer did percolate through from the 1950s (Rycroft, 1960). I probably didn't encourage such discussion because I had and still have a rather jaundiced view of the one-to-one therapeutic relationship, informed by my political opinions and sociological perspective. But I take his intellectual stance as a standard to follow: an empirical approach and an honest thinking-through of issues, based on ideas and facts, not personalities and feelings.

"At his memorial service I read the piece on 'continuity' from "The God I Want" (Rycroft, 1967), and feel it was well chosen by Jenny. Dad gave me a sense of the importance of continuity with the past, both through his interest in his own 'aristocratic' family background and his command of political and social history. He was brilliant at putting current events in the context of the past and at speculating over what might happen in the future. The connections he maintained with aged relatives, his relationship with Alice, and his willingness to chauffeur around young nephews and nieces visiting London showed his sense of family as a continuous experience. So did his maintenance of contact with our mother's sister Peggy and her children, two of whom attended his funeral, more than 30 years after his divorce from their aunt."

Catherine Merriman [b. 1949]

"I have no clear memory of Dad living with our family, just disconnected flashes, which include a sense that he was present. I have no memory of him leaving the family home. I just remember knowing, presumably because I had been told, that he was going to live in a separate flat because it would be 'nearer to his work'. But I do have clear memories of him as a weekend parent. I remember family lunches, when he played the piano in our playroom afterwards while my mother and perhaps others washed up. He played without sheet music, nearly always variations on the same haunting little tune that he eventually taught me but which I have now, to my regret, forgotten. He drove us out at weekends to the country: Monks' Green, South Mimms, was a favourite place. Both our parents were interested in animals and wildlife, as I was at that age, passionately, although Dad had a horror of touching bird feathers, because, he said, a bird had died in his hands from shock when he was a child. We used to creep quietly up to a little junk-laden pond at Monk's Green in the hope, several times rewarded, that we would catch sight of basking grass snakes slipping back into the water. Although it was my mother's tolerance, even enthusiasm, for keeping animals that predominated in those Lawn Road days, Dad was certainly interested, too. I remember an occasion when our rabbit developed a huge milk clot the size of a soap bar behind one of her teats, and Dad operated on her, breaking it up and cutting it out through the hugely distended nipple aperture, while I held the rabbit on her back in my arms. The operation was a complete success.

"Another early memory is of the game we children used to play with Dad while he was driving, and not, presumably, in a hurry to get anywhere. The game was to give him directions: 'turn left, turn right, straight on here', with the hopes of getting us lost somewhere in London. We never, to my memory, suc-ceeded in getting lost, but we did see overgrown bombsites in the East End and many other sights. I remember marvelling at how Dad always somehow knew the way home. I think maybe my happy memories of this game highlight the fact that Dad was best with children when there was something active to do. I don't think he was good at talking to children: he really wasn't interested in non-adult matters, and he didn't know how to pretend. But doing something practical with his own children, he could manage that.

"I think Dad had real difficulties following the lives of peo-ple, including his children, which took place outside his sphere of interest. As a child, unless some physical activity or an actual conversation was taking place, I could quickly sense his engage-ment with me fading. At one time this could be quite frighten-ing, because he would go into his 'silent rage' mode, turning red in the face and jingling the change in his pocket. I imagine this must have been at a time when he had many adult concerns worrying him. I learnt to say 'Dad' quickly, to pull him out, and then I would struggle to engage him more securely, to stop him slipping back and becoming frightening again. Family and his-tory were two subjects that could always reliably 'catch' him: anyone's family, including his own, and the history of practi-cally anything. I think I very quickly realized that these anger fugues weren't aimed at us children, but at the same time they left a damaging legacy. I always felt a pressure to actively entertain him, even in more recent years, which meant that throughout his life I found him harder work one to one than perhaps he should have been.

"If Dad was sometimes guilty of crimes of omission, this had an upside to it, especially when we were adolescents. He seemed to have infinite faith in the ability of us children to reach satisfactory adulthood without pep talks, lectures, warnings, or laid-down rules as to our behaviour or appearance. Maybe this faith was not faith at all, but a kind of unconcern, but the effect was the same. We were never nagged or harangued by him. Adolescents are selfish, and I think all three of us exerted our selfishness in different ways, without him ever complaining or even pointing it out to us. And he had more subtle and important virtues: he never criticized our mother in my hearing—as indeed I never heard our mother make more than the mildest criticism of him: even her expression 'benign neglect' came with a smile. And he imbued me, at least, with the belief that there was nothing I couldn't do, if I wanted to, and that anything I chose to do would be accepted, and indeed admired, by him. That is, I always felt that he was proud of me, a sort of unconditional pride that didn't depend on knowing exactly who I was or what, exactly, I was doing!

"I do wish, however, that he and our mother had been more clued up educationally. They were both, on the evidence, hopeless. I believe Julia wasn't sent to primary school when she should have been, causing the truant officer to call. Although she and I eventually went to a good local primary school, our secondary school, Battle Abbey, was dire in terms of academic standards. It seems to have been chosen simply because a cousin went there and an ex-headmistress had some psychoanalytical connection in her past. What makes this incompetence all the more frustrating is that neither parent had to pay for any of our education, since it came out of a trust fund my mother had inherited. We could have gone to good schools that we also enjoyed. Julia and I did, in fact, quite enjoy our schools, but Frank hated his, and nothing was ever done about his unhappiness.

"I also wonder at Dad's apparent lack of a sense of danger, to others as well as to himself. He took Julia and myself to Malta one summer when we were school-girls, and we all got horribly sun burnt. At the time I didn't think it was his responsibility to warn and protect us, but I do now. We were in our early teens, and he was in his late forties, a doctor and an experienced traveller. Another time, many years later, he came to stay with my family in Wales when my two children were small, and we hired a rowing boat on Llangorse Lake. When we got quite far out the water became choppy, and I became very anxious, realizing that none of us was wearing a life belt. My husband too could see the danger and made a turn for shore. Dad, however, was completely unfazed and somewhat amused at the anxiety that was curtailing the adventure.

"On another, more recent occasion, his disregard of personal safety was absolutely charming. He was staying with us, and we decided to go and visit Cyfarthfa castle in Merthyr. He would have been about 80. It was a very windy and wet morning, and as we drove towards the high stretches of the Heads of the Valleys road, it became obvious that we were driving through no ordinary high wind. The rain was horizontal, lashing at the car windscreen, and the noise was appalling. There was nowhere to stop, and when we got to the top of the hill, which is well over 1,000 feet, we decided that we'd press on anyway. In the streets of Merthyr dustbins were rolling across the road and branches flying through the air. Dad was a picture of enthusiasm, eyes gleaming, leaning forward from the back seat so he could see everything properly. His sense of excited invulnerability was catching; when we finally got to the Castle, I think we all felt a post-heroic elation. We were told that they would be closing in ten minutes because of fears that trees in the grounds might fall and block the driveway, but it didn't matter at all. We galloped round a couple of rooms, then, when they closed up, leapt back into the car and roared off, not home, but to a pub nearby to down a stiff drink and celebrate our adventure. I can't imagine any other of my aged relatives relishing such a morning, nor putting quite so much faith in us and fate.

"Jenny has always said that Dad claimed to think about all of us children at least once every day and being a father was, I am sure, a significant part of his inner life. There is one occasion in particular that, to me, exemplifies this. In the late 1980s my husband had a malignant melanoma and after a major operation became very ill with an infection and spent six weeks in hospital. The children were young and the hospital forty miles away. Dad rang regularly and after a few weeks, despite my protestations that I was coping, insisted on motoring down to 'take the driving load off me' for a weekend. I am afraid that, before he arrived, I viewed his determination as yet another burden to add to my list, and his driving, at the age he was then, was not a restful experience for a passenger. But I was, and still am, immensely touched by the urgent desire he clearly felt that summer to contribute and help out in such a fraught situation. It seemed a truly unselfish fatherly impulse, and I remember it now with warmth and gratitude."

Frank Rycroft [b. 1950]

"As the youngest of my father's three children I have very few memories of him living with the family, although chronology dictates that he was at our home, Lawn Road, Hampstead, during my earliest years. I was simply too young to remember much detail, although I do retain a background memory of his presence. I can, however, remember two specific incidents from those years.

"The first was hiding under the hanging coats in the lobby by the front door, waiting to surprise my father as he came home from work. This wonderful plan went adrift when my mother greeted him at the door and an animated conversation took place between them in the lobby, both of them unaware of my hidden presence. My surprise appearance was not greeted with enthusiasm: with hindsight, I think they were concerned that I might have heard things not for my ears. However, I had no idea, then or now, what they were talking about.

"The second incident I remember with some affection. It was evening, and I was in my bed, upset because my mother was going out, presumably with my father, and crying, unable to go to sleep as they wanted me to. Just why I was so upset is another question. However, I clearly remember my father sitting beside my bed for a prolonged period, stroking my head and offering quiet words of comfort, calming me in a patient and caring way.

"All further memories of my father relate to the period when he was not living at home. I have no recollection of the scene, remembered by my sister Julia, of us children running down the street waving goodbye at the car as he departed the family home—a description that I have found, slightly to my surprise, quite upsetting. All I do remember from this time relates to my mother rather than my father. I remember her calling me into the living-room at Lawn Road, away from playing with our neighbour's children in the street, and sitting me down very formally in the drawing-room to tell me that she and my father were to be divorced. I was completely unmoved by this statement and immediately asked if I could now go back outside and play with my friends. My mother seemed perturbed by my lack of reaction and told me that both my sisters had been very upset by the news. Over the years, I have sometimes thought about that scene and considered the reasons why it truly left me unmoved. Sadly, I have come to the conclusion that it was because it made no difference to me, since my father wasn't with the family anyway.

"The years leading up to their divorce must have been difficult for my parents as the period of 'limbo' between them seems to have continued for a considerable time. I remember with affection going to his flat, which I thought was very exciting, and being taken out to various London restaurants for treats. However, my most vivid memories of my father during those years were of desperately trying not to upset him whenever I was with him. I imagine we must have been guided by our mother to accommodate him and not upset him, but I think that we also realized the need for this approach instinctively through anxiety and fear.

"This was the period when, for no apparent reason, my father would retreat into himself in silent rages that he clearly struggled to control, which always started with the dreaded 'coin jingling' in his pockets. I would always be on the look-out for the first signs and do all I could not to trigger his displeasure and subsequent outbursts. With hindsight one can point to any number of pressures in his life at that time that might have led to this bizarre behaviour. However, as a small child I felt responsible, believing that his rage was caused by something that

I had done. Whatever the reasons behind it, I still feel that part of the cause was his impatience with the behaviour of children. My sisters and my mother describe his attitude to his children as 'benign neglect'. My view is somewhat more blunt. I think my father viewed children and their care as woman's work and, I regret to say, beneath him. I have no memories of father-and-son outings, no fishing, sport, or games; they simply didn't happen because he had no interest in being there or doing those things. His interests were much loftier. Although he would on occasion visit me at boarding-school and was always very generous with treats and outings, I can never point to moments of deep father/son connection. Our relationship always felt somehow formal.

"As we all grew older, I think our relationships with him improved. He was able to relate to us as adolescents with our own views and interests, and he seemed much more comfortable at that level. I know he enjoyed his children and took pride in showing us off. He was extremely tolerant and never sought to preach to me about what I should do with my future. I think he quite enjoyed the idea of having a non-intellectual son, and he never once criticized my somewhat bizarre choices of early employment, which included running a disco and driving lorries. He happily tolerated my staying with him for an extended period, with my then girlfriend and future wife Cherry, which with hindsight must have been very intrusive. However, throughout this stay he found it virtually impossible to connect or converse with us unless the subject matter was of interest to him. Any attempt at non-intellectual conversation with him was like trying to play tennis with someone who refuses to return the ball: the balls (subjects) are soon exhausted, and the game is over.

"I met a number of his women friends during these years, although I never got to know any of them well until his marriage to Jenny. The relationships always seemed to be complicated and problematic. I believe that he was at his happiest at the start of a relationship, when he was demonstrably adored and his lady was hanging on his every word. When this changed over time, as it must, to a more equal and rational partnership, he lost interest and felt neglected. I asked him once, only a few years ago, what had gone wrong between him and Chloe, my mother. His reply was, 'she stopped looking after me'. I have no way of knowing, and these things are never simple, but it is very easy to believe that this same syndrome was acted out again and again.

"My overall feeling towards my father and his life in relation to mine is, I regret, one of sadness at the waste—the waste of his failed first marriage, in particular, when he left a loving wife and family, and for what? If he had left to secure a loving and positive relationship elsewhere, then so be it, but he did not. I know he went on to become a well-known and respected authority in his field, a commendable achievement, which was rightly very important to him. And I know that we are all very proud of his achievements and significant contributions to his profession. However, in my view, nothing is more important than children and family, and those times with your children growing up should be the most precious of your life."

* * *

During the years after Charles moved out 'to live nearer to his work', he shared a flat for a while with Masud Khan. Their friendship began when Masud came from Pakistan to train in psychoanalysis, a rather exotic young man in his early twenties. Charles was by then close to qualifying, and he felt that people in the Society were not being particularly friendly or welcoming to the stranger in their midst, so he and Chloe began inviting him to visit at weekends. Masud was "extremely bright", and they enjoyed one another's intelligence. When the marriage began to founder and Charles was looking for somewhere else to live during the week, Masud was also separating from his first wife, and so it came about that they teamed up and rented a flat in Devonshire Place. It turned out to be rather a crazy arrangement. Masud drank a lot and was very "peculiar": at one time Charles discovered he had been steaming open his letters and reading them. Charles talked about him in the interview with Peter Rudnytsky, after Masud's death but before Wynne Godley's revelations about his disastrous analysis with Masud in *The London Review of Books*, February 2001:

I think his whole history counts as sad, ultimately . . . I must have decided he was mad, at some point. He was a psychopath, a creative psychopath. He wrote a paper on collage, and, as I look back on it, that is what Masud himself was. He was a picker-up of other people's ideas, which he didn't properly integrate. The whole of his mind was a kind of muddle of all sorts of people, including me, except that he hardly ever quoted me. Like many Moslems, he would get on to alcohol and start drinking too much. . . . Masud became an impossible person, eventually, and I gave up seeing him. [Rudnytsky, 2000, pp. 76–77]

However, I do remember an occasion near the end of Masud's life when we received an invitation to dinner and visited him in his huge flat near Kensington Gardens. He was very tall and dressed in a long black robe, looking both impressive and somewhat eccentric. The two men talked for a long time about shared memories and the sad situation in which Masud then found himself, in deteriorating health and estranged from most of his professional circle. Charles was at a loss for words when we left, and Masud put a hand on each of our heads and blessed us—a gesture that was at once touching and slightly comic.

Rosemary Gordon. A colleague who was friendly with Charles from these early days was Rosemary Gordon, the Jungian analyst and author, who first got to know him at the Maudsley, where he was a young psychiatrist and she was a psychologist. She told me,

"I can't remember how we met. We just liked each other, I guess, and we became interested in one another because we were both interested in analysis. I hadn't started training at that point.

"I had a Kleinian analysis to start with, with Hanna Segal. I liked her. I still do: I like her sense of humour. But I felt we were both hyper-intellectual. The interpretations came thick and fast. I enjoyed them, but they bypassed the feeling and the affect. I would sometimes tell her not to rush in with her interpretations. That's the Kleinians: their interpretations come too fast, so you get interpreted before you have experienced what you are talking about.

"I was interested in Jung ever since going to college. Going to Jung after Klein was like a return to myself. Going to a Kleinian was more because all my friends were in Kleinian analysis. It makes a lot of sense, in theory, and it adds a spice to Jung. Hanna Segal was very intelligent, and I am more likely to be intellectual than emotional, so I felt we were colluding in intellectual defences, and that was one of the reasons for getting out—that and the hurried interpretations. You talk about penises and breasts and all that without any sensation or affect. A lot of what I experienced later I didn't experience with her."

The connection that Charles and Rosemary formed as colleagues at the Maudsley was resumed when Charles and Masud were sharing a flat and Rosemary lived nearby. Charles enjoyed Rosemary's intelligence and liked talking to her, but she soon felt she knew Masud better: "I found him very loving and lovable. I was one of the few people he didn't quarrel with. I saw him a day or two before he died."

She was aware that Charles was "cut off" from other people by very strong defences, that "he wanted affect, wanted emotion, but couldn't relate to it or give it". When I reflected that he seemed to relate more closely to patients than to people he met socially, she said "I think it is likely he was helped a lot by his patients, because patients do something that the analyst sometimes can't. Sometimes the sort of experiences they have fit the experiences that the analyst has. I think we get as much from our patients as they get from us. Sometimes we get more from our patients."

Having a long interest in making "bridges" between Jungian and Freudian theory, Rosemary has kept track of Charles's contributions since she first knew him and was quick to seize on those aspects of his thinking that lead into the area of imagination. One could even be fanciful and draw a parallel between her progression through Klein and "hyper-intellectualism" to Jung and Charles's journey, via disagreement with Freud over the importance of the primary processes, to a point where symbolism and the imagination took on a central importance. As our conversation drifted into this area, she said:

"His book on dreams is very Jungian, in a way: his interest in the role of symbolism in healing, and what he says about the imagination. I think one of Charles's great contributions to psychoanalysis is his idea about the primary processes. He made two important contributions, to my mind: one is his book on dreams and the importance of the imagination and symbolism and the other is what he has written about the importance of primary process, re-valuing it, saying that it adds to experience rather than depresses it: his paper "Beyond the Reality Principle" (1962).

"In *The Innocence of Dreams* (1979) one feels that he got away from his hyper-intellectualism and suddenly saw value in the non-rational bit, which is dreaming and which has to do with creativity. He was obviously anxious to get closer to the creative.

"He was an original character, like Masud. A Freudian, but not with a closed system. Classical, but not strictly so. History meant a lot to him. He was interested in the origin of things—experience, theories, philosophies. He could be ironic. That's an anti-idealization defence and brings in a certain wickedness, you see the other side, and a certain wit. It brings in a new way at looking a something."

*   *   *

Rosemary's comment that Charles "got away from his hyper-intellectualism" when he wrote *The Innocence of Dreams* leads me back to the years at Kew, where the book was written, and the part of his story that I shared. I have already written quite fully in the introduction about the personal side of his need to get away from Hampstead and the professional scene in the quest for his own creativity. In retrospect I think that is partly what our marriage was about. At that time I had no involvement in the profession from which he was trying to distance himself. There was a long period when our life together was fairly idyllic, but over time I found myself in an increasingly impossible situation, as perhaps did every woman who became closely involved with Charles, including and especially Chloe. The subtext seems to have been that, as Pearl King suggested, "he wanted a mother"—a woman who would always "be there" for him, supplying the continuity that was missing from his childhood. The other side to this was that if one fell short of the ideal, he would "act out" his anger in fairly extreme ways, which included going off with other people who responded to the lure of being ideal. It is my impression that none of his three analysts succeeded in meeting his need at a level that might have laid it to rest or brought it within manageable range. However, being in touch with a deep, unfulfilled need in himself, he seems to have been well able to recognize and meet comparable needs in his patients. Among the few who came and talked with me after his death, there were at least three who gave me the impression of having been thoroughly rescued from an extremely bleak inner place and of having found enough nurturing to go forth and manage without him. I remember a conversation with him about this, at the end of which he sighed and said, "Himself he could not save."

In our marriage I was often sadly torn between feelings that I could have done better and other, less sympathetic feelings towards someone by whom I felt badly hurt. I had been a busy, sociable journalist with an active life and a lot of people around me. Over time, I discovered that there were limits to my capacity for quiet domesticity. My subsequent forays into traditional storytelling were felt by him as a betrayal, and the idyll collapsed. There was also something about the unevenness of power, in a marriage to someone 23 years older than myself, that combined with my own history to send me in search of help and landed me in a long-term analysis. After a while my part-time work with storytelling groups got me interested in Jung and started me on the path to training as a therapist. Charles was understandably not keen about any of this, but he came to realize that in following my new path I was working out something that I really needed to understand, and in the end he accepted it graciously. I think it was quite a surprise to us both that we managed to stay together in spite of a period I remember as "the wars". Our doing so had to do with deep needs in both of us: his, for a continuous home he could take for granted, with "someone there in the background", particularly when he settled in a room by himself to write; mine, for a comparable stability and continuity from which to venture on my chosen path. We were rewarded in the latter years by a mutuality of friendship that we could both depend on. He accepted my venture into psychotherapy with tolerance, and I did my best to keep the excited psychobabble of training away from him. We made a rule about not mentioning psychotherapy at meal-times. One time, when he found me reading a book about Winnicott at breakfast, he said, rather wearily, "You don't want to read too much of that stuff, you know. It's like trying to live on a diet of Smith's Crisps!"

He always took delight in the process that transforms situations into words, whether by him or by someone else—the creative, healing process of symbolization. He told a story about his daughter Julia when she was very young and he was anxious that she might be feeling crowded by the arrival of her two younger siblings: how he was reassured when he overheard her saying to herself as she was playing: "And there they were, three little babies lying in a manger!" In the last months of his life, when he didn't have the strength to walk as far or read as much as he wanted, he suddenly brightened on finding a new word for his situation: "I'm feeling *under*-whelmed!"

Aside from the very public performance he gave as a writer and reviewer of books and articles in the British and American press, the greater part of his time was spent in his consulting-room, engaged in the private, invisible work of a psychoanalyst and psychotherapist. He carried on this work on a daily basis for 50 years. His practice was always busy, and he saw a very wide range of patients, from distinguished philosophers and peers of the realm to office workers, would-be actresses, and the occasional farmer and monk. He saw his last patient on a Tuesday evening only five days before he died after the sudden onset of acute pancreatitis.

Samuel Stein, interviewing him the year before he died for his book *Psychotherapy in Practice* (Stein & Stein, 2000), asked if he had ever experienced doubts about his decision to become a psychoanalyst. Charles replied: "It has only happened when I've been hearing too much about psychoanalytical politics. In relation to patients, the answer is no, I haven't experienced any severe doubts" (p. 332).

I believe that his work with patients sustained him in a number of important ways. The fact that he stuck to the work of his analytical practice through thick and thin was in keeping with the sense of public duty that came from his upbringing. He approved of the proverb "Live each day as though it were your last and till your land as though you were immortal". Beyond this deeply ingrained sense of duty, he had a lasting fascination with human nature and the ways in which patients were able to make use of his skill and insight. Often when he came out of his consulting-room in the house where we lived in his last years I noticed the special glow and aliveness with which he would emerge from talking with a patient. I was reminded of this by Rosemary Gordon's observation that communing with patients probably nurtured him, as well as them, in ways that no other relationship did.

Looking back over this story of the hurt and angry child who became the urbane and gifted analyst, it seems to me that Charles's life was a heroic struggle against heavy odds and that perhaps he overcame the odds against him by entering into what Jung would call the "archetype of the wounded healer". This concept arises from a profound observation that a physician who recognizes himself to be a bearer of pain and sickness works at a deeper level than one who assigns all the illness to the patient. I suspect that Charles was fully aware of this dynamic to his work, though his natural reticence and social conditioning would have been against making an issue of it. He was, as I have said, naturally inclined to keep his own troubles out of the picture, well concealed behind the stylish mask. The Jungian writer Adolf Guggenbuhl-Craig describes the dynamics of the wounded healer archetype in his book *Power in the Healing Professions* (1971):

> The image of the wounded healer symbolizes an acute and painful awareness of sickness as the counterpole to the physician's health, a lasting and hurtful certainty of the degeneration of his own body and mind. This sort of experience makes the doctor the patient's brother rather than his master. Everyone has within him the health and sickness archetype. But it has a very special fascination for the physician with a true vocation. This is why he chooses the medical profession. The average doctor does not enter upon his career for the sake of an easy way to gain power and, perhaps, at the same time to help mankind. Doctors are often accused of being more interested in disease than in cure. This is a half-truth. Physicians are interested in the health–sickness archetype and wish to experience it. For a great variety of psychological reasons, those men and women who choose a career in medicine are attracted by the healer-patient archetype. Unfortunately not all those who choose are strong enough to continually experience both ends of the polarity. [p. 97]

Charles was strong enough: he kept going to the very end of the road. I conclude my story with this quotation as a tribute to his many years of unseen work as a dedicated analyst and psychotherapist, the bedrock upon which his more public thoughts and writings rest.

Note

1. *The Cloud of Unknowing* is an English mystical treatise of the fourteenth century, author unknown, influenced by the "negative" mysticism of Dionysius the Areopagite.

References

Anonymous (2001). *The Cloud of Unknowing*, ed. A. C. Spearing. London: Penguin.

Freud, S. (1901). *The Psychopathology of Everyday Life*. London: Hogarth Press.

Guggenbuhl-Craig, A. (1971). *Power in the Healing Professions*. Dallas, TX: Spring Publications.

King, P., & Steiner R. (Eds.) (1991). *The Freud–Klein Controversies 1941–45*. London: Routledge.

Nicholson, D. H. S., & Lee, A. H. E. (1917). *The Oxford Book of English Mystical Verse*. Oxford: Clarendon Press.

Rickman, J. (2003). *No Ordinary Psychoanalyst*, ed. P. King. London: Karnac.

Rudnytsky, P. L. (2000). Charles Rycroft: A science of the mind. In: *Psychoanalytic Conversations*. Hillsdale, NJ: Analytic Press.

Rycroft, C. (1960). On the defensive function of schizophrenic thinking and delusion formation. In: *Imagination and Reality*. London: Hogarth Press.

Rycroft, C. (1962). Beyond the reality principle. In: *Imagination and Reality*. London: Hogarth Press.

Rycroft, C. (1967). The God I want. In: J. Mitchell (Ed.), *The God I Want*, London: Constable. [Reprinted as "On Continuity" in: *Psychoanalysis and Beyond*. London: Hogarth Press.]

Rycroft, C. (1979). *The Innocence of Dreams*. London: Hogarth Press.

Rycroft, C. (1985a). Memoirs of an old Bolshevik. In: *Psychoanalysis and Beyond*. London: Hogarth Press.

Rycroft, C. (1985b). Psychoanalysis and beyond. In: *Psychoanalysis and Beyond*. London: Hogarth Press.

Stein, S. S., & Stein, J. (2000). *Psychotherapy in Practice: A Life in the Mind*. Oxford: Butterworth/Heinemann.

CHAPTER FOURTEEN

Further glimpses

R. D. Laing, Maryon Tysoe, Peter Fuller,
Vincent Brome

R. D. Laing

Laing was in analysis with Charles Rycroft for the period of his psycho-analytic training, beginning in 1956. His training supervisors were Marion Milner and Winnicott. While in training, he worked as a Senior Registrar at the Tavistock Clinic, having previously qualified as a doc-tor and psychiatrist in Glasgow. He missed a lot of lectures and semi-nars, becoming impatient at covering ground with which he was already familiar, and for this reason there was some strong opposition to allowing him to qualify. However, senior members of the Society who knew him well, including Milner and Charles, supported his ap-plication, and his membership of the British Psychoanalytical Society was granted. Laing kept an intermittent connection with Charles for the rest of his life: I remember occasional books and even recordings of Laing's poetry arriving through the post. Laing talked about his analysis with Charles as follows in a series of conversations with Bob Mullan, the documentary film-maker, for his book about Laing, Mad to be Normal *(Mullan, 1995). [J.P.]*

Rycroft was simply Rycroft. He was an urbane, intelligent man who had no major scenario that I could make out that he was laying on me. I realized what the name of the game was, so I went in and laid down on the couch and he didn't have to tell me what I had to do. I simply started talking, addressing myself to what I had been dreaming that previous night. He made very, very few interpretations of a psychoanalytical kind. Occasionally he expressed an opinion with a reservation that he was going to express an opinion. I had an undramatic analysis.

Being analysed by Charles Rycroft was undramatic? Was that proof to you that it was a waste of time?

No, no, I didn't feel that. I was thinking about the tone more than the content. . . .

Your time at the Tavistock, did you find it suffocating?

I didn't find Winnicott, Milner, or Rycroft suffocating. . . .

In the car this morning you were scathing about Melanie Klein and the way that it was, in the end, just nonsense. When did you realize that?

Oh, when I was there. Melanie Klein was giving clinical seminars about four-and-a-half-year-old boys. I haven't read the book that was subsequently published, quite a big volume of a case of child analysis. Well, she was going over this material at the time, and I realized this was a woman who couldn't say anything to me because of the way she treated people. If anyone raised a point in which they ventured, or dared, to give some possible alternative interpretation or something, it was simply impossible to disagree with her. She would simply say, "take that up with your analyst, for analysis. Your analyst will give you a personal interpretation of how you want to suck his penis or rip off her nipple, which you are displacing on to me." That would be her interpretation. Literally . . .

I wanted to be supervised by Melanie Klein just for the experience, so I asked Rycroft, and he said he would try to arrange it. . . . I wanted the experience of Melanie Klein acting as my supervisor on a case. I wanted that experience. It was reported back to me in the analytic session that Melanie Klein had refused to have me in supervision because Rycroft wasn't a proper analyst and therefore I wasn't having a proper analysis with him. Because Rycroft had been analysed by Melanie Klein's *bête noir*, I think, Sylvia Payne . . .

When you were under analysis with Rycroft, how did you conceive of that?

I was involved with it. . . . When Rycroft was in the context of a psychoanalytical session, I would begin to have the experience of what I imagined psychoanalysis was like: namely quasi-Freudian or quasi-Fairbairnian or quasi-Kleinian or some sort of eclectic mix of interpretations that I imagined was the psychoanalytic job of relating what I was saying in this respect or that respect to transference and him.

I was very interested to see what would happen in that respect: to discover what sort of transference I would be expected to develop in relationship to Rycroft and very interested to see what personal illumination of my life this experience could contribute. I didn't feel that there was anything the matter with me—only small things, like a bit of chronic wheezing. But I wasn't incapacitated. Rycroft in fact had very few things that he allowed himself, or that he felt like saying. He did say, after about a year and a half, that he wasn't sure what to make of it but that I didn't seem to manifest much of a transference to him, and this might be because of my particular phase of life. That's a point that was considered somewhat among analysts but not discussed terribly much in public— was there a right time for analysis?

Were you cynical at this time?

Cynical? What do you mean by cynical?

Well, I mean, Karl Popper would just have laughed aloud, wouldn't he, at Rycroft's excuse?

Yes, sure. But Rycroft regarded that he was putting his intelligence and time at the availability of someone else's life as expressed through this analytic situation. That could reflect back his personal viewpoint to another person that that person might not have himself, and that might be a useful contribution to their life. In other words, Rycroft was using his intelligent, educated, urbane, civilized faculties to give attention to you for this period of time. . . .

Neither Rycroft, nor Winnicott, nor Marion Milner as far as I know, or any of the analysts like Sutherland, or Balint who had a Hungarian background, conducted analysis in absolutely the caricature of the classical way.

Classical . . .

Mmm, which Freud never practised.

Your time at the Tavistock, did you find it suffocating?

I didn't find, Winnicott, Milner or Rycroft suffocating. . .

Was there a time when you saw patients as a classical psychoanalyst?

Oh, of course. I was in psychoanalytic training. I spent four years at the Institute of Psychoanalysis undergoing a classical analysis by the British Psychoanalytical Society, five times a week on the couch of Charles Rycroft, and was supervised doing classical analysis by D. W. Winnicott and Marion Milner and peripherally with other people, like Sutherland. . . . For over ten years I spend something like twelve hours of the week doing this out of about ninety hours a week in which I was seeing people one way or another, within the formal framework of the couch and the chair. . . Most of my time was spent in a room with people sitting in one chair and me sitting in another chair. . . My "patients" would want in a sense to get from me my view of them: well, they would get it, and they would go away and make the best or the worst of it. I mean, "I'm not saying that this is going to do you any good, but if you are coming to see me and if what you want to get from me is how I see your life and the situation you're in and you think that will help you, well, I don't mind giving you that. But I'm not promising you this is going to be therapeutic."

Reference

Mullan, R. (1995). *Mad to be Normal: Conversations with R. D. Laing.* London: Free Association Books.

Maryon Tysoe

Maryon Tysoe's pen portrait of Charles Rycroft is taken from an article published in New Society *on 12 July 1985, marking the publication of* Psychoanalysis and Beyond. *It is my favourite description of how he could be at a friendly, informal meeting.   [J.P.]*

Charles Rycroft's photograph in the new collection of his psycho-analytical papers looks like a stereotypical portrait of what he is: the son of a baronet, fox-hunter, and country gentleman—both aristocratic and formidable. His writings betray a highly critical and analytic mind, a powerful intelligence, a strong sense of irony—altogether, both intellectually and personally, an intimidating collection of characteristics.

Our meeting, then, came as a surprise. At the door of his consulting room in Wimpole Street stood a spare, neat, not over-tall man, with pale, thinning, fuzzy hair and one of those bespectacled, lived-in faces. He was smiling at me rather diffidently, and smoking a cigarette. Unexpectedly, his voice was gentle and hesitant, well-bred but not cut-glass.

The room, like the man, was unpretentious: furnished simply in dark wood, with glass vases dotted around, and a little clock from his childhood. There were two huge, battered high-backed arm-chairs for himself and his patients and, of course, the couch: not the leather, curvy type you see in films—more like a narrow bed, with two flat cushions for pillows, all covered in a mossy green needle-cord that clashed horribly with the chairs.

Prostrating oneself on the couch is, however, not mandatory. "Quite a lot of analysts", Rycroft says, "still talk as though they made a solemn, formal contract with any patient, saying that the patient was seriously ill, would have to come for several months or years, and *must* come five times a week and *must* lie on the couch, and I do none of those."

The dislike of authoritarianism is a key to much of Rycroft's thinking. When I asked him what he felt were his main contributions to psychoanalysis, he replied "Good heavens, isn't that difficult", and paused a long time in thought. "Insisting that psychoanalytical treatment is a personal relationship between two people, and *not* a scientist observing some*thing* else. So ideas like 'psychic apparatus' have been eliminated from my thinking." Why is that? "Well, it's all sort of mechanical, isn't it? I don't think you'd find the word 'material' in any of my writings, in the sense that 'the patient presented some interesting material *bearing on* . . .' I would say: 'He told me that . . .' It's quite a big difference, actually!"

Rycroft rejects Freud's mechanistic view of the mind, with an ego in constant opposition to irrational, neurotic forces that keep trying to break out as imaginings, dreams, fantasies. (This is what Freud meant by "psychic apparatus".) For Rycroft, imagination and creativity are not to be firmly squashed but are a vital part of being human. . . .

Peter Fuller

Peter Fuller, the art critic and Editor of Modern Painters, *was a younger friend with whom Charles had a lively, ongoing correspondence and many conversations around their shared interest in art, history, and psychoanalysis. Peter's Introduction to* Psychoanalysis and Beyond *(Rycroft, 1985), which he also edited, is a prodigious document, placing Charles's thinking in relation to that of Freud and the Freudians, and placing him and them in relation to the wider field of European thought. It incorporates interviews with Charles at the time they were working together on the book. In this opening section of the Introduction, Peter points to the radical nature of Charles's challenge to the orthodox Freudian view of symbolism.*

In the 1950s and early 1960s, Charles Rycroft's work as a writer, therapist, and organization man was well-enough known within the psychoanalytic community. Between 1947 and 1961 he sat on numerous committees of the British Psychoanalytical Society, and, as he has put it, "held several offices and wrote numerous scientific papers". Although the latter received "polite, sincere, but often uncomprehending praise", he came to feel that his voice carried little weight in the Society's affairs and that real power belonged to those of whose values he did not approve. His eventual departure from the Society in 1978 can have come as a surprise to no one, least of all himself.

As he makes clear, Rycroft left the Psychoanalytical Society after deciding not to try to change it from within. Why did he take this option? As the essays in this book demonstrate, he was not short on compelling theoretical arguments. But the weight of orthodoxy was such that any open confrontation with it inside the Society would have dragged him into precisely those rituals of polemic and pronouncement of anathemas that he was seeking to reject. In effect, he wanted to see the emancipation of psychoanalysis from psychoanalysts. He could not, therefore, put himself forward as yet another spokesman for an alternative, schismatic, therapeutic "school". He went quietly.

But his silence was meaningful. Indeed, he elaborated its meaning in his work with patients and the articles he continued to write for a "lay" public, whom he addressed through newspapers and non-specialist journals. The position he elaborated is nothing if not clear. Nonetheless, its impact has been dispersed through a plethora of publications. I hope that this book will both clarify and terminate the silence surrounding Rycroft's departure from the organized institutions of psychoanalysis. If Rycroft is right (and I believe he is), the arguments he is seeking to advance have considerable importance, not just for psychoanalysts, but for all of us: they constitute a major, innovative contribution to our understanding of ourselves and our species.

The reception accorded to Rycroft's first major paper, "Symbolism and Its Relationship to the Primary and Secondary Processes", presented in 1956, helps to illuminate his originality. At that time, the accepted psychoanalytic theory of symbolism had stood unchanged for forty years. In 1916 Ernest Jones, Freud's leading British disciple, had delivered his authoritative paper, "The Theory of Symbolism", which drew heavily and uncritically on Freud's own findings.

Jones had sought to reserve the concept of "symbolism" for a very narrow area of mental functioning. He insisted that the process of symbolization was invariably carried out unconsciously: the individual who made use of the symbol was not aware of what it symbolized. "Only what is repressed is symbolized," Jones wrote. "Only what is repressed needs to be symbolized." This, he said, was "the touchstone of the psychoanalytical theory of symbolism".

For Jones symbolism had a special, indeed an exclusive, association with the "primary processes", or primitive and maladaptive modes of thinking characteristic of the unconscious. Symbolism, according to Jones, "always constitutes a regression to a simpler mode of apprehension".

When Rycroft turned his mind to symbolism, however, he took a very different view. His concern was to rehabilitate the concept of symbolism; he presented it not as a regressive or defensive phenomenon, but, rather, as "a general capacity of the mind" which could be deployed in manifold different ways. In his view, symbolization had no particular association with the repressed, nor with primitive or unconscious modes of thinking. Rycroft argued that words themselves were only a special kind of symbol. ("Classical" psychoanalytic theory had seen verbalization as the hallmark of conscious, "secondary process" thinking.) Indeed, Rycroft insisted that "unconscious symbolic and imaginative processes underlie the development and maintenance of a sense of reality just as much as they do neurosis".

In putting these ideas forward, Rycroft took care to declare his "immense debt" to Jones's classic paper. But twelve years later, Rycroft *himself* was to criticize the tendency in psychoanalytic writing to make appeals to authority in order to legitimize the ancestry of theories, or to ward off charges of unorthodoxy. The truth is that Rycroft's paper is not so much an extension or revision of Ernest Jones's as a reversal of its principal insights and arguments. The two papers take up mutually exclusive positions. If Rycroft's conception of symbolism is right, then Jones's is wrong, and vice versa.

How was Rycroft's revolutionary communication received by his psychoanalytic colleagues? There was a certain amount of pecking, scratching, and fluttering of the wings in the theoretical dovecots of the Society, almost all of it designed to protect the orthodox position. Meanwhile, Jones wrote to Rycroft saying, "You are of course right in pointing out that my use of the word 'unconscious' has since been superseded, and that my formulations need bringing up to date in the way you have excellently attempted." But then the awkward matter was largely forgotten. To the best of my knowledge, Jones never publicly acknowledged that his "classical" theory of symbolism required a revision, or even a defence.

Nonetheless, I think that most of those outside the psychoanalytic movement who read both Jones and Rycroft on symbolism today would concur with Jones's privately expressed view that Rycroft had got it right. Symbolism is such a pervasive characteristic of human psychological and cultural life that Jones's attempt to restrict the concept to a very particular usage seems arbitrary, even perverse. Similarly, experience indicates that symbolism is intimately involved in the "highest" (e.g. aesthetic, religious, and scientific) as well as the "lowest" (e.g. instinctual or sexual) modes of thought; nor can we really believe that its use in the latter is always unconsciously determined. It is not just that Rycroft appears to have logic and common sense on his side: his way of discussing psychoanalytic ideas renders them compatible with insights arising from quite different kinds of discipline, and, indeed, from the experience of life itself. Nonetheless, this incident epitomizes Rycroft's relationship to psychoanalytic orthodoxy.

For example, his most recent, and in my view his finest book, *The Innocence of Dreams* (1979), is a thorough-going reversal of Freud's pioneering classic of psychoanalysis, *The Interpretation of Dreams* (1900). Indeed, Rycroft's arguments against Freud's view of dreams are similar to those he put up against Jones's concept of symbolism. For Rycroft, dreams are not necessarily disguised expressions of repressed wishes, the royal road to the unconscious, nor analogies for psychopathological symptoms. Rather, he sees them simply as the way we think while asleep. Characteristically, Rycroft's conception of dreaming, unlike Freud's, is in keeping with contemporary non-psychoanalytic thinking on the subject.

References

Freud, S. (1900). *The Interpretation of Dreams. Standard Edition*, 4.

Jones, E. (1916). The theory of symbolism. In: *Papers on Psycho-Analysis*. London. Ballière.

Rycroft, C. (1956). Symbolism and its relationship to the primary and secondary processes. In: *Imagination and Reality*. London: Hogarth Press, 1968.

Rycroft, C. (1979). *The Innocence of Dreams*. London: Hogarth Press.

Rycroft, C. (1985). *Psychoanalysis and Beyond*, ed. P. Fuller. London: Chatto.

Vincent Brome

In his last years, membership of the Savile Club in Brook Street, W1,
was a valued part of Charles's social life: he dined there at least once
a week. A friend with whom he often kept company at the Savile was
Vincent Brome, the biographer and novelist, whose unconventional
thinking he greatly enjoyed. Vincent's description of Charles, as en-
countered at the Savile, is taken from the obituary he wrote for The
Guardian, *1 June 1998.   [J.P.]*

Some people found Charles Rycroft ... a formidable person to
meet because of his craggy face, lack of small talk, and searching
intelligence. Hidden away, perhaps too deep, was a compassionate
man who became a psychoanalyst to some of the most distinguished men and women of our day.

Rycroft was born into a uniquely British milieu, his father being
a baronet, foxhunter, and country gentleman. After Wellington he
took an honours degree ... at Trinity College, Cambridge, and
became a research student in modern history. When Trinity presented him with £10's worth of books as a prize, he chose Russell's
Freedom and Organisation, Marx's *Capital*, and Freud's *Psychopathol-*
ogy of Everyday Life. The three books permeated his early thinking.
The Communist Party, into which he was recruited as a student,
held him for a while, but psychology prevailed.

In his third year he applied to the Institute of Psychoanalysis to
train as an analyst. It was the institute's policy to emphasize medical training, and he was accepted provided he took a medical
degree first. He always remembered his interview with the rigorous Ernest Jones, who discovered that Rycroft came from an upper-
class family. "You will be going to St. Bartholomew's in that case,"
Jones said. Puzzled, Rycroft asked what made him think so. "Oh,
that is where all the upper-class dilettantes go."

He qualified medically at 32, finished his analytic training, and
married his first wife, Chloe Majolier. They had two daughters and
a son. His second, childless marriage to Jenny Pearson came much
later.

In the two decades after the war, Rycroft played an important
role in the politics of the British Society for Psychoanalysis and
its academic research. . . . Disillusion with hard-line psychoanaly-

sis began in 1953. He found the strife within the Institute of Psychoanalysis time-wasting. Rycroft always remembered the precise day he decided to get out; it was 5 May 1956, Freud's centenary. . . .

From the days of his defection from the Institute he began to unravel Freud's model of the psyche. He came to approve of the shift away from distribution of libidinal tension to object relations theory. This meant that analysts no longer focused on the observation of mental processes but gave closer attention to relations with their patients. His book, *The Innocence of Dreams* (1979), exemplified his deviation.

He became the leading critic of psychoanalytic literature in 1953 when David Astor appointed him chief reviewer in *The Observer*. His imprimatur on any book carried great weight.

The ambition to be a writer had persisted from childhood, and 1968 was a prolific publishing year. Psychoanalytic papers apart, he produced two books, one of them a classic of its kind. *Anxiety and Neurosis* set out to dispel the idea that all anxiety is irrational and neurotic. On the contrary, the capacity for anxiety was a biological function necessary for our survival; it was a form of vigilance by which nature kept us alert to threatening or unexpected experiences.

Imagination and Reality (also in 1968) attempted to bridge two schools of psychoanalytic thinking: that which believed in the sovereignty of internal processes and that which pressed the role of current social factors. The book examined, defined, and classified the role of imagination and its relations with reality. It also explained the popularity of murder stories in terms of the oedipal complex, with the victim an example of the reader's own hostility towards his parents which had to be punished.

Deeply read in history, literature, and psychoanalysis, Rycroft could be the most enriching conversationalist. He was one of the most popular members of the Savile Club, but he had to be drawn out. He hated anything resembling heartiness or gossip and remained slightly aloof. However, his haggard face could suddenly radiate as he quoted Karl Kraus on his profession: "Psychoanalysis is that kind of illness of which it thinks itself the cure." A wry smile accompanied by the remark: "I have learnt to co-operate with the inevitable."

Known among his friends as a survivor, he always regretted that he had not put himself to the ultimate test, but would not specify what that was. He claimed that one of his work's main themes was people under pressure in extreme situations. Certainly he suffered a number of such experiences, one of which approached breakdown.

Misled by first impressions, there were those who felt that he lacked the spontaneous warmth required by the ideal analyst, but he will always be remembered by many grateful patients and is a great loss to both his professions.

CHAPTER FIFTEEN

The last word . . .

Reminiscences of a survivor: psychoanalysis 1937–93

Charles Rycroft

This article, published in the British Journal of Psychotherapy, 11 *(No. 3, 1995), was originally given as a Graduation Address for the School of Psychotherapy and Counselling, Regent's College, in December 1993.*

I must confess that one of the reasons why I accepted the invitation to speak to you this evening is that I have always been much attached to Regent's Park, which I have known well, perhaps even intimately, since October 1937, which was when I started medicine at University College in Gower Street and started my training in analysis with Ella Sharpe in Kent Terrace. As my analytical session began at 5.30 p.m., it was possible and convenient to walk daily, five times a week, across Regent's Park from Kent Terrace.

The previous year, two Cambridge friends and I had applied for training at the Institute of Psychoanalysis and been accepted, after interviews with Ernest Jones, Glover, and Rickman, on condition that I did medicine. This condition was insisted upon, I now think, for two reasons: to ensure that I could not start practising analysis until I was over 30 and to test out whether I was really serious about becoming an analyst. Ernest Jones suspected me of being a dilettante and did indeed call me one during one of my interviews with him.

I should explain that in the 1930s Freudian psychoanalysis was regarded as deeply subversive. In progressive, advanced circles, Marx and Freud were regarded as the arch-enemies of capitalist society and middle-class morality, and to announce that one wanted to become an analyst was, indeed, a gesture *pour épater les bourgeois*. In fact, of course, British psychoanalysis in the 1930s was more an offshoot of Bloomsbury than a wing of any revolutionary movement, but I did not realize that at the time, despite the fact that it was Karin Stephen, a sister-in-law of Virginia Woolf, who pushed, prodded, and dared me to apply for training.

Of the years spent in analysis with Ella Sharpe, I can remember more about Regent's Park than I can about my sessions in Kent Terrace. I do remember that Ella Sharpe thought highly of me, which was flattering but embarrassing, and also that she worried about me, which was an alarming and novel experience for me. What I did not know until very recently was that she already had the heart disease of which she died in the mid-1940s, and that she had suicides in her practice. One of the hazards and/or rewards of being a survivor is, incidentally, that one sometimes discovers— stumbles upon—information about one's analysts that explains things about them that had previously been opaque. It was only when, a couple of years ago, I read Margaret Little's account (1990) of her own analysis with Ella Sharpe that I realized that Sharpe had only been interested in the Oedipus complex and infantile sexuality, and that loss, bereavement, grief—subjects about which I then urgently needed enlightenment—did not enter into her theoretical scheme of things.

The Second World War began in September 1939. University College left London and so did Ella Sharpe—and the walks in Regent's Park were interrupted for some years. But in 1941 I resumed analysis, this time with Dr Sylvia Payne. Several friends commented at the time that there was something bizarre about transferring from one analyst called Sharp to another one called Pain.

Payne was in fact quite different from Sharpe. Now best known for having negotiated the so-called "gentleman's agreement" that enabled the British Psychoanalytical Society to accommodate such divergent and incompatible tendencies as the Freudians, the Kleinians, and the Middle or Independent Group, Payne was a pillar of practical common sense. She was quite prepared to see relatives, to prescribe sedatives, to be helpful about practical problems of being a medical student in wartime—and at the same time she had an intuitive understanding of dreams. What I did not know at the time was that various periods of illness she had were almost certainly a result of the strain she suffered trying to make peace between Anna Freud and Melanie Klein; I only appreciated that when in 1987 I read Phyllis Grosskurth's (1986) life of Klein. Nor did I realize at the time that Payne could be indiscreet; I only discovered that some twenty years later when a protégé of Payne came to me for analysis and regaled me with anecdotes about myself and my analysis.

I qualified in medicine in 1945, did six months at the Maudsley, a few months as a locum at an old-fashioned mental hospital, and started my analytical practice in 1947, a year before qualifying as an Associate Member of the British Psychoanalytical Society. My first patients were the overflow from Payne's and Winnicott's practices.

In 1951, before I was eligible to be a training analyst, I was appointed a Member of the Training Committee and its Acting Training Secretary—the inactive or non-active Training Secretary being Winnicott, who had recently had a coronary thrombosis. I thought at the time, and still think, that this appointment had little or nothing to do with any merit I might possess or promise I might be showing; it was due to two factors: first, very few analysts had qualified during the war years, so there was a vacuum above me into which I was sucked; and, second, officers of the Society, though nominally elected by the whole Society, were in fact nominees of the leaders of the three groups. So I was nominated as delegate or representative of Payne and Winnicott, while other members of the committee were delegates of Anna Freud and Melanie Klein.

Being a member of a committee of an organization that was based on a truce between potentially hostile factions proved an educational experience. Sometimes a discussion would for no apparent reason come to a grinding halt; it would later become apparent that neither Anna Freud's nor Melanie Klein's delegates had been adequately briefed; they had no idea what their leaders thought about the matter under discussion, so the discussion dried up and had to be postponed until the next meeting. And trade-offs occurred. The "A" group wanted the rules bent so that Dr X, who was over-age, could train; the "B" group wanted the rules bent so that Dr Y, who was over-age, could train. Their applications were synchronized and considered at the same committee meeting: both X and Y became analysts.

Another thing struck me forcibly at the time. I had more children than the rest of the committee put together.

In one way Dr Payne's tolerance and broadmindedness unwittingly did me a disservice. I entered the analytical movement without appreciating the passionate intensity, the absolute certainty, with which many analysts held their views. Too many did not have opinions that were open to discussion and possible modification but, instead, had unalterable convictions—including the conviction that anyone who disagreed with them had not had a sufficiently deep analysis. As a result the so-called scientific meetings were all too often not discussions but collisions. I once read a paper to the Society about a woman who had dreamed that the moon fell out of the sky into a dustbin (Rycroft, 1955). During the discussion Melanie Klein expressed her regret that I had not had a sufficiently deep analysis; at the time I took this as an insult to Dr Payne. I heard later than some of the audience had construed my paper as a conscious, deliberate allegory about Klein; it wasn't, but it's a pleasing idea.

Another disconcerting discovery was that too many leading analysts were not therapists but fishers of men. They did not set out to cure neuroses but to acquire converts, disciples, and followers. This attitude was, of course, part of the ideology of the analytical movement. Its aim was to spread the true faith; it granted prestige to training analysts, who were judged by the quality and success of *their* analysands—all fair enough in a way, but it did, and perhaps still does, mean that too many patients-turned-analysts did not become their own persons but, instead, became pawns, extensions, reincarnations of their training analyst.

In the late 1950s and early 1960s I engaged in a strategic retreat from the analytical movement, retiring from committees and offices, avoiding taking on new training cases, and eventually ceasing to attend the fortnightly scientific meetings. There were, I think, two reasons for this withdrawal.

The first was exasperation with the perpetual bickering between, first, the Anna Freudians and the Kleinians, and, later, between Winnicott and Klein. The latter exercise in mutual non-comprehension had a most peculiar flavour about it. It was not just that they had different ideas about infancy, mothering, early ego-development, and object relations, but that Winnicott always seemed to be pleading to be understood and appreciated by Klein. When I discovered that throughout this period Mrs Winnicott was in analysis with Mrs Klein, and that some years previously Mrs Klein's son had been in analysis with Winnicott, I began to wonder what I was doing sitting in on a family quarrel.

At the time I thought it was a bit wet of me to be got down by all this feuding and bickering, but I feel better about it now, having in 1991 read Grotstein's description of this period as "one of the most dreadful, shameful and regrettable chapters in the history of psychoanalysis" (Grotstein, 1990).

The other reason for my withdrawal—the last straw that made me vow never again to attend one of the Society's scientific meetings—was a meeting in 1964 at which the late James Home read a paper called "The Concept of Mind" (1966). In it he argued that psychoanalysis is not a causal theory and one of the natural sciences, as Freud had always maintained, but a semantic theory and one of the humanities or moral sciences—an idea that was not quite original then and has since become widely known and accepted. But it was not Home's paper but his audience's reactions to it that appalled me. Speaker after speaker got up to assert his belief in psychic determinism, in the natural-scientific base of psychoanalysis, each eagerly making a Declaration of Faith and Loyalty and dissociating himself from the heresy being propounded by Home. The only two speakers to support Home were Peter Lomas and myself.

In 1964, then, I last attended a meeting of the British Psychoanalytical Society, and that was that—or, rather, would have been that, had it not been for two apparently fortuitous invitations from publishers to write books for them. I say "apparently fortuitous invitations" because I suspect I had a guardian angel looking after me, but I do not know who he or she was or whether he was a figment of my imagination.

One of these two invitations came from Penguin, who asked me to write a book on anxiety for them, which I duly did (*Anxiety and Neurosis*, 1968a). The other was from the late James Mitchell, who wanted me to compose a dictionary of psychoanalysis to include in a series of dictionaries he was bringing out. I agreed to do this on condition that I could include the word "critical" in the title. The *Critical Dictionary of Psychoanalysis* came out in 1968, only 13 months after its conception over the telephone, and is still in print. It and its various successors have kept me in touch with analytical and psychotherapeutic thinking to this day.

I have, however, never had the slightest wish to attend a Scientific Meeting of the British Psychoanalytical Society again, nor to rejoin the Society—I stopped paying my subscription in the early 1970s—and any doubts I may have had about the wisdom of my withdrawal were assuaged when last year I encountered the following quotation from Bion, who continued to attend them longer and later than I did: "You can't go to a Scientific Meeting without becoming full of contempt for the subject—you wouldn't think that what was being discussed was the most exciting and original theory of the human mind ever devised" (in Hill, 1992). This is Bion, not Rycroft. If I had written it, it would have read "exasperation" not "contempt".

I must add that all this time—indeed, until 1990—I was seeing patients in the Harley Street area and taking a daily walk in Regent's Park. Long before it became public knowledge, I knew that there were herons in the Park, as one evening at dusk I had encountered one flying down Harley Street pursued by angry smaller birds mobbing it.

Finally, I can't remember ever attending and speaking at an occasion quite like this before, but it reminds me of Speech Day at school, when some aged Field Marshall, Peer of the Realm, or, even, on one occasion, the last surviving son of Queen Victoria, would deliver a speech in which they pressed upon us sage advice on how we should conduct our future lives and careers. I shall make no attempt to emulate them, but two thoughts do occur to me as relevant to the present occasion.

First, I hope you, who are going on to practise psychotherapy, will never forget that your clients, your patients, have bodies as well as minds, and that the symptoms and problems for which they consult you are reflections, derivatives, and manifestations of the great human problems implicit in whatever stage of the life cycle they are in.

And, second, I hope that those of you who are going to become counsellors will never forget that your clients exist within society— a society of which they are both beneficiaries and victims, of which they are both protected members and casualties.

These two points can also be made another way. Winnicott has famously said that "there is no such thing as a baby", meaning that babies make no sense without a mother. Similarly, there is no such thing as a mind without a body, and there is no such thing as a person without society. We are all members of one another.

References

Brome, V. (1982). *Ernest Jones: Freud's Alter Ego*. London: Caliban.

Grosskurth, P. (1986). *Melanie Klein: Her World and Her Work*. London: Hodder & Stoughton.

Grotstein, J. S. (1990). Introduction. In: M. Little, *Psychotic Anxieties and Containment*. Northvale, NJ/London: Aronson.

Hill, J. (1992). A brief personal memoir of Wilfred Bion. *British Journal of Psychotherapy, 9* (1): 70–73.

Home, H. J. (1966). The concept of mind. *International Journal of Psycho-Analysis, 47*: 42–49.

Little, M. (1990). *Psychotic Anxieties and Containment*. Northvale, NJ/London: Aronson.

Rycroft, C. (1955). On idealization, illusion and catastrophic disillusion. *International Journal of Psycho-Analysis, 36*. Also in: *Imagination and Reality*. London: Hogarth Press, 1968; London: Karnac, 1988.

Rycroft, C. (1968a). *Anxiety and Neurosis*. London: Allen Lane/Penguin, 1971: London: Karnac, 1988.

Rycroft, C. (1968b). *A Critical Dictionary of Psychoanalysis*. London: Penguin. Second edition: London: Penguin, 1995.

INDEX